Deep Living

Deep Living

*A practical path to
happiness and fulfillment through
honesty, courage, consciousness,
and self-responsibility*

James Swank

Lyryll
Berlin

Published by
Lyryll
an imprint of
Coaching GbR Swank
Lieberoser Strasse 18
13439 Berlin, Germany

For more information
visit our website
www.jamesswank.org
or e-mail
info@jamesswank.org

ISBN 978-3-00-036071-8

Printed by Lightning Source.
Printing location on last page.

Disclaimer: We offer the contents of this book solely as information.
Experiment with these ideas and suggestions at your own risk. Proceed carefully
and get professional assistance if necessary. The author and publisher accept no
liability for what you choose to do with this information.

Acknowledgments

Many people helped me learn the things I needed to learn and do the things I needed to do to reach the state in which I was able to develop the Deep Living Practice and my way of working with people.

I consider several people my primary teachers in the area of personal growth and in my professional development as a bodyworker/therapist/group leader/ coach. These are, in roughly reverse chronological order, Paul Lowe, Kathy Kain, Hal Meyers, Luann Overmyer, Jeru Kabbal, and Christine Day. They were all instrumental in my becoming who I am today, and my gratitude to them is boundless.

I consider a very large group of people my secondary teachers. Many of these teachers and therapists provided crucial aspects of my personal development or taught me things that have become part of my professional practice. I've chosen not to list names as there are so many. I would rather not mention any, than disservice one, by not including his or her name. I am eternally grateful to all of you who have taught me and supported me.

Then there are my fellow students. I learned so much from so many of you and want you to know that you are a part of who I have become and I appreciate your role in my life as fellow travelers on the path.

Harbin Hot Springs provided a home and place to develop and transform. I am grateful to Ishvara for starting it, and all my fellow residents for both making it what it was, and the roles they played in my development.

My deepest gratitude goes to the thousands of clients I have had throughout the years. You have both supported me and taught me the vast majority of what I have learned.

I would also like to thank the authors of the countless books I read, many of which had profound effects on my development. That you took the time and effort to share what you have learned is an amazing gift and I am grateful to you.

In terms of my writing this book, I would like to thank Kimberly Bradley, who copyedited the manuscript. Besides making it much more grammatically correct, she has also helped make it clearer and more direct.

My final thanks goes to my partner Sarah. She made the book possible by making sure I had time to write while she managed all the practical details of our lives and our business. She was the first to read the manuscript, and the suggestions and corrections she made were invaluable in creating the finished product.

My love to her and our son Sylvyn, it is to both of you I dedicate this book.

Table of Contents

You are the answer

Introduction

When I turned 40 years old in 1995, my life fell apart. This collapse motivated a search that led me to a deep understanding of myself and human behavior in general. It was the beginning of a process through which my experience of life radically altered, and I became aware of many things that had previously eluded me. It was the beginning of a new way of living that led me to a deep sense of happiness and fulfillment.

For most of my life I was lost, confused, angry, fearful, and profoundly unhappy. Through what I have learned, I have come to love myself, love life, and experience an amazing sense of clarity about myself and the world around me. I've gone from being someone who was dark, cynical, and sarcastic, to someone who is caring, grateful, and in awe of life's perfection. I have found a personal sense of truth that guides me through life with joy, grace, peace, simplicity, and a feeling that I have found and am fulfilling my purpose. Having found this, it is very clear to me that this feeling of happiness and fulfillment is the most valuable thing to obtain in life, after our basic requirements for survival.

In my search, I looked in many different directions. I learned and experienced many things. Some were extremely valuable, some were useful as stepping stones, and some I eventually saw as diversions, though at the time I thought they were valuable.

In this book, I offer the lessons that were instrumental in my transformation; what supported me in finding my true sense of self, and the feeling of joy and simplicity I experience in day-to-day life. I want to tell you the things that I learned that were most effective for timely and permanent transformation, so you can take advantage of them and find the most direct route to your own experience of joy and fulfillment, while avoiding many of the paths I found less effective.

In my search, I studied many religions and philosophies; eastern and western, esoteric and practical, traditional and alternative. I became particularly attracted to Hinduism and yoga and became a yoga teacher. I also studied several forms of Buddhism, Taoism, Paganism, and a variety of meditation practices, both traditional and more modern variations coming out of the Human Potential Movement.

Besides looking for philosophical answers, I was also looking for practical answers on how to heal my body and my psyche. I experimented with a wide variety of therapies and forms of healing and bodywork from many different traditions. When I found a form of therapy effective, I studied it. I was particularly drawn to osteopathy and studied several osteopathic techniques, including becoming a registered practitioner of Ortho-Bionomy. I was also attracted to aquatic bodywork, gained certification as an aquatic bodyworker, and I developed a distinctive form of therapy using osteopathic techniques in the water.

As I became more skilled, I applied to and was accepted by a healing center, where I was able to practice what I was learning professionally. As my practice developed, I became very interested in our emotions and studied psychology and behavioral sciences with particular interest in the new developments in cognitive science, gestalt therapy and trauma resolution.

I became very interested in how we heal, and explored perspectives on healing including certain aspects of Western medicine, Chinese medicine, Ayurveda, Shamanism, and many esoteric methods out of the "New Age" movement. In my desire to understand relationship and sexuality, I studied several forms of modern Tantra with a number of different teachers.

I dove into spirituality, going to satsangs, meeting gurus, and studying with many spiritual teachers. Along the way, I found several teachers whose work I found extremely valuable with whom I spent as much time, and learned as much from, as I could.

An amazing synergy developed between my personal and professional practices, in which I was constantly confronted professionally with what I needed to address personally. It was through this combination of personal and professional practices, and the influence of my teachers, that I both learned and developed the practice through which I found happiness and fulfillment, and the method to support others to find deep happiness and fulfillment as well.

Here I present a combination of the most effective practices that I learned, combined with a way of looking at the world through which you will learn to reach a state where you are deeply feeling your authentic feelings in response to what is happening in the present moment. You will come to see that there is a deep inner truth within each of us that is quite different than who we were taught to be, and that we are constantly making choices, usually unconsciously, that, in most cases, support the sense of self that was created by how we were taught to live, instead of this deep inner truth. I will show you how you can become aware of these choices and learn to make the choices that more directly support you living your deepest truth. Through becoming connected to your deep inner truth, you will obtain the happiness and fulfillment I describe.

I have found that our feelings are our path to truth. I show a way to feel feelings that supports transforming behavioral patterns, that taps into vast sources of information that are extremely valuable in making life choices, and that guide us to a deep connection to our inner truth, which will bring us into a state of happiness and fulfillment that is beyond anything I could have imagined before I experienced it. This is an amazing state where life is incredibly rich, and in this state, you will experience a sense of clarity, empowerment, stability, and joy. It is this state I am referring to when I use the term "Deep Living".

Moment by moment, we are all having an experience. I have found that by focusing our awareness on that experience and making choices that create as deep and rich an experience as possible, not only do we feel as wonderful as we can possibly feel, but the things we do that create those feelings are the exact things we need to do to fulfill our purpose in the world and participate in life in the most responsible way, both individually and socially. Throughout the book I will refer to our "greatest potential" or our "maximum potential". By this I mean when we are feeling as wonderful as we can possibly feel while living our purpose and contributing our perfect part into the joint creation that is life on earth.

The purpose of this book is to help you create a personal practice that will bring you ever closer to your maximum potential. By "personal" practice, I mean a practice that you design specifically for yourself. Everyone will have a different path to develop the skills to reach their greatest potential. When I refer to this overall practice, I call it the "Deep Living Practice" or capitalize the word "Practice". This helps differentiate your overall Practice from the many individual practices of which your overall Practice will be comprised.

Along with teaching you how to create an effective Deep Living Practice, I also present a way of looking at life, and the world, that I refer to as the "Point of View." I also capitalize "Point of View" so you will know that I am referring to this particular perspective. The Point of View is a fundamental part of what I offer in this book. It provides a viewpoint that is essential to support the transformation your Deep Living Practice will provide.

I do not believe the Point of View is the right way, or the only way, of looking at life. Part of the Point of View is that there is no right way of looking at life, and that beliefs tend to create more problems than they solve. I encourage you to take the Point of View as a hypothesis and experiment with how your life changes as you look at your life from its perspective. You will find that the Point of View is an extremely valuable tool that supports transformation by providing a bridge between your current belief system, which is instrumental in how you are presently experiencing your life, and your deepest inner truth.

I did not create the Deep Living Practice and the Point of View by myself. They are a combination of what I have learned from several different sources that I have adjusted, altered, and augmented through the lessons I learned in my personal and professional practices. My personal and professional practices were laboratories in which I could develop and test the information and the practices I recommend, and to personally experience how they affect different people in different situations. My personal and professional practices have been the conduits that have taken the information I am presenting from the theoretical to the practical, and are the basis of how effective the Point of View and the Deep Living Practice are.

This is not an easy path. In creating the Deep Living Practice I strove to make it as practical and effective as I could to support timely and permanent transformation. When I started my search, I was looking for enlightenment and a quick solution to all of my problems. Over time, I found a persistent step-by-step approach to be much more effective. There are many challenging obstacles to overcome on the path from who you have been taught to be (who you think you are) to your deep inner truth (who you really are). I have found by breaking those challenges down into smaller manageable parts and focusing on the next step on your path, while also working on the skills that will allow you to make those steps, you will achieve the greatest results.

Since 2005, I have been sharing this information in private sessions and small groups. I make it as easy to learn as I can. I find this information extremely practical, and I try to teach it in a practical way, so interested people can learn it and benefit from it as efficiently and effectively as possible. In this book, I will jump from subject to subject, telling you small pieces at a time, letting you know what I am going to tell you, reminding you of what I have already told you, all with the goal of bringing you to a point of understanding, and then deepening that understanding. I ask you to bear with me and, at least the first time, read this book in the order I present it. After that, I encourage you to reread and jump around. I will be presenting a huge amount of information, so be careful to not let it overwhelm you. I've kept most of the chapters short, and I suggest you take at least a moment between chapters to let the content sink in. The real understanding doesn't come from the book. It happens inside you, and deepens over time.

I offer many, many possibilities—far too many to do in a short period of time—so take your time. You might start a few of the basic practices as you read the book the first time. Then, if you have decided you want to follow this path, use what you have learned by reading the book to create the Deep Living Practice that is perfect for you. Experiment with the information I provide here. It is essential to learn from your experience rather than to just accept ideas.

Many aspects of this Practice are quite challenging. Be gentle with yourself. It doesn't work to push yourself too hard. On one hand, you need to make your Practice a priority and apply yourself if you want to get results, but on the other hand, this is ultimately a Practice of self-love, so being too strict with yourself, or pushing too hard, will defeat your purpose. You will not reach happiness and fulfillment through struggle and hardship. You can learn to create a balance where you are actively pursuing your Practice in a nourishing and loving manner.

If you choose to adopt the Point of View, and experiment with the practices and exercises I suggest, I feel sure you will experience transformation, and that you will come closer to the feeling of happiness, clarity, power, and fulfillment I experience, and the deeper you go into it, the deeper you will experience these feelings. As you read this book, you will see that the choice to adopt this Point of View, and pursue the Deep Living Practice, is at the core of the results you will obtain. Your gains will be proportional to your commitment to your Practice, and, as you will come to see, your commitment to your Practice is actually a commitment to your deepest inner truth.

The vast majority of the specific practices I recommend are things you will be able to do by yourself, and these are the parts of your overall Practice where you will have your greatest development. You will find that you need help for some parts of your Practice. Don't let this stop you. I suggest ways to get the help you need. Being connected to the world around you is an important part of the Deep Living Practice. Getting the help you need is a way to start connecting. I have found that, if you really make the choice to do something, support will be available if you make yourself available for it. Intimacy is also a vital part of the Deep Living Practice, and the connections you make with the people you share your Practice with will very likely enrich your life.

Earlier I mentioned that I had found my purpose. My purpose is to support and encourage people to find happiness and fulfillment in their lives by helping them find their deepest inner truth and through that, the fullest and deepest experience of life available to them. It is my goal, through writing this book, to do exactly that for you.

James Swank
2011

– Chapter 1 –

Our Conditioned State

My basic premise comes from the experience that there is an aspect of each of us that is pure and untouched by the world around us. This aspect came into our bodies during the process of conception, gestation, and birth, and that this is who we really are. Various names for this aspect include the spirit, the soul, our essence, our deepest inner truth. Whatever you call it, my experience is that connecting with this aspect of ourselves is how we can obtain the greatest possible feelings of happiness and fulfillment available to us in this life.

But very few people are in touch with this part of themselves. In fact, we are taught not to be in touch with this part of ourselves. Each of us is taught to be the person the people who are teaching us think we should be, and they are trying to be the person the people who taught them thought they should be. The result of this is thousands of years of unconscious develop-ment. As our consciousnesses have been evolving, more and more of us are becoming aware of this disconnect between the life we are taught to live and what will bring us joy. Increasing numbers of people are feeling dissatisfied with their lives and are looking for something else. Through this book, I am offering a path to find this truth within yourself.

This is a spiritual path, but it is a practical spirituality. It is about experi-ence, not about belief. Belief is in fact one of the many things that keep us from being in touch with our true selves. I'm even reticent to use the word "spiritual", because for so many people it is so tightly entwined with belief. That most spirituality guides us to believe in something besides ourselves is another example of how deep and effective this condition of trying to be something we are not exists within us. When I use the word "conditioning", I am referring to all of the things that we have learned, and have happened to us, through which we have created our ideas about who we are and from which we have derived our sense of self.

Obviously this is a necessary process. We need to learn how to be in the world. What has happened, though, is that most of us have been conditioned in a way that keeps us from experiencing our deepest truths. Some parts of our conditioning are very necessary and help us live in the world in ways that are in line with our truths. Unfortunately much of our conditioning teaches us to be something we are not. The part of our conditioning that works well for us, we can put aside and leave alone. It is the part of our conditioning that keeps us from experiencing our true selves that we need to address in order to find joy, happiness and fulfillment in our lives. In the following pages I will discuss how we become conditioned, the effects of our conditioning, and how we can start the process of undoing our conditioning to find the path to our deepest truth.

Our true self comes into the body in the womb. Each of us finds ourselves in a body that is still in the process of developing and that we do not know how to operate. Learning how to operate this body becomes our focus. This process is more or less challenging based on genetics and the environment of the womb we are in, but for the most part, all our needs are taken care of. This remains the case until we are born.

Our birth process becomes the foundation for our experience on earth. Even in its most natural state, it is an intense transition. Going from an environment where it is dark, warm, quiet, protected, and where our needs are automatically met, we are pushed into a very different reality, and for the vast majority of us, very little attention is paid to our experience of this transition. Through the use of drugs, surgery, forceps, rough handling, bright lights, loud noises, separation from our mother, and a wide variety of other interventions, most people become traumatized by their birth experience.

In this traumatized state, we are confronted with many new challenges and intense sensory stimulations that we need to process and organize.

Obviously there are almost as many different ways for all of this to occur as there are different people. My point is that most of us begin our lives in some level of shock, and a sense of being overwhelmed by what we are confronted with, and that this has a huge, fundamental effect on our lives.

From this beginning we find ourselves in a situation that we need to learn to survive in. We are in bodies that we don't know how to operate. We have instincts that take care of the basic necessities, but we are also surrounded by giants who do whatever they want with us whether it is in line with our instincts or not, and most of them are not very good at interpreting our needs. At the same time, we are amazing creatures with the ability to learn, so we start to figure things out as quickly as we can.

Much of what we figure out is based on our surroundings and what is happening to us. We start to develop patterns and strategies of how to survive, and feel good, considering our circumstances. We do this to the best of our still developing abilities. Many of the choices we are making to develop these patterns and strategies are in response to what we are feeling. Our primary motivations are feelings like hunger, pain, cold, and separation. As we develop, we also begin to feel things like helplessness, frustration, and loneliness. When we feel nourished, comfortable and connected, we are not very motivated to change. As we begin to feel ability, accomplishment and pleasure, we are motivated to develop these feelings more deeply, but the drive to develop the feelings we like is not as strong as it is to avoid the feelings we don't like. We develop many of our strategies when we are feeling the things we don't want to feel.

As we become older and more aware, more and more influences affect us. We have more experiences to base our decisions upon. We are able to learn from observing others. People tell us things. We start to develop an idea of what life is like. Still, for most of us, it is the negative that primarily drives the process. It is the many times each day we hear "no" and "don't do that" that have the strongest effect on us. One book I read said the ego begins to develop the first time we hear the word "no". Now there is a right and a wrong, a good and a bad, and much of this information of what is right and wrong, and good and bad, comes from the people we are dependent on for our survival. We have a tendency to take this information very seriously. It becomes integrated into our ideas of how we should behave, what is allowed and not allowed, what is possible and impossible.

Let's consider the source of this information. It is mostly coming from people who are telling us to behave the way they were taught to behave. Most people don't question, or consider, their behavior. They either pass on what they were taught, or if they did not like what they were taught, they do the opposite. It is very rare that much consciousness is involved in this process. Most people also have the tendency to be quite self-involved; so much of what we are taught is based on what will serve the person telling us as opposed to what will serve us.

This process continues for the first five or six years of our lives by which point our basic ideas about ourselves are formed. This, of course, is a gross simplification of a very complex process, but I want to get across a few basic points about it. First, that there is a part of us that is who we truly are. Then, that through a process that is largely environmental and situational, we start to develop beliefs about what life is like and how we need to behave. The early parts of this process take place while we are still developing, so as we become able to be more conscious of our behavior, many of these patterns are already in place. Many of our behavioral choices are based on trying to avoid feelings we don't want to experience. We make these choices while we are small, dependent and helpless. Much of the instruction we get is in how not to behave and it is coming from people we are dependent on. We come into consciousness with much of this conditioning already in place.

Although this process is basically set by the time we are six years old, it continues with new information that gets added to our basic conditioning, with our basic conditioning creating the context in which we process the incoming information. We begin to have a much greater realm of input, including teachers, religious figures, media, and all the other cultural influences that tell us how we are supposed to behave. We also start to have our own ideas, but by this time our ideas are already coming from the deeper levels of conditioning we have been subjected to. In some cases we rebel against our conditioning, but if we are against something we are still being heavily affected by what we are against. We develop strong ideas about who we are, how we should behave, a moral code, ideas about what is possible for us, what is expected of us, and what we are entitled to. We begin to think that this conditioning, based on conscious and unconscious choices, patterns, strategies and reactions, is who we are. Again, I am hugely simplifying a very complex process. My goal is you accepting the hypothesis that it is highly likely that through your conditioning you think you are this set of beliefs, choices, strategies, reactions and behaviors while in truth you are something else. Let's look at what that might be.

-Chapter 2-

The Truth

Most people read a book like this because they are unhappy. There are a wide variety of experiences of this unhappiness, ranging from where you feel your life is a total disaster and you can't face another day, to where everything is just the way you think it is supposed to be, but still you are not quite satisfied. Something seems to be missing. The vast majority of people I have met exist at some level of unhappiness. I have met very few truly happy people.

My explorations have shown me that the cause of this unhappiness is our conditioned state. Most people are trying to be who they were taught to be, instead of being who they really are. The experience of trying to be someone you are not creates the feeling of unhappiness. Most people experience their conditioning as the truth, but as soon as you begin to look at this, it becomes clear that many different varieties of conditioning, many different systems of belief, and many different personal truths exist, and obviously not all of them can be true. This led my search for happiness to become a search for truth.

In this search, I found many people who told me they knew the truth, but it always required faith. I would have to believe something that I had not experienced. In my search I also came across people who said they did not know the truth, and they taught how to live with grace in a state of not knowing. In my searching and experimentation I found that the systems that taught me to believe in something also taught me how to behave; what was right and wrong, and what was good and bad. In other words, they were trying to control my behavior. On the other hand, those who were teaching how to live in a state of not knowing the truth were teaching awareness and self-responsibility.

I experimented with different beliefs. Belief is very powerful, and in my explorations I had many incredible experiences that, at the time, seemed to confirm what I had chosen to believe. There is also an incredible power of a group of people getting together to believe the same thing. It feels wonderful, but underneath I always had a lingering doubt to which the only answer was faith.

My life was much better than when I had started my search, but still, when I was alone with my uncomfortable feelings and doubts, I came to see that I had just traded in one set of beliefs for another, and though I was less unhappy, I had found a system of belief that gave me a better experience, I still had not found what I was looking for. Although it is extremely seductive, belief is not the truth.

Ultimately I became attracted to those who were teaching how to live in a state of "not knowing" by focusing on awareness and self-responsibility. I felt that these teachers were trying to set me free, but they were also telling me that I was responsible for everything I was feeling. This felt like an incredible burden and was also a terrifying notion. It is much easier to believe in something than to take responsibility for your life. Ultimately it was the quality of the feeling that won me over. Even though these teachers said they did not know the truth, they were able to guide me to a feeling that felt truer and realer than anything else I had experienced. My explorations had shown me that you might not be able to know the truth, but that you could feel it.

I have found that truth is an experience. It feels a certain way. When you have this experience it touches you deeply. Your mind may doubt it, but the feeling is there. It is indescribable, but you will know it when you have it. Once you experience this feeling of truth, you will have the possibility of the happiness I describe. I don't want you to believe this though. The point of this book is to help you have this experience yourself.

This is not an easy path. It is much easier to believe in something. There are many things out there to believe in that may give you a better experience of life than the one you currently have. Most people want to believe in something. We are all free to make our own choices about what we want to do with our lives, although through our conditioning many of us are not aware of this freedom. I am offering a very effective path for those of you who would like to get the maximum potential out of life.

My experience is that there is truth and we don't know what it is, but we can feel when we are coming closer to our truth, and the feeling is one of indescribable happiness. We can use the feeling of unhappiness as a guide to show us that we are not living our truth. Our conditioned state keeps us from our truth, and keeps us in a state of unhappiness. We can obtain a greater experience of happiness by moving towards our truth. Our maximum potential is living our truth, and the results of living our truth are feelings of joy, happiness, empowerment, and fulfillment.

Some ultimate truth of all things may exist, but that is not the concern of this book. I am trying to guide you to a deeper experience of your personal truth. By doing this, we can all come closer to what is actually real, but more important, is that each and everyone of us can live our lives with more clarity and joy.

The crux of the issue is the conflict between who you think you are and who you really are. Who you think you are exists in your mind. Who you really are—your truth—exists as an experience. My goal is to guide you to experience your truth, and if you choose to live your truth, support you to break away from your conditioning so you can have the deep experience of living you deserve.

This is not a black and white process where you are either 100 percent in your conditioning or 100 percent in your truth. It is a process of shifting your focus from your thoughts to your feelings. As you do this, your experience will change, deepen and become more wonderful, and as you continue to do this, your experience will continue to change, deepen, and become even more wonderful. You will begin to experience life as more wonderful than you could ever imagine it being.

Here we come to an important point. We begin to see that our imagination is strongly connected to our conditioning. We are limited by our imaginations. Take it as a hypothesis that you can't even imagine your truth. Part of this process will be to expand and explode your imagination about what is possible and how your life can be. This is all about experience. You will experience many things that do not seem possible. You may have a tendency to downplay and dismiss them. This is another example of your conditioning controlling your life. I encourage you to pay attention to your experience, not to your thoughts and ideas.

A concern I hear from many people, and an example of how our imaginations limit us, is the belief that it would be impossible to function in the world if one were to let go of their conditioning. My experience is that the opposite is true. It is much easier to function in the world without our conditioning blinding us to our truth. Later I will go into the many reasons for this, but now I would like to point out how, during this process, you will often think one thing will happen, and then you will experience something else. This Practice is about learning to trust your experience as a guide to your truth as opposed to your ideas and beliefs.

We can look at our truth as our purpose. The feelings of unhappiness, or things not being quite right, are the result of us not doing what we are here to do. The happiness I am referring to is a deep sense of feeling that everything is exactly as it is supposed to be. This is what we feel when we are living our purpose. This is what we feel when we are living to our maximum potential.

–Chapter 3–

Why?

As we have already seen, we are looking at a conflict between the mind (expressed as who we think we are) and our feelings (which will lead us to who we really are). I am interested in supporting you to choose to listen to your feelings. I'm not saying the mind is a bad thing. I feel just the opposite: our minds, our brains, are incredible. How our brains work and express themselves as minds and consciousness is a vast subject that we are just barely beginning to understand. I feel what I have been doing these past years is making a tiny step in the process of learning how to use this amazing gift we have been given.

In this vein it is important to address the mind. If your mind does not support the choice to shift focus to your feelings, it is not going to happen. For this reason it is important to have a point of view that supports the mind, to in turn support the choice to make your choices based on your feelings instead of your mind. As incredible as the mind is, one thing that it does not do well is make life choices. Let's look at why.

We'll start with perception and the nature of reality. When you come down to it, we don't know anything for sure. Absolutely nothing. Authorities in any subject will tell you, if you really pin them down, that they are not absolutely sure, beyond a shadow of a doubt, that what they know is true. If they don't admit this, they are either lying or considering unsubstantiated belief as truth. What we do is perceive that things have a tendency to work in a particular way; then we create a story that supports that way of things working, and use that as a theory or hypothesis to operate upon. This works pretty well. The state of our cultures' science and technology is an expression of how well this works. But there is always a margin of doubt and exceptions to the rule. Exploring these exceptions that don't fit into the accepted explanation results in advances in science and technology, but still there is always this area where we don't really know. Trying to figure it all out is a wonderful activity that attracts some people, but I feel it is a continuous game. No matter how much we figure out, there will always be something else to figure out. If we do eventually figure everything out and know everything about nature, consciousness, reality, the universe, our selves, etc. wonderful. Until then, our highest potential is in how we operate within this state of not knowing.

Most people are not very comfortable with not knowing. This discomfort is responsible for much of how things in our culture have developed the way that they have. While a relatively small number of people dedicate themselves to figuring out how things work, the vast majority search for something to believe in that will give them the illusion that they know what is happening, or at least divert them from their insecurity in not knowing. My experience is that allowing this insecurity is the beginning of the path to finding your truth, and through finding your truth, you learn to function extremely well in a reality where you don't know anything for sure.

I'd like to talk about metaphor. If you accept that we don't really know anything, you might consider that there is only metaphor. We are creating metaphors all the time. We function in metaphors. Even how we interpret what we perceive with our senses is a metaphor. Look at how different cultures perceive things differently, particularly cultures with vastly different technologies or belief systems, and how these differences in perception affect their experiences of reality. We will look more deeply at the effect of how we perceive what we perceive, and what might be possible in the realm of perception, but my point for the moment is, that though we rely on what we perceive, we would do well to remain open to the possibility that our perception may not be totally accurate, and that there may be things that are having an effect on us that we do not perceive. If this is the case, we might consider that the metaphor that we use to operate may not be the one that serves us best. This brings us to the Point of View. It is an attempt to create a metaphor that allows us to function more effectively and with more joy. If, after all, our experience of reality is linked to a metaphor, why not choose the one that works best?

In the years I spent learning all of this, I was exposed to many different metaphors, and learned different things from them. One of my teachers was very interested in the subconscious, and used looking at life and considering the effect of the subconscious to give a sense of the world and our conditioning within it. He told us that the vast majority of our brains' activity was subconscious. Somewhat like how a small percentage of an iceberg is visible, but where 10 percent of an iceberg is visible and 90 percent under the surface, less than .01 percent of our brains' activity is conscious, and more than 99.99 percent unconscious. He used various metaphors to help us understand the role of the subconscious in our lives.

One of these was that the subconscious is a bodyguard. Its primary concern is our safety. It runs all the systems in our body and makes choices based on what will keep us safe and secure. In that major aspects of our subconscious develop in our first years of life, he also used the metaphor of a four-year-old child. His experience was that the subconscious relates to the world in a very childlike way. This makes sense, as it is the choices we make with our conscious mind that define mature behavior.

He also looked at the subconscious as an autopilot. It learns how to do things, and when it is satisfied it is doing them correctly, it just continues to repeat the patterns. This is very useful as we can learn to do complex tasks, like playing an instrument or driving a car, without having to use our conscious mind, but as we will see later, this can also be dangerous. A good example of the relationship between the conscious and subconscious mind is when you go to a country where you have to drive on the other side of the road. Until you get used to it, you have to use your conscious mind to override the automatic behavior of your subconscious mind, which wants to drive on the side you are accustomed to, and will automatically switch back if you stop paying attention.

Another of this teacher's metaphors for the subconscious mind was a computer. It stores data and runs programs based on the information it has stored in its database, this database being what we have experienced, i.e. our memories. So if we put this all together, our subconscious is a childlike computer running automatic behaviors based on our memories with the goal of keeping us as safe and secure as possible. This is not a bad thing, but you will notice that feelings of happiness and fulfillment are not mentioned, and are not of particular concern to our subconscious.

This teacher then discussed the nature of memory at great length. He described how memory is not a reliable source for the decisions our subconscious is making, both because our memories are frequently inaccurate, in that they are affected by our conditioning as they are being made, and that by relying on them, we are frequently not seeing our current situation clearly. This results in us being lost in a behavioral trance controlled by our conditioning and our memories. Here, we mostly indulge in automatic behavior primarily triggered by fear of what may threaten our ideas of safety and security, which are in themselves the product of our conditioning and memory. Then he would tell us how, through this, fear becomes our primary motivating factor. In that our subconscious is primarily concerned with our safety and security, it is constantly watching for what may threaten us. But since it is using memories as a source of information, we are often afraid of things that don't actually pose a threat. He would describe this by comparing a memory to a photograph. A tiger can hurt you, but a photograph of a tiger can't hurt you. One of the childlike aspects of the subconscious is that it treats our memories as real.

This is a lot of information and a complex metaphor. What I would like you to take away from it is that most of us are allowing our subconscious to make many of our choices, and the choices are frequently based on our past experiences and motivated by fear.

As this is happening within ourselves, the same thing is happening within our culture, and has been developing as we have evolved as a species. We can look at this both individually and collectively. My teacher's metaphor paints a picture of our individual states, and we can look at the thousands of years of civilization to get a picture of our collective state. If you do, you will see that fear is most often the primary motivating factor, both individually and collectively.

Let us discuss fear for a moment. Fear is an essential part of our biological makeup. As we have seen, the subconscious is primarily concerned with our safety and security, and fear is the tool it uses to keep us from danger. What isn't working is that (through these processes I am describing) we have become afraid of things that don't actually pose a threat. We need to make a distinction between the useful fear that keeps us out of actual danger, and the imagined or conditioned fear that keeps us from things we only think are dangerous. My experience is the vast majority of fear most people experience is the imagined kind, so when I use the word "fear", I will be referring to the imagined kind. If I am referring to fear of actual danger, I will call it "useful fear" or "rational fear".

Your relationship to fear is a major aspect of the Point of View that I am presenting, and key to finding freedom and happiness. We will look at this in great depth. For the moment, however, we are focusing on the effect of fear (both real and imagined) on our culture.

We have an instinct for survival that dictates many of our actions, but as our brains evolved, we began to develop both the ability to override our survival instincts, and fear for things beyond what was immediately threatening our survival. We see through the history of religion and belief that it developed primarily in response to our fear of the unknown. Starting at the tribal level, a story would develop to explain why things were the way they were, and some people would take on the role of the keepers and interpreters of that story. When the fear of the unknown became acute, they would be whom you would go to for answers.

This changed radically as we became better at survival and we began to develop surplus goods. The history of religion and government show that it is completely entwined with the existence of surplus or wealth. It was with the growth and increase in wealth that hierarchical religion and government developed and expanded. At some point in this process, the people who had taken the role of responsibility began to separate themselves from the rest of the people, and began to use fear to control and manipulate them. This is a huge subject that could fill lifetimes of research, but at even the most cursory glance it becomes obvious that the goal of religions, governments, belief systems, culture for that matter, is to create people who behave according to a specific set of rules.

This is our cultural conditioning, and if you look at most cultural conditioning, it is based on creating obedience in its believers. Many different cultural conditionings are in effect on the planet. Most of them are based in controlling the behavior of the adherents. If you begin to study them, you will find aspects designed to create feelings of dependence, duty, disempowerment, helplessness, and a wide variety of other feelings that do not serve the individual. Any thoughts you have that it has to be this way are just part of this conditioning. Something else is possible.

Through this chapter I would like you to have a deeper sense of the state that most of us are in, both individually and culturally. I find an understanding of it useful in the process of disconnecting from it. This individual and cultural conditioning is deeply imbedded in our systems, and breaking free from it is not easy, but it is possible, and the benefits of doing it are indescribable. It is like waking up and seeing that most everyone else is asleep. If you find your mind asking how you could live like that, realize that this is your conditioning speaking, and the truth is that it is much easier to live if you are more aware of what is actually happening.

In my search for happiness I came across many different possible paths and soon began to see that most of them were belief systems that were ultimately trying to control me. In the midst of this I found several teachers who were trying to set me free, and they were all saying more or less the same thing. They used different approaches and metaphors, but all of them were trying to guide me to the same place, where I am in turn trying to guide you.

Over the years I have created my own metaphor and approach. If this approach appeals to you, great. If not, great, but even if not, I encourage you to choose freedom. We are literally slaves to our conditioning, and the state of the planet is the result of this. My experience is that the most effective thing you can do is to find your truth, which is your freedom. The only things that are keeping you from this freedom are your ideas and beliefs about yourself that are the products of your individual and collective conditioning. Let's change that.

Just as a note, though I learned much from the teacher who shared the metaphor of the subconscious, enough to feel it useful to share this extremely abbreviated version of it, I don't use this term in my practice anymore. I prefer to use the term "unconscious" for those aspects of our mind we are not conscious of, and will from here on.

-Chapter 4-

The Point of View
and the Deep Living Practice

To present my information as efficiently and effectively as possible, I am
breaking it down into two parts. One is a way of looking at life that I will
refer to as the Point of View, and the other is a personal practice that I
will refer to as the Deep Living Practice.

The Point of View is food for the mind. It is essential to address the
concerns of the mind if we want to break away from the effects of our
conditioning. This Point of View showed me that there was an alternative.
It showed me that things did not have to be the way I thought they were.
It created a context in which I was able to transform my life from one of
suffering to one of joy. This Point of View is a large part of what this book
is about. What I have already written is part of this Point of View and I
will continue to expand upon it. If you adhere to this Point of View you
will always know what path to take in order to come closer to your truth,
instead of continuing to allow your conditioning to control your life.

I am very aware of the dangers of belief, and I can see how this Point of
View can be seen as a system of belief. I encourage you to look at this
Point of View as a tool. It is a transitional phase. It is very hard to see
your conditioning from the state of believing it. We can look at this Point
of View as a bridge between who you think you are and who you really
are. It gives you a perspective outside of your conditioning to help you

see your conditioning for what it is, and the possibility to make choices outside the influence of your conditioning. For this it is extremely valuable, but it is important not to take it too seriously. One aspect of this Point of View is that it is not true. It is a tool designed to help you find your truth.

The other part of what I offer is the Deep Living Practice. I encourage you to choose to begin a personal practice to find your truth, your power, your joy, and your happiness. One of my teachers used to say over and over, "Your true gains come from your personal practice." This is also my experience.

There is no set Practice that I recommend. Your Practice is personal and my ultimate goal is to support you to be able to create a continuing Practice that will allow you to keep coming closer and closer to your personal truth and experience the joy in life that this affords. There are some basic things that I find useful for most everyone I work with, and I will suggest you start with these, but I will be making many suggestions and presenting many effective exercises and specific practices I have learned and developed over the years. I encourage you to experiment and play with these to find out what works for you and what supports you the best. Later I will also make suggestions how you might organize your overall Deep Living Practice at different stages of your process.

It is useful to look at your commitment to your Practice. The more energy you put into your Practice, the more you will get out of it. We will be looking at many "fine lines" as we continue, and this is the first. On the one hand you need to pursue your Practice actively in order to achieve results, but on the other hand it is a Practice to find joy and happiness in your life, and you can't do this if you are too strict with yourself, or pushing too hard. One of the goals of the Deep Living Practice is to learn to walk these "fine lines", but for the moment, just be aware and watch your relationship to your Practice.

Looking at relationships in your life is part of the Deep Living Practice, so looking at your relationship to your Practice itself is a great place to start. It doesn't have to be hard. That idea comes from conditioning. I encourage you to have fun with your Practice and be playful. It may be outside your imagination how to do this, but open up to the possibility, and I will do my best to help.

Many aspects of the specific practices I suggest are very challenging. Many of the most effective practices are the most challenging, but they all can be fun if you allow them to be. One of my favorite analogies is that of the roller coaster. You can be on a roller coaster screaming in joy and delight, or screaming in mortal terror. It's the same you and the same roller coaster, only two different ways to be in relationship to what is happening. Part of what the Deep Living Practice will show us is that we have a choice in how we are in relationship to what is happening, and it will teach us to exercise that choice. A good place to start is with the Practice itself.

At the beginning I encourage you to designate some amount of time each day for your Practice, and then continue to experiment with doing more or less until you find what works for you. Realize that this is a continuous process and keep adjusting the amount of time you put into it to maintain a feeling that you are actively pursuing it without pushing too hard. If you can start to have fun with your Practice you will naturally want to spend more time with it. Also as you begin to experience the results, you might feel like doing more. At the same time, if you feel like taking a break, take a break.

I also find it very useful to integrate your Practice into your life. You don't have to set much time apart to practice. While some of the exercises and beginning practices are easiest to do alone in a quiet environment, most of the practices can best be done while you are going about your life, and actually many of them are more effective that way. Play with this and experiment.

As we go forward I encourage you to accept the Point of View as a hypothesis and play with it in relation to what you are experiencing in life. If you do this, you will see it is a path to a greater sense of freedom and possibility than you have previously experienced. Start to create, and develop, your Deep Living Practice in order to translate the ideas I am conveying into experiences. Even though I am expressing myself in ideas, I am writing this to share an experience, and in order to have that experience, you will need to play with these ideas.

-Chapter 5-

Honesty, Courage, and Consciousness

In my search for happiness and contentment, many of the paths I explored offered practices that I did not find very effective. Some would ask me to do things I found impossible, like giving up my conditioning by simply deciding to in an instant. Others would offer a practice that took many years to achieve results. Some were extremely expensive. Some paths were very vague and I found most teachers quite remote. I am interested in offering a way that is as easy to understand and accomplish as possible. This is not to say that it is easy, but I have created an approach that anyone can do if they apply themselves.

One of the ways I have accomplished this is by breaking the process down into achievable parts, and by making sure we focus on the things that will have the greatest permanent effect in the shortest amount of time. I have found that the most effective way to begin your personal Practice is to focus on honesty, courage, and consciousness. I have made this the core of the Deep Living Practice. Let's look at each of these aspects briefly.

When I talk about honesty I am referring to your personal truth. We have discussed how we are conditioned to believe we are someone we are not, and that there is another aspect that is who we really are. This is what is honest. Everything else is a lie. This may seem like a radical way of looking at things, but it is a very effective way of looking at life, if you want to find your truth. You can't accept the lie if you want to find your truth.

This also makes honesty a very challenging practice. My experience is that it is a gradual process. We start with the concept, and as we apply it, we find deeper and deeper levels of dishonesty within us. One thing that makes this practice so challenging is that most of us are conditioned to be dishonest. We live in a very dishonest culture. Look at politics and media. Most all of us have experienced dishonesty as a successful strategy. My experience though is that, in the long term, honesty is essential to happiness.

Your conditioning is not your truth; therefore it is a lie. Truth is a wonderful feeling. This is a feeling you will never have if you are living a lie. If you are living a lie, real intimacy is impossible. As you dive deeper into this practice you will find that most thoughts you think are lies. Most words out of your mouth are lies. Our conditioning is embedded so incredibly deeply in our systems. The practice of honesty is the choice to become free of your conditioning.

The practice of honesty can frequently result in some devastating moments. The realization that you can't trust your thoughts or that you are incapable of speaking your truth can be shattering, but if you stay with your practice of honesty you will see that the results are very much worth it. Once you get over the initial challenges, living honestly is incredibly easy. You don't have to think to be honest. As you become more honest, you are able to see dishonesty in others much more clearly. It is with honesty where the Deep Living Practice really begins.

The next basic aspect of the Deep Living Practice is courage. We have already begun the discussion of how most of us let fear control our behavior. This is something we will continue to look at in great depth. Courage is not the absence of fear. Courage is the practice of not allowing fear to control your behavior. This is a core part of the Deep Living Practice, and courage is very much a practice. It is not that you were given some amount of courage at birth. The more you practice courage, the better you get at it.

Courage is what makes wonderful lives. If you look at the biographies of people who have had great effect in the world, you will see that it is the acts of courage that made their lives what they were. The practice of courage is essential to fully taking advantage of the potential of your life. When we start to look at the nature of fear, we see that the other side of fear is excitement. We can use the metaphor of the roller coaster again. When we fight the experience we feel fear, when we accept the experience we feel excitement. We will go deeply into how to create a Practice that will allow you to live courageously, and transform a fear-based existence into an exciting life.

The third primary aspect of the Deep Living Practice is consciousness. This aspect is really the most important. Ultimately this becomes a practice of consciousness. I have found that no matter what the problem is, being more conscious is usually the solution. Consciousness is a hard thing to define, but at the moment we will consider it as simply paying attention. I will be offering you many ways to effectively practice consciousness, but at the beginning of the Deep Living Practice, I find it most effective to focus on honesty and courage.

–Chapter 6–

Self-Responsibility

To find power, joy, and fulfillment in your life, you must take complete self-responsibility. Taking complete self-responsibility means that you accept that the choices you are making, both consciously and unconsciously, are what are creating your experience of reality. At first this struck me as an esoteric concept, but as I explored and practiced self-responsibility over the years, I have found it to be one of the most practical pieces of information I have learned. Self-responsibility is a practice. The more you do it, the better you get at it, and your experience of the effects of taking responsibility for yourself will continue to grow and deepen.

In giving away our responsibility, we give away our power. This is a challenging concept for many people, and quite a few have decided not to take responsibility for themselves, simply because they don't want to. As I mentioned earlier, many people want to be told what to do. They want to be given something to believe in that will solve all of their problems. My experience is that by giving up our self-responsibility we give up our power, our freedom, and our ability to make choices based on what will bring us to our maximum potential.

The way to begin the practice of self-responsibility is to resist the temptation to blame outside sources for what you are experiencing. As you start to pay attention to what is going on in your mind, you will probably notice how powerful this temptation is. Many aspects of our conditioning encourage us to give up responsibility, and therefore give up our power.

Our conditioning is largely concerned with keeping us weak, obedient, and controllable, and leading us to give up responsibility for ourselves is one of the major ways our conditioning achieves this.

Part of taking complete self-responsibility is accepting that it is impossible to do something that you do not want to do. This is a difficult thing for many people to accept, but if you really consider it, and are willing to take responsibility for yourself, you will see that whatever it is that you are doing, at least 51 percent of you wants to be doing. If you are reading this book, it is because at least 51 percent of you wants to be reading the book. As soon as 51 percent of you wants to be doing something else, you will be doing that. It is easy to lie to yourself, and tell yourself you want to be doing something else, but if you are doing anything, at least 51 percent of yourself wants to be doing it. Sometimes we are conflicted. Part of us may want to be doing something else, but believing in that smaller part of yourself that is just wanting, instead of the larger part that is actually doing, is deluding yourself and keeps you from realizing your truth. We will look at the ramifications of this in great detail, but for the moment, consider accepting it.

Taking self-responsibility is part of growing up, and many people don't want to grow up. They feel they need a parent figure to take responsibility for them. When we leave our actual parents, our conditioning teaches us to shift our feelings of dependence to another parent figure, and encourages obedience instead of the independence and the self-determination of self-responsibility. Most couples I work with have parent projections on their partners. Many people have parent projections on their bosses, teachers, religious leaders, or therapists.

I would like you to consider taking complete self-responsibility even though part of you may not want to. The feelings of freedom and power you will experience through taking self-responsibility are so much more wonderful than the feelings of safety and security you may experience through giving it up. Once you have experienced the feeling of self-responsibility, you will become aware of how tight and limited you feel when you don't take it. Most of us have never had the experience of self-responsibility. This constricted, closed, childish feeling of having someone take care of us is all we know and all we want.

We have a tendency to find the familiar comfortable, but when we expand our experience, we often find that there is much more available for us than we knew was possible. Then the familiar feels extremely limiting and not comfortable at all. This is a Practice of experience, so I encourage you to give it a try and have the experience for yourself.

By taking complete self-responsibility you reclaim the ability to transform your life. If you want to reach your maximum potential, if you want to experience the happiness and fulfillment of living your deepest truth, taking responsibility for what you are experiencing is an essential part of the process.

–Chapter 7–

Feelings

After we have decided to find our truth, one of the first things we look at is our feelings. It is through feeling our feelings that we find our truth. My experience is that most people do not know how to feel their feelings. Most of us have been taught not to feel our feelings. We are taught to use our minds, but not encouraged to feel deeply and let our feelings guide us. The process of learning to feel and interpret your feelings is a key aspect of the Deep Living Practice.

Most people have been taught to repress their feelings. They do this as best they can, then occasionally their feelings get too powerful for them to repress, and their feelings burst out. Interestingly, I have found that allowing our feelings to burst out uncontrollably is also a way to *not* feel our feelings. I refer to this as "going over the top" of your feelings or "going unconscious" with your feelings. This means, for example, that if anger is coming up, and you start to yell or go hit a pillow or a person, you are doing this to avoid really feeling your anger. If sadness comes up and you break into hysterical crying, this is a way to avoid actually feeling your sadness. The pressure of the feeling builds. You do something to release the pressure. Then you don't have to keep feeling the feeling. I also sometimes refer to this state of going over the top of a feeling as "collapsing" into the feeling. I use these different metaphors to help describe the way a person avoids a feeling. The key is that they are doing something to avoid feeling the feeling.

I've discovered a very specific state in which you are fully allowing what you are feeling without going over the top of it, or collapsing into it. Learning to come into this state is one of the most valuable things you can learn in life. This is one of the first things I teach people who come to work with me. Learning to feel your feelings is a key step to finding your truth.

I've worked with many people but have yet to have someone come to me who already knew how to feel their feelings. Some people pick it up very quickly; others take a while. I have not met anyone who wanted to learn it that was not able to. While it is nice to have someone help you learn how to feel your feelings, it is not necessary. You can learn this by yourself. The important part is knowing that this state exists and then choosing to find it. We will discuss how to learn to feel your feelings later in the book.

The teacher who taught me the importance of learning to feel your feelings only told me about it, and then sent me off to find how to do it by myself. One of his helpful remarks was that it was a knack, like riding a bicycle. This is a good analogy, and like riding a bicycle, once you get it, you've got it. You know how to do it, and you can do it whenever you want, though the more you practice, the better you get at it. It is also a good analogy in terms of doing it by yourself. You can learn to ride a bicycle by yourself, but it is much easier with someone helping. I have found that if you make a determined choice to do something, the help you need will be there. I highly encourage you to make the choice to feel your feelings. It is a crucial part of the Deep Living Practice.

Feeling your feelings is also part of being honest and self-responsible. Many of us find it challenging to be honest with ourselves, not to mention with others, about what we are really feeling. This is a result of the conditioning that feelings are messy and best avoided. You might be tempted to blame others for what you are feeling. This is the time to practice self-responsibility. Start considering the idea that you are responsible for everything you are feeling.

It is not easy for most people to learn to feel their feelings. It usually goes against their conditioning. Learning to feel your feelings will be one of the steps you will be taking to break away from your conditioning, and stop allowing it to control your behavior. Once you learn to feel your feelings, you can learn to interpret them. A huge amount of information is available in your feelings. After you learn to understand your feelings, you can allow them to guide you. Whereas your conditioning does not guide you towards happiness, fulfillment, your truth and your maximum potential, your feelings will take you directly there.

I make a distinction between feelings and emotions, and as you will see as we continue, an important part of this Practice is being aware of what you mean by the words you say. When I use the word "feelings", I mean the sensations we are experiencing in the moment. When I use the word "emotion", I am talking about the labels our conditioning puts on those feelings. For most people anger and hate are bad, joy and caring are good. Lust can be good or bad depending on the situation. These are judgments that are heavily affected by our conditioning. I use these words (anger, joy, lust, etc.) when I am talking about feelings, as they prove useful in guiding attention to different qualities of feeling, but I would like you to consider that feelings are just feelings, there are no good or bad feelings, only conditioned judgments of feelings, or judgments about what people do when they are feeling certain feelings.

If you remember, a major part of how we develop our patterns and strategies is in finding ways to avoid things we do not want to feel. I have found that the way to break free of these patterns and strategies is to choose to feel these feelings. By doing this we achieve the practical experience that feeling the feeling is not as bad as we thought it was going to be. It is certainly not worth the consequences caused by what we do to avoid the feeling. It is part of what makes this Practice challenging. In the early stages, it is based on feeling feelings that you have spent most of your life trying not to feel.

I developed much of this work through my study and practice of trauma resolution. I found the principles behind the form of trauma resolution I studied had applications far beyond the applied practice. It is in this zone of truly feeling a feeling where trauma resolves. After working with this for many years, I found that it is in this state of really feeling your feelings, where life is incredibly rich. This is what I am referring to when I use the term "Deep Living".

Once you learn to allow your feelings, you will see that they are constantly changing. My experience is that as soon as you truly allow a feeling, it changes into another feeling. Life is a very dynamic experience where one feeling arises out of another in response to what is happening. I use the word arise because this is how it feels to me. Each feeling comes up from a deeper place within us than the previous feeling. It is important not to hold on to whatever you are feeling and let the new feeling take over. It is when we resist a feeling that we get stuck with the frustrating experience of fighting a feeling that wants to arise. Once we learn to allow the flow of our feelings, the next step is to learn to interpret them. It is like learning a new language. Again, I believe it is one of the most valuable things you can learn in life.

Earlier I mentioned that the mind is not good at making life choices. Your feelings, on the other hand, are excellent at it. They will guide you to an incredible experience of life. Everything becomes simple and clear. Confusion only exists in the mind. You will begin to experience your feelings as an inner voice. This is the voice of your truth, and when you find your truth, you have what you need to live the life you were meant to live.

–Chapter 8–

The Pelvis

As we start to allow our feelings, many people become very uncomfortable and scared. People tell me they feel overwhelmed and their feelings are too much for them. Our feelings are our experience of life, so when I hear this, I am hearing the person tell me that life is too much for him or her. If we want to have the full experience of life, we need to address this.

One of the most powerful techniques to support you to stay present when you have intense feelings is to connect to your pelvis. This may sound too simple, but it is extremely effective and a core aspect of the Practice. It is also one of the first specific practices I recommend for most people, as it allows them to start experiencing their feelings without becoming overwhelmed. The pelvis is a very powerful part of our bodies. We will discuss the reasons behind this more later, but for the moment I am interested in starting the practice of bringing your attention there.

With the term "pelvis" I am referring to the area that starts where your legs connect to your body and goes to the top of the bones you feel when you put your hands on your hips. This area includes the hips, genitals, anus, and buttocks, and is defined by the bony structure that supports it. Most people pay very little attention to this part of the body, and culturally we are encouraged to cover it, not talk about it, not touch it and not look at it. It is considered taboo. There are reasons for this. Our conditioning has developed to keep us feeling helpless, powerless, and obedient. Keeping us disconnected from our pelvis makes us feel this way.

Here is the first of many specific practices and exercises I will present as part of the overall Deep Living Practice. As I mentioned, I am much more interested in you experiencing, rather than just absorbing, my information. It is through these specific practices and exercises that you will have these experiences. When I label something a "practice", it is something I recommend that you do frequently and integrate into your life. These are skills that you can develop that will help you get more out of your life. Many early practices are foundations for later practices. I will go more deeply into how to develop your overall Deep Living Practice as this book progresses. Exercises are more short term and meant to give you a specific experience. Once you get that experience you can move on. There will be many exercises and practices in the book, and I encourage you to do them if you want to get the most out of the information I am presenting.

> *Practice: Feel the Pelvis*
>
> *As a first step, close your eyes and feel your pelvis. What feelings arise in you? Many people feel emptiness or numbness when they do this. This is the feeling of disassociation. Some people feel tension. This is common and over time I will show you ways to relax here. This may seem too simple to do any good, but if you do this frequently you will begin to notice more feelings and that the feelings change over time. Do this for at least 30 seconds at least four to five times a day.*

As you become more familiar with your pelvis you will begin to notice you feel different things in different parts of your pelvis. It is particularly useful to learn to bring your attention to your pelvic floor. This is the area between your sitting bones from the bottom of your genitals to your tailbone. A specific point in the pelvic floor that I encourage you to focus your attention on is called the perineum. This is the tiny area right between your anus and your genitals. I will talk more about the importance of this area later, but for the moment let us start the practice of putting our attention there.

> *Practice: Feel the Perineum*
>
> *Bring your attention to your perineum. Feel how you are feeling there. Do this for three to five seconds three to four times an hour. It is much more effective to do these awareness practices*

frequently for short periods of time than to do them infrequently for longer periods.

If you have a hard time connecting with your perineum, I suggest you spend some time touching it to support the process. Lie down naked and touch your perineum with the tip of your middle finger. Make small slow circles gently massaging your perineum. Play with the feeling of touching your finger with your perineum instead of your finger touching your perineum.

Here is a more dynamic pelvic practice.

Practice: Balance and Center

Sit and bring your attention to your pelvis. Feel your sitting bones on the seat beneath you. Gently rock side to side, feeling your weight shift from one sitting bone to the other. Let the rocking motion become smaller and smaller until you feel your weight equally balanced between your two sitting bones. Then begin tilting your pelvis forward and backward in nice big movements. Move with your breath allowing your spine to arch as you inhale and tilt the top of your pelvis forward, then round as you exhale and tilt the top of your pelvis backward. After three to four repetitions of these big movements, allow each repetition to get smaller and smaller, until you find a sense of center. As you are almost at center you will probably feel a tendency for your spine to readjust in relation to your pelvis. Allow this to happen. Then take a deep inhalation and, as you exhale, let your spine and torso relax into your pelvis. Get into the practice of doing this when you first sit down, and then occasionally if you are sitting for long periods.

Here is an exercise that will bring your awareness to your pelvis.

Exercise: Pelvis Visualization

You can read this first and do it from memory, have someone read it to you, or record it and do it as you listen to the playback.

Come into a comfortable seated position and close your eyes. Do the Balance and Center Practice. Bring your attention to your pelvis. Feel the bony structure of your pelvis. Feel how it makes the shape of a bowl. Direct your attention to this bowl. Now we are going to create a metaphor of how your pelvis feels. We are going to create the metaphor of a landscape. If you find this hard to do, just feel how it feels to try to do it. After trying several times you will probably be able to do it.

As you feel the bowl of your pelvis, allow an image of a landscape to come into your imagination. What kind of landscape is it? Spend some time imagining this landscape and fill it with details. The more details the better. What is the terrain like? Is there vegetation and what is it like? What is the sky like? What time of day is it? What time of year? What is the weather like? Is the landscape inhabited? Stay with it for several minutes and continue to notice the details. After a few minutes, imagine yourself in this landscape. How does it feel? What is the mood? Move around and explore the landscape of your pelvis. See if you can discover more details while constantly being aware of how it feels to inhabit your pelvis. Now look for your perineum. What aspect of your pelvic landscape is your perineum, and how does it feel to discover it and be close to it? Stay with these feelings for a few moments.

Open your eyes and write down a brief description of the landscape of your pelvis including the most memorable details and feelings you had during the exercise. Be sure to include what your perineum was and how you felt about it. I find this exercise a very effective way to get someone to describe their relationship to their pelvis. Do this exercise every month or so and notice how the landscape and the feelings change as you continue your Practice.

I can't emphasize enough the importance of being able to be firmly in your pelvis. It is a basic part of the Deep Living Practice and will allow you to stay centered, balanced, calm, and present no matter what is going on in you or around you. Remember that this is a practice. The more you do and master the practices I suggest, the more results you will experience in your life. All of the things I recommend are highly effective and I strongly suggest you choose to do them. Find your self. Find your truth. Find your maximum potential.

–Chapter 9–

Internal Dialogue

In the Deep Living Practice we find the truth of who we really are and let go of the conditioning that informs who we think we are. On the path to this truth, we will be learning to feel and interpret our feelings. At the same time it is necessary to actively bring our attention to our conditioning and choose to disconnect from it. This becomes another element of our Practice.

Our conditioning expresses itself in our thoughts. Again, I am in no way against the mind. I find the mind and brain incredible beyond description. We can do many wonderful things like design, plan, imagine, create, communicate, the list goes on and on, but as I discussed in a previous chapter, our minds have been conditioned in such a way that they make life choices that do not support our happiness and maximum potential. An important part of the Deep Living Practice is to learn to tell the difference between what aspects of your mind support your joy and happiness and what parts don't, then learn to support the parts that do and either let go of the parts that don't, or transform them so they support your goals.

This is challenging because it is very hard to see your conditioning from inside your conditioning. Adopting the Point of View is helpful in letting go of your conditioned state. Learning to feel your feelings and let them guide you gives you an alternative to being guided by your conditioned state. What I would like to look at now is identifying your conditioning so you can begin the process of making the choice of where it serves you and where it does not, instead of blindly believing in it.

An excellent way to begin the process of identifying your conditioning is to bring awareness to your internal dialogue. By "internal dialogue" I mean the voice in your head that, in most of us, is constantly thinking, figuring, commenting, judging, fantasizing, imagining, singing, babbling, and doing all the other things our minds do. Some people have multiple layers of internal dialogue going on simultaneously. Many people think they *are* their internal dialogue. Our first step is to let go of this idea. You are not this stream of thoughts. This stream of thoughts is largely the product of your conditioning, and to separate the supportive from the non-supportive parts of this, we must start paying attention to it.

Practice: Create a Witness

The first step in bringing awareness to your internal dialogue is to create a new voice in your mind whose role is to pay attention to the other voice, or voices, in your mind. We will refer to this voice as the "witness". When we start this practice there is very little difference between the witness and the other voices, but over time our witness will change and our relationship to our witness will change. Do this as often as you can until you relate more to the witness than to the other voice, or voices, of your internal dialogue.

Practice: Splitting Focus

To create a witness in our internal dialogue, we need to split our focus. Splitting focus is an extremely powerful and effective life tool that we will be using in several parts of our Practice. It is worth practicing for its own sake, as becoming good at it will make creating a witness, and quite a few other practices, much easier. This is something we all do frequently, but if we begin to practice it consciously we can get much better at it. I recommend integrating this practice into your life and doing it while you are waiting, traveling, or in situations where you have some time between activities that require more directed attention.

To do this practice, simply pay attention to more than one thing at a time. An easy way to start is to do it across senses. Listen to one thing while looking at something unrelated, or feel something with your hand while tasting something with your mouth. As you continue the practice, start focusing on two different things with the same sense. This is a bit more challenging but quite achievable with a little practice.

Continue challenging yourself by paying attention to more than two things at a time and using multiple senses. You will notice that as you do more challenging things, you will start to feel some strain. This is the same kind of strain as when you exercise a muscle, so treat it that way. You need to feel a little strain to grow, but don't push yourself too hard. As you get better at splitting focus, play with both how long you can maintain paying attention to multiple objects, and how many different ways you can split your focus simultaneously. This is a foundational practice of consciousness. There are no limits to how good you can get at it, and though it may not be apparent to you, the gains that you obtain through this are well worth the time put in developing the skill.

Exercise: Speak Your Internal Dialogue

A useful exercise to support getting in touch with your internal dialogue is to say your internal dialogue out loud. When you are alone, and not concerned about being heard, sit and face a blank wall. Say the things running through your mind out loud. Most people find this difficult to do, but stick with it until you are able to do it. At first just say whatever is on your mind. As you get more comfortable with this, begin to listen to what you are saying. Do this exercise for at least 15 minutes at a time. Do it several times until you are able to do it easily. It can also be interesting to record this and listen to it later to get into the practice of observing this voice.

As you become aware of your internal dialogue you will notice that there is a difference between what is going on in your mind and what you say to others. In line with the honesty part of the Deep Living Practice, it is vital to share your internal dialogue. For most people this is a scary proposition and requires courage. This is an interesting transitional time, as what you will be sharing is not who you really are, but you will be becoming more honest about your conditioning. It is essential to accept and feel the effects of your conditioning if you are going to let go of it.

Practice: Sharing Your Internal Dialogue

This is an exciting practice that requires other people. Some people enjoy doing this with friends, but for others it is too scary and they prefer to do it with people they do not know so well. It may seem hard to organize this, but it really isn't. Just approach someone and explain the practice; then set a fixed time to do it. Many people will be afraid to do this, but I have found that there are also many people who really want the opportunity to be more honest and to be with people who are practicing honesty. I have seen many long-term friendships and relationships begin with this sharing practice. You may first want to try it with one other person, but it is also very effective to practice in small groups. If you decide to do this practice in a group I suggest the group be a maximum of eight people. When the groups get larger than that, they become unwieldy.

When doing this practice, I suggest starting with eyes closed and tuning into your internal dialogue. When you feel ready, open your eyes and begin to share what is going on in your mind as honestly as you can. Avoid the temptation to think about what you want to say and just talk. This is also an excellent time to practice listening when others are talking and noticing your reactions and responses to what they are saying, which you can then share as honestly as possible. Practice stopping editing what you say and being as direct as you can.

This is a powerful practice that offers the potential to learn many things about yourself as you continue with it. For most people it starts as a practice of courage, as they are afraid to talk at all. Once you become more comfortable, start using your witness to watch what you are saying, and see if you are being as honest and direct as you possibly can. Many times we have lies in our lives that we have told so many times we have accepted them as true. If this is the case, see if you can notice them and be honest instead. Notice if you use modifying words to make what you are saying less direct. Look if there are things you are afraid to say. Look at why you are saying what you are saying. Frequently we have a hidden agenda, and we are saying what we are saying to manipulate how people perceive us and what they think of us. There are many opportunities to practice honesty, courage, and consciousness as you are sharing your internal dialogue.

Play with staying in the present with what you are saying. Avoid telling stories. Share what you are feeling. Pay attention to the difference between someone sharing their feelings and talking about their thoughts. You will start to notice how interesting feelings are and how much less interesting most thoughts and behavioral strategies are.

Start to practice really paying attention to people when they are talking. Notice if they are being honest and direct, or if they are indulging in behavioral strategies. Watch how some topics make people quite reactive, and see if they take responsibility for their reactions, or if they blame others for what they are feeling.

These sharing groups are a great place for many aspects of our Practice. I will go into this more later. It is also a very useful way to cultivate a group of people to practice with. You can achieve much by practicing alone, but ultimately this is a Practice of how to be in the world. The world is full of people, so I highly recommend you find some to play with. Creating sharing groups is an excellent way to establish relationships with people.

We got a bit ahead of ourselves with the potential of sharing groups. For the moment I would like to keep our focus on sharing our internal dialogue. By doing this we will become more aware of the effect the dialogue is having in our lives. We will begin to see how automatic and reactive much of our behavior is, and we will start to get a sense of all the bits and pieces that create our mental construction. It can be very uncomfortable to face some of these things, but it is essential to recognize and accept something if you are going to transform it. Most of us are unconscious of the effects our conditioning has on us, and in that unconsciousness we are powerless to change it. I highly encourage you to become aware of your internal dialogue and start learning about your conditioning.

-Chapter 10-

Choice

As we get deeper into our practice of self-responsibility, we begin to see the importance of choice. We see that the choices we make create our experience of reality. As we realize this, it becomes obvious how important it is to be conscious of our choices.

If we go back to looking at how our conditioning develops, we see that as we are learning how to be in the world we make choices, based on our experience, on how to behave in order to get the things we want and avoid the things we don't. Most of these choices are based on feelings. We want to feel nourished, loved, cared for, entertained, and safe. We don't want to feel hunger, pain, helplessness, fear, loneliness, boredom, or threatened. As we develop, we figure out how to create the best life we can.

These choices are highly affected by whatever environment we are in. Some strategies work in some situations and don't work in others. The choices behind these strategies become fundamental aspects of our behavioral patterns. If you are in a family with lots of siblings, you may choose to become loud in order to be noticed, whereas if you are around someone who has a tendency to be violent you may choose to become quiet in order not to be noticed. We are quite amazing beings, and usually we make choices to create effective strategies, although some people create better strategies than others. Where this stops serving us is that most adults continue the strategies that worked when they were children, even though the conditions have changed. Most people don't even see them as strategies and behavioral patterns. They think that this collection of choices they made as children is who they are.

This is why our practice of consciousness is so valuable. Most of us have forgotten that we are making the choices behind our behavior. Most of us are unconscious of this whole process. Bringing consciousness to these choices, and making different choices, is the basis of the Deep Living Practice. It is how we can permanently transform our lives. Our choices are behind our concept of who we are and our perception of reality. By becoming conscious of these choices, we can create a perception of reality that supports our happiness, fulfillment and ability to reach our full potential.

A major part of developing an effective Deep Living Practice is learning to identify the choices behind what you are experiencing as real. We learn to do this through a combination of practicing honesty and learning to feel our feelings. Then we need to learn how to make different choices and which different choices to make. This will involve courage, consciousness, and learning to feel our feelings and let them guide us.

As we proceed with our Practice, our goal is to create situations where you are confronted with the choices you made when you were young, and then have the opportunity to make different choices. These are the moments when transformation happens. Much of the early Deep Living Practice is to prepare to be aware of these moments when they arise, and to be able to make conscious choices when they do. This is easier said than done, but it is something you can learn to do. The more you practice it, the better you get at it, and when you have mastered this, you will be able to create an experience of life that is unimaginably wonderful. It is unimaginable because your imagination is limited by your conditioning, which was created by the choices you are still unconscious of. If you pursue this Practice, you will frequently expand and sometimes explode your imagination. Then you will experience what I mean.

This is a good time to bring up the subject of being present, meaning being conscious of what is actually happening in the moment. Most people are not very present. We have the tendency to rely more on our experience of what has happened in the past to make our choices, rather than relying on what we are actually perceiving at a given time. We tend to put more focus on our internal dialogue than we do to the input of our senses. Our conditioning also affects our perception, which keeps us from perceiving with clarity.

As with so many things, presence is an experience, and many people have many different experiences of presence. My experience of presence has changed and deepened radically over my years of practice. I found that the experience of presence I gained through trying to be present was not very deep compared to the experience of presence I gained through looking at my choices not to be present. I will go into this in detail later, but I bring it up now for two reasons. One is to support the understanding that one of the main reasons our choices are not serving us is that they were made in the past and were based on what was happening when they were made. Part of the Deep Living Practice is to learn to make your choices based on what is happening now instead of what happened when you were a child. The other is to realize that to transform yourself, you must make your choices in the present. Many of us are addicted to automatic behavior. We go through life unconsciously reacting to what is happening, paying no attention whatsoever to the choices we are making. To transform we must become aware of the choice we are making in the moment, and have the experience of the effect of making a different choice.

The Deep Living Practice is all about choices. It's about being honest and taking responsibility for your choices. It is about having the courage to experiment with making different choices, even though your conditioning is telling you not to. It is about being conscious of when you are making choices, which is all the time, and becoming aware of what choices you want to experiment with. It is about feeling the experience caused by the choices you make and finding which choices will bring you the experience of your deepest truth and maximum potential.

As you continue this Practice, you will often feel that you come to a fork in the road. There will be the familiar path that you usually take. You will decide not to take it, but very often you will not know how to take a different path. This point comes up frequently when I work with people. The unsatisfying answer I give to the question, "How do I do it?" is, "It is the choice to do it. Find the choice within yourself." I will explain this more later, but if you want to find these choices, it's time to start looking for them.

-Chapter 11-

Starting Your Practice

When you first begin the Deep Living Practice, I suggest you split your time between fundamental practices and active practices. Fundamental practices support you in doing the active practices more easily and effectively. The active practices support you to come closer to your truth and your maximum potential.

I have already suggested some practices that bring your consciousness into your pelvis. The purpose of bringing your consciousness into your pelvis is to support you to be able to feel your feelings, so let's jump right in.

> *Practice: Pay Attention to Your Feeling Centers*
>
> *We begin our practice of feeling our feelings by paying attention to parts of our body where feelings express themselves most clearly. The center of the chest is where most people are able to feel most easily, so this is an excellent place to begin.*
>
> *Consciously choose to pay attention to what you are feeling in your chest. This is most effective if done frequently for short periods of time. At first the feelings may be subtle, but as you continue the practice they will become extremely obvious. We will focus on interpreting feelings later. For the moment just focus on feeling them.*
>
> *Different people feel in different ways, but certain areas are easier to "feel in" than others. These are the throat, the chest, the solar plexus, the belly, the genitals, and the perineum. Different people get in contact with these feeling centers in different sequences,*

and some people have strong feelings in other parts of their body as well.

There is no right way to do it. It is a process of getting more in touch with your feelings by focusing on the areas where you feel the most. One aspect of this practice is learning to pay attention to these feeling centers instead of paying attention to your internal dialogue. I suggest you connect the Feeling the Perineum Practice to this one. We have a tendency to perceive our consciousness as existing in our head a little above and behind a point between our eyes. By bringing our attention to the perineum, we can notice all the other feeling centers between our head and our perineum to support the path to full-body consciousness.

I suggest you do all of the early practices and exercises in the order I present them and stay with them until you can do them easily. After that it is up to you to create your own Practice. I will continue to give you suggestions on how to do this, but the first step is to learn to feel your feelings and let them guide you. There will be more about this later, but for the moment let's focus on paying attention to our feeling centers.

I am a big fan of making lists. Get a notebook to support your Practice and start making lists in it. I will be suggesting many specific lists for you to keep as we progress, and I will be telling you how to work with your lists. For now, get the notebook, so it is ready when you need it.

Part of the Deep Living Practice is to learn to be calm, clear, and conscious no matter what is going on around us. This meditation provides a foundation to reach this state.

Practice: Connecting Meditation

I find this meditation useful to reach a state where I feel calm, centered, balanced, and connected with the world. I will share this meditation as I do in beginning groups. Think of this as the long version. Once you have learned it, feel free to abbreviate and change it. The point is not to do the meditation; the point is to reach the state the meditation brings you to. Use the meditation as a place to start, but as you work with it you should be able to reach the state more and more quickly. Using this meditation as a basis I can reach this state now in a breath. I encourage you to learn to do the same. For the first few times I suggest you have someone read it to you, or that you record it and do it as you listen to the playback.

This meditation begins with the Balance and Center Practice. I will include it for your convenience.

Sit, with eyes closed, and bring your attention to your pelvis. Feel your sitting bones on the seat beneath you. Gently rock side to side, feeling your weight shift from one sitting bone to the other. Let the rocking become smaller and smaller until you feel your weight equally balanced between your two sitting bones. Then begin tilting your pelvis forward and backward in nice big movements. Move with your breath allowing your spine to arch as you inhale and tilt the top of your pelvis forward, then round as you exhale and tilt the top of your pelvis backward. After three to four repetitions of these big movements, allow each repetition to get smaller and smaller, until you find a sense of center. As you are almost at center you will probably feel a tendency for your spine to readjust in relation to your pelvis. Allow this to happen. Then take a deep inhalation and, as you exhale, feel your spine and torso relaxing into your pelvis. Imagine your body like a stack of dinner plates where each part fits into and is supported by the part beneath it. Relax into yourself. When your body is in alignment, you will feel supported by gravity instead of pulled on by it. Through our Practice we can find physical, emotional, and mental alignment.

Let your attention come down to your pelvic floor. Then slowly allow your attention to focus on your perineum. Keep your attention on your perineum and split your focus so you also imagine a field like a grid about a meter below you. Imagine that this field is very connected with the earth. If you have a hard time imagining or visualizing, keep trying and feel how it feels to try. You can develop this ability in time. Feel the qualities of this field as they are connected to the earth deep below. I experience the qualities of this field as extremely slow movement, warmth and deep glowing red against dark brown. Imagine a root growing down from your pelvis to connect with this field. Let your attention go down this root and out into this field. Imagine the other people or things around you are also connected to this field. Play with feeling the things surrounding you through this field.

When ready, let your attention come back toward the root connecting you to this field. Feel the quality of the energy of this field coming up the root towards your body. Allow this energy to come into your body through your perineum. Allow this energy to fill your body, then start to move up through your body. As this energy moves up your body, see if there are any blocks or places where this energy does not flow freely and make note of them. These will open up and change as you continue your Practice. Allow this energy to come up to your chest and imagine it radiating out through your chest. Imagine this energy creating a field at chest level and let your attention go out into this field. With eyes still closed, play with feeling the people or things around you through this field.

When ready, let your attention expand to include the field of energy beneath you feeding energy up through a root into and through your body, out of your chest, and connecting you with what is around you. Stay with this and split your focus to include the top of your skull. Relax the top of your skull. Let your attention go straight up above the top of your skull. As your attention goes up and up, feel how the quality of energy continues to get lighter and brighter. Continue to imagine your attention going higher and higher and the energy getting lighter and brighter until you experience brilliance and a sense of oneness. Again, if you do not experience this at first, continue to play with it and your experience will continue to change. After connecting with this brilliance, allow your attention to come back down. Let your attention continue to come down, bringing this white bright energy with it, until your attention comes back to the top of your head. Let this energy come into your skull with your attention and let it continue to come down through your head, into your neck, and down into your chest where you can allow it to mix with the energy coming up from the earth through your perineum, and then allow both of them to radiate out of your chest together. Let your attention go out into this field at chest level and feel how the quality of energy is different now that you have included this energy from above. Again, play with feeling and connecting to the people and things around you through this field.

When ready, let your attention expand to include both energy flows from their source, moving through you and out into the world around you. Feel how this feels.

◇◇◇   ◇◇◇   ◇◇◇

When you are finished, slowly open your eyes and notice the connection between how things look and how they were feeling while your eyes were closed.

Some of you may be skeptical of the value of this kind of guided meditation. I was when I started my search. I encourage you to experiment with it anyway. Look at it as a tool or a metaphor through which you can have useful experiences that are replicable, and you can gain access to streams of information that are extremely valuable. It is time to start expanding your imagination to what is possible. I am not going to ask you to take anything on faith. I am going to guide you to experiences and let you make your choices based on what you are feeling. This meditation is part of what will take you there.

So much of the Deep Living Practice is about saying "yes". We spiral into level after level of experience of this. At first it is about saying "yes" to the Practice itself. Over time you will see that this means saying "yes" to yourself. The Practice can seem like a mountain. At first it feels like it takes some effort to reach the peak. This peak is the "yes" I am talking about. Once you reach it there is still much to do, but everything is much easier. The Practice becomes about relaxing into yourself. When you get close to this peak you will very likely experience resistance, if you are not already. Resistance is a big subject and we will address it later. Now I would like to talk about a crucial part of the Practice and one I encourage you to begin right away. This is self-inquiry, and it is important enough to deserve a chapter of its own.

−Chapter 12−

Self-Inquiry

A core part of the Deep Living Practice is self-inquiry. This is an extension of creating the witness; where we take time to reflect on what we are doing, how we are doing it, and what we may want to do differently. This is something we can integrate into our lives and do in the moments between the things that require our active attention, but this is also something where I find it is valuable to dedicate some time to practice every day.

Practice: Develop a Sitting Practice

Spend some time each day sitting in a quiet place. Have your notebook at hand so you can take notes. I suggest you do this practice at the end of the day, but you can do it any time. Start by tuning in to how you feel in the moment. Notice how you feel physically. Adjust your body so it feels as comfortable as possible. Make notes of any physical discomfort. Spend a few moments tuning into your pelvis. Feel your sitting bones on the cushion beneath you. Feel your pelvic floor. Deeply inhale, and as you exhale, relax your pelvic floor as much as you can. Notice any feelings you are having. Allow them as fully as possible. Notice if you are resisting feeling any feelings. Make notes of feelings you feel you are not able to allow. Notice your internal dialogue. Are there any thoughts that you feel you are unable to let go of? Take notes. Then review what you have done since the last time you sat. Look at what has happened in your life. Look for automatic behavior. Look for times you were reactive. Look for the deeper motivation behind the choices you made. Look for times when you allowed fear to control your behavior. Look for opportunities where you could have made other choices. Note the things you want to change.

Look at how your Practice is going. Notice your progress. Notice what is more and less effective. Consider if there are any changes you want to make in your Practice and make them.

Then spend some time just sitting. If you are uncomfortable with this, do some of the consciousness or intuition exercises we will discuss later, but eventually you will reach the point where you will receive great pleasure from just sitting and feeling what you are feeling in the moment. As you come closer to your truth, the earlier part of this practice will just take a few moments, and the majority of the practice will be spending time tuning into yourself. This will be an opportunity to let your feelings guide you. As you learn to feel your feelings, you will notice that as you think about the events of your life, your feelings will change. In time you will learn to interpret your feelings into actions that will bring you closer to your truth and maximum potential. Through this sitting practice we learn to do this in a quiet and controlled environment where it is easiest. With practice we can learn to be able to do this anytime and anywhere, no matter what is going on around us.

Many people who are on a path to find themselves practice meditation. You can look at this self-inquiry as a meditation practice. I have found that the way many people practice meditation serves more as a coping mechanism than as a tool for transformation. Of course, if you need your meditation as a coping mechanism, don't abandon it too quickly, as it is one of the healthier coping mechanisms. Yet, I encourage you to look at any existing meditation practice you may have and see if it is really the best method, or would the time be better spent looking at why you need a coping mechanism and addressing those issues.

Several times I mentioned taking notes. I find this very useful. Part of developing a successful Practice is breaking things down into addressable parts, and taking notes is part of this process. I also suggest you make lists. As you are witnessing your internal dialogue, you will probably think of many things you need to do. We tend to become haunted by such thoughts. When you think of such things, see if there is anything you can do about it in the moment. If there is, do it. If not, put it on your list and do it when you can. This may seem simple, but it is a useful step in breaking away from the control of the mind, and just the first of many ways we will use lists.

Part of what we get out of our practice of self-inquiry is understanding our conditioning. It is helpful to see what has influenced your ideas and beliefs, and it is even more useful to become familiar with the things that have happened to you, and the choices that you have made, that are the roots of your behavior. By practicing self-inquiry, we can start to understand our behavioral construction and begin the process of dismantling it. One way of doing this is to start to look for fixed points.

In my professional practice supporting people, I began by working physically and was focused on helping my clients get out of pain. As my practice developed I came to understand that emotional pain was as much of an issue for many people as physical pain, and I learned how to help people get out of emotional pain. This led me to working with trauma and I learned an effective method of trauma resolution. As my practice continued, I began to see that it was the mind that was having the greatest effect on what the person was experiencing, and learned to help people change their minds, and through this, change their lives.

I came to see people as a combination of physical, emotional, and mental elements interacting to create what they were experiencing as reality. I also saw that we have a built-in tendency to heal ourselves. Our systems want to move toward balance. I came to see that people's symptoms were usually the result of some part of their systems that had stopped moving toward balance. Part of a person—sometimes physical, sometimes emotional, sometimes mental, frequently combinations of these aspects that, for some reason—had become fixed. These fixed points were getting in the way of the person's natural tendency to heal. I found that if I could find the reason the point had become fixed, and support movement, the person would move toward balance and healing.

I use these principles in my personal and professional practices. I have come to see that when we have fixed points in a system, all the other aspects of the system have to organize around the parts that don't move, and they become defining factors of the system. We can look at our conditioning as a series of fixed points, and look at the Practice as a way to locate these fixed points and create movement to support our system to find its natural balance. A useful part of our practice of self-inquiry is to locate these fixed points so we can address them.

Our fixed points can show up physically, emotionally, or mentally and it is useful to locate them, make a list, and work on clearing things off of your list. I mentioned that I found the mental system the most powerful of the three. As you begin to look at your fixed points mentally, you will see that these are your ideas and beliefs about what is true or real, and this is where it is most effective to focus your Practice. At the emotional level, the fixed points show up as feelings we are repressing or resisting. We will address resistance shortly. Trauma also shows up as a fixed point. We will discuss trauma later, but note for the moment that it can have physical, emotional, and/or mental aspects. We can learn to address fixed points at the physical level. I find the discomfort or disease they cause can be very distracting and they are frequently a manifestation of an emotional or mental issue, and can be a guide to locating them.

I have very few rules when I am working (rules are usually fixed points), but there is one I find useful, and it pertains particularly to the practice of self-inquiry. The rule is to not allow yourself to say "I don't know." There are several reasons for this. The first is that it is usually not true. Usually, it isn't that you don't know, it is that you don't want to know. The basis behind the practice of self-inquiry is the choice to find out. By saying, "I don't know", you stop the process of finding out, so I encourage you to not say this, or if you do, add, "I don't know, but I'm going to find out." On the path to understanding the construction of our behavioral patterns it is necessary to explore the deeper motivations beneath our behavior. This will be a future topic, but until we get there, stop saying, "I don't know."

As you pursue your practice of self-inquiry, you will be diving into the deeper layers of your conditioning, and very quickly you will see that things stop making sense. Don't let this stop you. When we enter the world of feelings and deeper motivations, we leave logic behind. Consider whatever comes up, even if it seems unlikely or impossible. This Practice is about letting go of your sense of reality, so don't cling to that sense.

Here I would like to suggest another practice to jump-start the process of opening up the mind and exploring deeper levels of what we are feeling.

Practice: Journaling

This is a popular practice I find useful when one is starting to explore what is really going on in their mind. Get another notebook for this practice. Keep it by your bed. When you wake up in the morning, first thing, take the book and start to write down your internal dialogue. Whatever is going on in your mind, even if it is, "I don't know what to write. I don't want to write. Writing is stupid..." or whatever else you may be thinking. Write at least three pages. You will notice that after writing for a while you will access a deeper part of your consciousness and start to get in touch with useful information. You might not get this at first, but if you stay with it, you will, and as you continue this practice, you will be able to tap into this deeper level of information more easily. I encourage you to do this practice for at least a month, though many people come to really enjoy it and stay with it much longer.

Your self-inquiry is an integral part of the Deep Living Practice and will change and develop over time. It is an opportunity to practice honesty, consciousness, and self-responsibility. I highly encourage you to devote time to it.

−Chapter 13−

Some Things to Help You Feel Better

When you first begin, the Deep Living Practice can seem rather daunting. Adopting a new way of looking at the world, doing unfamiliar practices that you have not yet mastered, and realizing how powerful and complex your conditioning is may feel like simply too much. I encourage you to stay with it, and offer some things in this chapter that may help you through this process.

First, I would like mention that the Point of View is not as complex as it may seem. You may notice that it has the quality of feeling right, almost like you already knew it, but you didn't know that you knew it. The most challenging part of accepting the Point of View is letting go of previous beliefs. After understanding the Point of View, most people comment on how simple it is. Once you accept it, there is a very satisfying feeling of always knowing the appropriate thing to do or way to behave.

The early practices are really worth learning. These are incredibly valuable life skills that I wish I had learned as a child. It may take some effort to learn these fundamental skills, but your life will be so much easier once you have. I have no doubt you will see the value of the time you have invested in yourself.

One of the most difficult times is when you begin to realize how deep and massive your conditioning is—when you start to look at honesty and see how dishonest you really are; when you start to look at the role of fear in your life and see how pervasive it is; when you start to make lists of things to transform and see that they go on for pages. I know all of this can be challenging, but please don't let it discourage you.

An encouraging word: as you learn these skills, everything gets easier. An important part of the Deep Living Practice is to learn to break things down into achievable parts so you can experience making progress. Once you have experienced how well it works, you gain more confidence in the process, and this makes it even more effective. You can build momentum that will easily carry you through things that may seem impossible to accomplish now. Remember, this is a practice, and the way to practice is to start by mastering easy challenges and then build up the difficulty as you feel ready. This requires patience, which is also a valuable life skill that we will develop as part of the Practice.

One way to support patience is to let go of goals and expectations and to focus on what is actually happening. Practice letting go of ideas of how things will be in the future and focus on your daily and weekly gains. The value of this is twofold. First, you will feel happy at the progress you are experiencing as opposed to being disappointed by what isn't happening. More importantly, at this point, any expectations or ideas of how things will be in the future can only come from your conditioning, so paying attention to them is a waste of time. Remember, our imagination is tied to our conditioning, and we will be expanding and exploding our imaginations. At this point we have no idea of where our truth will lead us, and thinking we do will only get in the way of the process.

Another benefit is how much better your Practice will make you feel. This is not a practice you do for a long time and then have a sudden change. This is a practice of incremental growth. This is one reason I find lists so useful. After you have taken care of several items on your list, you will feel much better. As your Practice develops, you will start to feel better than you could have imagined you could ever feel. Once you have experienced this a few times you will have a major shift in your reality. The fact that there may be hundreds or even thousands of things on your list to take care of will cease to be an incredible burden that you can't imagine ever being free of. It will transform into an amazing opportunity to feel better than you could ever imagine feeling over and over again, even beyond the foreseeable future. Let go of the idea of reaching a goal. If you can feel better than you could ever imagine feeling every few months, isn't that enough? If you reach the end, great. If you keep feeling better and better for the rest of your life, that's great too.

This brings up another aspect of the Point of View. Nothing matters. This is a challenging concept for many people, but a crucial one. In our conditioned state, we think things matter. As we let go of our conditioning we experience that they really don't. In the vast scheme of the universe, what is happening to you right now has very little significance. When the conditioned mind hears that nothing matters, the most frequent response is, "So then what is the point?" When we let go of our conditioning, we realize that the fact that nothing matters is the basis of freedom. We are here to have an experience. If we have one experience, great. If we have another experience, great. If we learn from our experience, great. If we don't, great, we can have another opportunity to learn from our experience again, or not.

This is an entry point to a more advanced aspect of the Deep Living Practice, where we see that there is no right or wrong or good or bad outside of our conditioning. Things happen, and have consequence, but this only creates opportunities to learn, grow and have other things happen, which will also have consequence. We can learn not only to be at peace with this, but see the incredible potential and freedom in it. I encourage you to consider the idea that things don't matter as much as you might think they do.

A step on the way to realizing that nothing matters is to not take things too seriously. Being serious comes from thinking that things matter. Begin this practice with yourself. Practice not taking yourself so seriously. A step in this direction is to realize that you are not your behavior and to begin the process of disengaging from it by not taking it so seriously.

We have discussed the difference between who you think you are and who you really are, and your behavior is an artifact of who you think you are. Practice looking at your behavior from the perspective of your witness and play with disengaging from the importance your behavior puts on what is happening to it. This can be a very useful area to explore. Also realize that other people are not their behavior, either. They are also a deep inner truth believing they are something else. If you can look at people this way, you will be seeing them much more clearly, and be less likely to get your behavior entangled with their behavior. We will be exploring this much more later.

-Chapter 14-

The Practice of Honesty

When we first think of honesty we think of telling the truth, but as we consider it, we soon come to see we do not know the truth, and that the quest for our truth is what the Deep Living Practice is about. This starts with the realization that our conditioning is not our truth, and therefore is a lie.

This may seem like a radical way of looking at yourself, but I find accepting this a necessary step in the process, even though it can include some shattering realizations like; almost every thought in your mind is a lie, or almost every word out of your mouth is a lie. Our conditioning tells us one thing, and our truth tells us something else, so the transition from one to the other can be quite bumpy.

As you start to practice honesty you will see how your mind will tell you stories about why you are doing what you are doing. If you investigate more deeply you will find that deeper motivations that are more honest than the stories you are telling yourself are almost always driving your behavior. Being able to find these deeper motivations is one of the things you will learn in the Deep Living Practice. Here is an exercise to point out our tendency to tell ourselves lies.

Exercise: What Are Your Priorities?

This exercise is in two parts. For it to work you must do the first part before you read the second part.

Part 1: Close your eyes and think about what is important to you. What are the most important things you want out of life? In your mind, make a list of the three top priorities in your life.

◇◇◇   ◇◇◇   ◇◇◇

Part 2: Now with eyes open, think about what you do in the average week in terms of how many hours you spend involved in different activities. What do you spend the most hours in the week doing? What do you spend the second most hours of the week doing? What do you spend the third most hours of the week doing? These three things are your top three priorities. It does not matter what you think your priorities are, or what you want them to be, what matters is what you actually spend your time doing. If you remember when we discussed self-responsibility, we said that you are always doing what your really want to be doing. When you can be honest with yourself, and look at the real reasons why you are doing the things you are doing, you will be deepening your practice of honesty.

Realize that as we deepen our practice of honesty, and feeling our feelings, things stop making sense. Part of the motivation to tell ourselves the lies we do about why we are doing what we are doing is the desire to live up to our conditioning and have our lives make sense in the context of our conditioning. Let this go and be open for anything. You are not who you think you are, so stop trying to be.

Another way to live more honestly is to look at the secrets you keep. Having secrets is inherently dishonest. If you are keeping secrets you are presenting a false version of yourself. If you want to live your truth you must stop having secrets. I know this is challenging and may seem impossible for some of you, but it is possible to live completely honestly. Doing it just may be beyond your imagination.

Secrets have consequences. They become fixed points that your life has to organize itself around. You need to remember secrets, and they have a tendency to plague you. Relationships built on secrets are not real, and will eventually become progressively uncomfortable. Intimacy is impossible if you have secrets. As well, the effort to keep secrets creates behavior that is not trustworthy.

You may decide to keep some secrets. Just realize they will keep you from the experience I am trying to share with you. I know that many people who keep secrets can't imagine that life could be better without them, but open up to the possibility. More often than not, the only thing you lose by sharing secrets is the ability to have people keep thinking of you the way you want them to. The way you want them to think of you comes from your conditioning, so telling your secrets becomes an effective step in letting go of your conditioning.

Many of us also keep secrets from ourselves. Sometimes we tell a lie so many times we are not sure if it is a lie anymore. We also block out parts of our memory. Our practices of self-inquiry and journaling help us be more honest with ourselves.

Once we are honest with ourselves it is important we share the information with others. Part of the practice of honesty is the practice of transparency. We will go into this more later, but I would like you to start to consider now, that even though it has the exact opposite reputation, vulnerability is where we find our deepest power. The practice of honesty is the path to the power of vulnerability. Your conditioning tells you this is not true, but your conditioning is designed to keep you a powerless and obedient participant in a culture that is not concerned with your happiness. Look at how popular dishonesty is. Our parents lie to us "for our own good". The media lies to us. Politicians lie to us. Businesses lie to us. We are taught to lie. We lie to each other. Lying frequently gets us what we want. Dishonesty is pandemic in our culture. Look at how often our entertainment is based around the effects of a lie; the vast majority. This is how we become conditioned to abandon the personal power we will experience if we live honestly, transparently, and vulnerably.

An interesting aspect of this is how many people have been taught to equate honesty with obedience. Frequently when someone is called honest or dishonest, the label actually refers to obedience and disobedience. Honesty and obedience are two totally different things that have nothing to do with each other. I am a huge fan of honesty. I am not a huge fan of obedience. The connection between honesty and obedience is an example of how our conditioning is embedded in our language. I encourage you to become aware of how often our language supports our conditioning.

Honesty is a core aspect of our Practice, and our relationship to it will change and deepen over time.

> *Practice: Tell the Truth*
>
> *If you catch yourself saying something that isn't true, stop, say you were saying something that wasn't true, and tell the truth the best you can.*
>
> *When sitting in self-inquiry, review what you have said recently, see if you said anything that wasn't true and if you did, contact the person and tell him or her the truer version. This also ties into the practice of courage.*

As you deepen your Practice, look for more subtle levels of dishonesty. One that I found in myself was seeing that a major motivation behind the things I chose to say, and the way that I said them, was to try to affect how the person thought of me, which was both manipulative and dishonest because I was trying to get him or her to think I was better than I thought I was. This is a beginning example of looking for the deeper motivation behind our actions, which is where the practice of honesty will lead us.

When you become more honest and start to share your secrets, you are also likely to discover many people around you already knew the truth, or at least were aware you were hiding something. One of the benefits of sharing your secrets is that you start having contact with people who accept you for who you are, instead of having to hide the truth from people who would judge you for being who you are. Another benefit of honesty is that as you become more honest you become able to see dishonesty in others more clearly. This is an example of how the Deep Living Practice makes life easier.

The more we disengage from dishonesty, the more we see that it wasn't as successful a strategy as we thought it was. When we stop it altogether, it becomes extremely clear how huge the consequences of dishonesty are, and how these consequences invariably create unpleasant experiences. Don't take my word for it though. Start practicing honesty and begin to experience it for yourself.

–Chapter 15–

The Practice of Courage

Now I would like to focus on the practice of courage. The first thing to understand is that courage is not the absence of fear. Courage is the choice to not let fear control your behavior. Let's begin looking at this choice by looking at fear.

As we explore our deeper motivations we will see that fear is behind the vast majority of behavior in most people. There are two types of fear. The first is the fear that protects us from harm. This is why we have fear and this fear is useful. The other kind of fear is the fear of feeling things we don't want to feel. I am much more interested in this.

Considering fear's huge role as a motivating factor, it is interesting to note that very few people are aware of their fears or put any effort into understanding them. Most people I work with can quickly become aware of the role fear has in their lives, but don't seem motivated to explore it. Most people have an undefined cloud of fear that guides them. One use for our practice of self-inquiry is to identify specific fears so we can address them individually. This is part of breaking our conditioning down into manageable parts.

As we examine fear, we see that the fear of feeling things we don't want to feel is the primary tool our conditioning uses to control us. This is why the practice of courage becomes such a crucial aspect of breaking free of our conditioning. As part of your practice of self-inquiry, while looking at the deeper motivations for your behavior, start to look for fear of feelings. As you identify fears, try to define them as specifically as possible. First classify these two types of fear. In most people I work with, well over 90 percent of the fear they allow to control them is that of feeling feelings. If, as you are classifying your fears, they fall in the first category of something that would actually harm you, make a choice if you are happy with your relationship with it, and see if there is something you want to do to change it.

An example of this is the fear of heights. This is a reasonable fear. There is the danger of hurting yourself if you fall, but if your fear is excessive it may get in the way of your enjoyment of life. You may benefit by changing your relationship to this fear, so it is no longer disproportionate to the actual danger. This is a useful practice, but it is much more effective to focus on the fear of feeling feelings. This is the kind of fear that keeps you from approaching someone you are attracted to, because you are afraid of feeling rejected, or you are afraid of doing something because you fear you might fail.

An interesting aspect of this kind of fear is that it usually creates the outcome that you are afraid of experiencing, just without the feeling you are avoiding. If you don't approach the person you are attracted to, you get the same result as if you were rejected, you just don't have to feel the rejection. If you don't try the thing you'd like to try, you will never do it and don't have to risk the feeling of failure. I mentioned before how we create our reality, and these are examples of how allowing fear to control us creates a rather unpleasant reality. Once you start to examine your fears, you will see that if you allow them to control you, you will create your absolutely perfect personal hell. When people feel stuck in their lives, it is usually this level of fear that is behind the feeling.

The answer to all of this is courage. It is amazing how transformative the practice of courage is. My experience is that the most effective way to develop courage is to dive right in.

> *Practice: Courage*
>
> *This is one of the most effective practices to do if you want to change your life.*
>
> *Make a list of everything you are afraid of. This is an ongoing process. Keep adding to the list as you discover new things and*

*removing things when you no longer have fear. Separate the list
into two lists; one list of things that will actually cause you harm
and one list of things you are afraid to feel. Put the list of things that
would cause you harm aside; you can address it later if you would
like. Focus on the list of things you are afraid to feel. Re-order the
list, putting the things you are least afraid of first and progressing
to the things that you are more afraid of. As you add new things
to the list, put them in their proper order. Do the things on the list.*

When I first did the Courage Practice, I did at least one thing I was afraid
of every day. I suggest you do the same. This was the practice that made
the biggest change in my life in the least amount of time. If you do this
practice, your relationship to fear will radically change. You will begin to
see that fear and excitement are the same feeling. Your experience will
change depending if you are resisting or accepting the feeling. Remember
the metaphor of the roller coaster. Screaming in terror is resistance, laugh-
ing with joy is acceptance. If you wholeheartedly dive into this practice,
your life will change from one of fear to one of excitement. Over and over
you will have the experience of fear changing to excitement in an instant.
By having this experience with the things that you are only a little afraid
of, you will start to see that you could possibly have the same experience
with the things you are extremely afraid of, and develop the courage to
do things that are unimaginable within a period of weeks.

An important lesson we learn from this practice is that things almost never
turn out the way we think they are going to. Over and over again I would
be doing something I had avoided for years only to find that suddenly
my feeling would shift to, "What was I afraid of? This is what I always
wanted." Remember how our conditioning is created by all the "no's" we
hear as children and develops into a twisted mirror image of what we
really want. Confronting our fears is a crucial step in finding our truth.
Your conditioning is using fear to keep you the person you were taught
to be, instead of the person you really are.

As you continue to study your fears, also start looking at desire. Fear
and desire frequently come from the same root, and as we dive into this
practice we see that many of our deepest desires are our deepest fears and
visa-versa. Here is an exercise that can help you explore this and also will
help create your fear list.

Exercise: What Are You Afraid Of? What Do You Want?

I find this exercise most effective when done with a partner, although you can do it by yourself if you like.

Sit facing one another and give the supporting partner your notebook. Close your eyes for a moment and do the Balance and Center Practice. When ready, open your eyes. Your supporting partner asks, "What are you afraid of?" You answer with the first thing that comes to mind. Your partner writes it down in your notebook for future reference. Repeat this process over and over. Your job is to say the first thing that comes to mind without thinking. The supporting partner does not respond and keeps a neutral expression if possible. Continue this for at least 15 minutes, preferably longer. Usually after a while you will drop into a deeper level and you will start to get some very useful information.

Repeat this exercise with the question "What do you want?" Notice how we tend to desire what we are afraid of and be afraid of what we desire.

It is with the Courage Practice where most people start to get major results, and as you get results your confidence builds, you invest more energy, and you get even more results. Looking back, I see that making this list and doing this practice was the turning point for me in making the choice between a life controlled by fear and conditioning, and a life of freedom and joy. Making that list and doing those things was when I actually began to find myself.

–Chapter 16–

The Practice of Consciousness

The practice of consciousness is the most valuable part of the Deep Living Practice. Ultimately the Deep Living Practice *is* a practice of consciousness. In the beginning I encourage people to focus on honesty, courage, and self-responsibility, but it is never too early to start doing some fundamental practices to develop your ability to be more conscious. I have found that being more conscious invariably creates a more pleasant experience of life, and that the solution to most every problem is to be more conscious.

In my early years of practicing consciousness I found most of the information I got and the practices I was encouraged to do rather vague and ineffective. I practiced many different forms of meditation and, though I am grateful for what I learned and experienced, in retrospect, I do not find them as direct and effective as what I subsequently learned and teach now.

To start, look at consciousness simply as paying attention. The early practice of consciousness is all about your ability to pay attention and what you choose to pay attention to.

Practice: Capacity for Consciousness

This practice can be done when you are sitting quietly, but it is also one you can integrate into your life and practice anytime, anywhere. Simply see how much you can pay attention to at the same time. For example, if you are sitting in a restaurant, how much can you be aware of? How many tables are there? What are the people at the tables doing? How are they dressed? Where is the wait staff and what are they doing? Are there any smells? What can you hear? Be aware of as much as you possibly can.

Practice: The Shape of Consciousness

As you become aware of what you are being conscious of, you will notice that your consciousness has a shape. For most people it is a sphere that they are at the back of. Play with this and notice that there is an area where you are more conscious, and an area where you are less conscious, and some things you are not paying attention to at all. As soon as you become aware that your consciousness has a shape, you realize that this shape is not fixed. It is very fluid. You can choose what you are being conscious of and what you are not being conscious of.

Play with the shape of your consciousness. Play with different shapes, or areas of focus.

Put yourself at the front of your sphere of consciousness and put all your focus on what is happening behind you.

Change the sphere into a horizontal cylinder and put a tight focus on an object somewhere in front of you.

Shrink your consciousness to the size of your body and pay as much attention as you can to what is going on in your body, but as little as possible to what is going on outside you.

Expand your consciousness to fill the room you are in. Pay attention to every little bit of it. Push your consciousness up into the corners at the ceiling and the floor, or if you are outside, see what happens as you allow your consciousness to include more and more space.

You will probably start to feel fatigued, at which point you should stop. Developing your consciousness is like developing your body. Do it until you feel a little strain and then rest. I also suggest frequent short practices over long exhausting ones.

Make up your own practices for the things that attract you. At the beginning I suggest you keep playing with the size, shape, and focus of your consciousness, and then let it develop in whatever way you find most fun.

Practice: Depth of Consciousness

Continue the practice of narrowing your focus. Stay with it and deepen it. Focus on a very specific thing and open up for information to start coming to you. Don't worry if it is right or wrong, or

*where it is coming from, just open up. Deeply focus on an object
or a person or part of a person: his or her knee, for example. As you
do this, pay attention to whatever you are feeling and whatever
thoughts are in your head.*

These three practices will exercise and build your capacity for consciousness, but where the practice of consciousness is most effective is in your choice of what you are conscious of. We have a limited capacity for consciousness. Remember the exaggerated iceberg with less than .01 percent visible and more than 99.99 percent beneath the surface. It is wonderful to increase your capacity for consciousness, but even if you were to greatly increase it you would still just have a very small percentage available. Realizing this, it is apparent that learning the most effective use of what we are able to be conscious of is the most effective practice of consciousness. This is a primary focus of the Deep Living Practice.

The Witnessing the Internal Dialogue Practice I recommended earlier is where we start choosing what to be conscious of. The Pay Attention to Your Feeling Centers Practice is the next step. When you are not present, it is because you are choosing to be more conscious of your internal dialogue than you are of what is actually going on around you. Through these two practices you can get in touch with the choice of what you are conscious of.

For most people the focus of their consciousness is automatic and they feel it is out of their control. My experience is that it is not. You can learn to direct your consciousness. When you can do this your life is indescribably better. If you are not able to direct your consciousness, it is your conditioned state that is choosing what you pay attention to, and your conditioning chooses what will reinforce your conditioning. Create a witness and listen to your internal dialogue to help you become aware of it and experience that a choice is involved. As our next step I encourage you to practice whether you allow your internal dialogue to affect your life choices or not.

Practice: The Maniac on the Corner

*You may feel it is a little early to start this practice, and if you find it
too hard, stay with some of the practices I just mentioned until you
get better at them. This practice can take quite a while to master,
so I mention it early so you can start exploring the concept. This
one will completely change your life.*

You have been learning to feel your feelings, and as you get better at it, this practice will become much easier. This practice is an extension of the Witness Your Internal Dialogue and Pay Attention to Your Feeling Centers Practices. It starts with you noticing when you are paying attention to your internal dialogue. When you notice you are, choose to pay attention to your feelings, your feeling centers, or the input of your senses. This will probably be very challenging at first, and you may only be able to do it for a few seconds. Don't worry, just stay with it. You may also find this practice exhausting. Don't worry, just do it for short periods of time, but do it often for short periods of time.

I call this practice "The Maniac On The Corner" because as you continue with this process your relationship with your internal dialogue and your conditioning will change. Particularly through your self-inquiry you will learn how the life choice advice coming from your conditioning through your internal dialogue is responsible for most of the unpleasant experiences in your life. Start to relate to your internal dialogue the same way you would relate to a crazy person standing on the street corner yelling at you and telling you what to do with your life. You may feel compassion for him or her, and he might be hard to ignore, but you wouldn't consider doing what he was telling you to do. At first, not following the direction of this voice makes it scream all the louder, and it frequently takes a lot of courage to not follow its direction. But as your practice develops, this voice will get quieter and quieter and easier and easier to ignore.

I suggest you split your time practicing consciousness between about 30 percent developing the capacity and depth of consciousness and about 70 percent learning to choose what to be conscious of. I will be providing many more specific practices as the book progresses.

The practice of consciousness is the basis of a wonderful life, as are the practices of honesty and courage. The possibilities in expanding and directing consciousness seem limitless and I find they are one of the most exciting aspects of life. I find that learning how to direct your consciousness is, by far, the most valuable life skill and it is a major focus of the Deep Living Practice.

–Chapter 17–

Resistance

A major part of the Deep Living Practice is the process of making the choice to be who you really are as opposed to who you think you are. For most people this happens over a period of time and consists of making many choices concerning different aspects of the self. At first we are still choosing to be who we think we are. Through the various practices I recommend, we break this choice down into smaller manageable parts and address them one at a time until the majority of our self is choosing to be who we really are.

During this process we need to address the part of ourselves that sides with our conditioning. Our conditioning believes in itself and resists change. By accepting and examining this resistance we gain the ability to let it go.

We are learning to feel our feelings. Most of us will feel resistance when certain feelings arise. Learning what resistance feels like and what to do when you experience resistance is part of learning to feel your feelings. We resist our feelings in various ways, and each type of resistance has a certain quality. In this chapter we will discuss a few of the more common ones so you can learn to identify them.

Practice: Working with Disassociation

One of the most common forms of resistance is disassociation. Our system unconsciously chooses not to feel something. Frequently I ask someone what he or she is feeling and the answer is "nothing." This feeling of nothing is the feeling of disassociation. We are always feeling something, we just need to pay attention and learn what the feelings are. Other feelings of diassociation can be emptiness, numbness, or feeling spaced out. If you remember, we want to allow feelings instead of repressing them, so if you are feeling resistance, feel it. When you truly allow a feeling it will change. If you feel resistant, be honest about it, recognize it, then feel it as deeply as you possibly can. When you learn to do this you will start to feel the feeling you are resisting rise up in you. Allow this too. We want to learn to allow our feelings fully, but not stay attached to them. When the next feeling comes up, let it come. It is important not to have any expectation of what the next feeling will be. Frequently you will be surprised. Allow whatever comes up, and through this learn about yourself.

If you have a hard time allowing your feeling of resistance, exaggerate it. It can be an effective way to support making a different choice. Exaggerating patterns is a very useful technique that we will use frequently. Be careful not to resist your resistance. This creates a lock that is very hard to break. If you notice yourself doing this, choose to allow your resistance and look for what is underneath it.

Another common form of resistance is stubbornness. Stubbornness has a very particular feeling. It is a childish reaction and when you are feeling it you will feel very young. You can exaggerate the feeling of stubbornness by crossing your arms over your chest, sticking out your lower lip, and stamping your foot. If you do this you will probably feel like you are somewhere between three and six years old. If you are feeling resistance, check and see if this childish feeling accompanies the resistance. If it does you are being stubborn.

For many of us, when we were very young and relatively powerless, being stubborn was one of the only strategies available for us. Many people learn stubbornness when they are young and continue to use it when they are older. It is a very childish way of being in the world. It is about shutting out all input, digging in your heels, and blindly putting all of your energy into your "no". It is an unconscious and irresponsible way of interacting with whatever is going on around you.

Practice: Choosing Not to Be Stubborn

The trick with stubbornness is to realize that it is an ineffective and childish way to interact with the world that will result in feelings of powerlessness, frustration, and disconnection from the people around you. Once you realize this I encourage you to make the choice not to support it. The practice is to pay attention so you notice when you are being stubborn, identify your stubbornness by the childish feelings that accompany it, and then do whatever your stubbornness is telling you not to do.

Feel how you are feeling when you are doing whatever it is. It is very likely that you will feel helpless or powerless like a child. You may feel you are being taken advantage of. Stay with the feeling. It may be hard to stay with this feeling, but practice bringing your attention to your pelvis and staying with it. As you do this, look for any anger or resentment you might have about being helpless or powerless or being made to do something you don't want to do. This may be challenging. You will have to stay with the initial feeling for a while. This will probably be uncomfortable, but stay with it. Be open for any feeling that might arise and allow it as it does. With stubbornness it is very likely that, if you stay with it, you will find anger. When you find it, allow it. Anger is a very powerful feeling. We can use it to transform our lives. We will discuss anger shortly, and you will need to learn more about anger before you can complete this practice, but you can already start working on your choice not to support your stubbornness.

Some people are quite attached to stubbornness and get a feeling of strength out of it. I refer to this kind of strength as force, and will discuss it soon, but I can tell you that you will not achieve any sense of power, joy, or fulfillment through force or by using stubbornness as a strategy. For those of you who use stubbornness as a primary strategy it can be very challenging to let go of, but it is necessary if you want to find your truth.

A frequent way we express resistance is with the phrase, "I don't want…". "I don't want…" almost always comes out of your conditioning, so pay careful attention to whatever words come after "I don't want…". You will get useful information about your conditioning. Often, but not always, you actually want the thing that you are saying you do not want. This comes from how our conditioning develops around the many "no's" we hear as children. Consider the possibility that it is your conditioning saying "no", and that you really want it, you just don't know you want it. Though this is frequently true, it is not always the case, but even when it is not, it is still worth some inquiry into why you don't want it. It might be some aspect of your conditioning such as judgment, fear, or shame that is behind the thought that you don't want whatever it is. The more powerful the feeling of not wanting the thing, the more likely it is connected to your conditioning.

Now I would like to discuss some other ways that resistance expresses itself. Frequently when you are approaching feelings that you have repressed and your conditioning is resisting, it will create feelings designed to keep you from feeling the feeling you are choosing to feel. Sometimes you will get extremely tired and you will feel like it is impossible to keep your eyes open. Sometimes you will feel like you need to go to the bathroom. Sometimes your mind will start racing and you will think of many reasons to not do the thing. You will feel skepticism, doubt, shame, fear, or even unrelated things to distract you as you get closer to a feeling that will really change your life. Your conditioning will try everything it can in order to keep you from feeling the feeling in order to stay in control. You will think of many reasons not to do whatever it is. I encourage you to stay focused on the one reason to do it—to find your truth and to let go of all the lies that have been driving you.

When you get very close to a powerful feeling you have been repressing, you will often feel nausea. This is actually a good sign. It means you are very close to changing your life. If you experience this I encourage you to allow the nausea and keep moving toward the feeling. Many people feel like they are going to vomit right before the big feeling comes and occasionally people do. Don't to let it stop you. Have a bucket to vomit in and some towels nearby and keep going. This is about you finding your life. Don't let your conditioning discourage you with some discomfort or a bit of a mess.

Finally, resistance frequently expresses itself as pain. This can happen physically, emotionally, or mentally. If you are experiencing pain at any of these levels, use your self-inquiry to explore the possibility that it may be a manifestation of resistance. If you find something, see if you can allow the thing you are resisting. If you can do this it will probably bring up an uncomfortable feeling. If you can fully allow the feeling, frequently the pain will disappear. When my professional practice was primarily concerned with pain relief, this was one of the most effective ways I supported people to get out of pain.

You may get the sense that the Deep Living Practice is a very intense process, and it is. It is also a highly effective process. I wish it were easier, and I do everything possible to make it as easy as I can, but if you choose to make it a priority and apply focus and energy to it, it is doable. Through my years of supporting people, I have learned a way to approach feelings that makes this process much more achievable. Let's look at this next.

–Chapter 18–

The Rhythm

The next step in learning the Deep Living Practice is exploring reactivity. When someone is being reactive, his or her response to what is happening is out of proportion to the stimulus. Many people are frequently reactive and tend to become so when their resistance is challenged; for example, if someone tries to get you to do something you don't want to do, or someone says something you don't want to hear. In subsequent chapters, we will look at what is behind reactivity, the effects of it in our lives, and what we can do about it. But for the moment I would like to focus on how we can come into relationship to reactivity in a way that minimizes it and allows us to work with it.

When I studied trauma resolution, I found that trauma tends to create reactivity. As a practitioner, resolving trauma means you must approach trauma in your client without causing him or her to become reactive. I learned that this can be done using what I call a rhythm—a pattern of behavior that involves carefully approaching the clients issue, paying attention to the feelings that arise, and letting these feelings guide you. From now on I will refer to this as the Rhythm. Learning this Rhythm was one of the most valuable things that I have learned in my life. After learning it, and becoming adept at working with it in my years of practicing trauma resolution, I began to notice that I was using it in many other situations as well, both in my professional practice and also in my daily life. Using the Rhythm, I was able to approach people and situations without creating reactivity. In my personal practice I realized that I could approach challenging feelings without becoming overwhelmed. When, in the process of developing the Deep Living Practice, I began examining exactly what I did and what effects it had, I was amazed to see that I was using this Rhythm almost constantly in most all aspects of my life. Learning and mastering the Rhythm is a key element of the Deep Living Practice.

You can use the Rhythm in many different ways. Once you have learned it, you can apply it to whatever you are doing in many variations. I find this exercise an effective way to begin. It is also a way to develop your sensitivity and your ability to feel your feelings.

Exercise: Moving Through Energetic Boundaries

There are two ways to do this exercise and they both require a partner.

In the first version you sit comfortably, while your partner stands as far away from you as the room allows, or as far away as you can communicate without yelling if you are outside or in a big room. Close your eyes for a moment, do the Balance and Center Practice, then tune in to your feelings. Your partner's job in this exercise is to do exactly what you tell him or her to do to the best of his or her ability.

While paying attention to what you are feeling, ask your partner to move toward you very slowly. As she moves towards you, you will notice that feelings come up. If you do not feel anything, you are disassociating. If that is the case, repeat this part of the exercise periodically until you begin to feel something. If you do this, in conjunction with the rest of the Deep Living Practice, you will eventually begin to feel. When I began my search I was extremely disassociated and was aware of very few of my feelings. Through this Practice I have become extremely sensitive. Frequently the first thing many people feel is a little fluttering in their chest. Others feel their throat or jaw tighten, or get an uneasy feeling in their stomach. If you stay with this, these subtle reactions will develop into full-blown feelings. This exercise will work even with the least intense feelings.

As soon as you feel something, tell the person to stop. Then tell her to move backward slowly until you no longer feel the feeling. Next have her move forward until you feel it again. Then backward again until you do not feel it. This time have her move forward very slowly and as soon as you start to feel the least little bit of the feeling have her stop, and then just stand there and wait. After about thirty seconds tell her to move slowly forward again. It is very likely that she will pass the point where you felt something before, and you will not feel anything, or the feeling will be greatly diminished.

These feelings are the result of your partner crossing your energetic boundaries. We all have quite a few of these boundaries and learning to feel and transform them is a great way to learn the Rhythm. Once you have found and shifted one, keep moving forward until you find another. As I said, we all have quite a few of these, if you only find two or three you need to work on your sensitivity. The consciousness practices will help you with this.

The other variation of this exercise is to have your partner sit, while you stand and move through his boundaries. In this version, get feedback from your partner. When you feel something, ask if he feels it too. When the feeling shifts, ask if he feels it shift. You will be moving in the same pattern as the first version of this exercise, just this time you are moving yourself without the other person telling you how to move. You make your choices when to move based on what you are feeling, and you check in with your partner to see if he is feeling the same things you are feeling.

The pattern you are moving in—move forward, feel something, wait, move forward—is the most basic form of the Rhythm. Do this exercise frequently until you are able to feel these boundaries and dissipate them using the Rhythm.

As I said, there are many, many applications of the Rhythm. Let's use the body to look at a slightly more sophisticated version of it.

Exercise: Exploring Tight Muscles

We can use the Rhythm to explore and relax tight muscles in our bodies. I find this a much more effective way to work with muscles than stretching. If you accept our premise of self-responsibility, you will see that if a muscle is tight, it is because some part of us wants it to be tight. Finding this part and making a different choice is the most effective way to let go of tightness. Stretching, on the other hand, is one part of us choosing to be tight, while another part fights the tightness. It is like being in a car and pressing the brake and the accelerator at the same time. It uses a lot of energy, it is exhausting, and it is not comparatively effective.

To use the Rhythm in this situation you slowly move in the way you would if you were stretching, but as soon as you feel resistance in your body, you stop. Wait about 30 seconds, then slowly move forward until you feel resistance again, and stop. Here we will add another step to the Rhythm. This is a crucial step that greatly increases its effectiveness. After you feel the resistance and stop, pull back and create a tiny gap between the part of you that wants to move forward and the deeper part that is resisting. When the gap is just right you will start to feel the feelings behind the holding in the muscle. Allow the feeling fully. As you do, the muscle will relax. Then you can move forward to the next resistance. Although you are not doing much physically, this can be a very intense process so don't push yourself too hard.

You can also do this with another person, where you are using the Rhythm on him or her to explore the tightness in the body. For example, have your partner lie on her back, then you lift her leg until you feel resistance in her muscles. Use the Rhythm to slowly move her leg through the resistance, giving her plenty of time to feel her feelings. If you do this, remember, the purpose is to explore the tightness and allow the feelings. It is not about how far you can move the leg, although you will probably be amazed at how far the leg will move.

These two exercises will get you started learning the Rhythm. Several different skills are necessary to become adept at using the Rhythm. We are already familiar with some of these and some are new.

The Rhythm is not fixed. It may sound that way as I described it, and the way I described it is a common example of how it goes. It is a good model to use to start, but as you learn the Rhythm you will see that there are many variations you can apply in different situations. Sometimes you can make great leaps forward; other times you will see that the resistance you are working with is too great in the moment, and that by not even trying, you are applying the Rhythm over a greater time span. The best way to learn the Rhythm is to focus on the basic skills required.

The ability to feel what you are feeling is essential to the Rhythm. If you are applying the Rhythm when you are with someone else, you will also need empathy. Empathy is your ability to feel what someone else is feeling.

Empathy is another aspect of the Deep Living Practice, which we will explore and develop as we continue.

Part of becoming proficient at the Rhythm is learning to be resolute in your choice to move forward. This also requires the ability to split your focus. Part of you is completely behind your choice to move forward, while another part of you is totally focused on feeling your feelings and letting them guide you in moving forward, stopping, creating the gap, and waiting. This can be tricky at first, but with practice, you will learn.

To master the Rhythm you need to learn to create the perfect gap between your determination to move forward and whatever is resisting the movement. If the gap is too small, the resistance will dissipate very slowly, or not at all. If it is too big, you disengage from the process and nothing will change. When you get the gap just right, you will feel it. It has a very distinctive feel that is different in different situations, but is usually accompanied by a feeling of expansion and relaxation, though strong feelings are also often released at the same time.

You will also need to learn how to wait. When it is time to wait, you need to be able to come into a state of mind as if you were willing to wait forever. I previously mentioned waiting 30 seconds. When you first start you can use 20 to 30 seconds as a rule of thumb, but to get really good at the Rhythm, the person you are working with needs to feel as if you are prepared to wait as long as it takes. The slightest feeling of impatience on your part will affect the process. I find the best way to achieve this state of complete availability is telling yourself that you will steadfastly wait forever. Even to the point where you might imagine spiders spinning their webs on you. Then the very first time you start to wonder if you have waited long enough, you stop waiting, and continue. Sometimes the wait will be less than a second, other times the wait can be much longer, even to where you see that there is no point continuing in the moment.

This may sound complicated or beyond what you are capable of now, but if you start with these basic exercises, and focus on learning these skills, you will pick up the Rhythm quite quickly. I have taught the Rhythm to many people and it is really not so hard to learn. Many of the other exercises and practices we will be doing will also help you get better at the Rhythm.

There are limitless applications of the Rhythm in life. I encourage you to look for them and use them to practice the Rhythm. They exist at all different levels from the physical, to the emotional, to the mental. You can use the Rhythm as you touch someone's cheek. You can use the Rhythm as you approach a powerful feeling within yourself. You can use the Rhythm as you explain something to someone who is resisting what you are saying.

This is a key element in the Deep Living Practice. We will be exploring many specific ways to use the Rhythm and more sophisticated ways to use it. Through learning the Rhythm, so many things that may seem difficult or impossible will become achievable. Learning the Rhythm has improved my life immeasurably, and if you take the time to learn it, I have no doubt it will do the same for you.

–Chapter 19–

Resourcing

Through my work in trauma resolution, I also learned the valuable skill of resourcing. By "resourcing" I mean supporting someone to have the resources available to feel stable, conscious and aware of what is happening in the moment. This is an essential aspect of trauma work because a person in the trauma state feels threatened by dangerous situations that have happened in the past. In the trauma state we lose touch with what is actually happening. To make this clearer I will tell you some of what I have learned about trauma.

The study of trauma and trauma resolution is a huge subject beyond the scope of this book. Here, I am presenting a few things I have learned about how trauma affects our behavior and a way of looking at trauma that supports the Deep Living Practice.

When something starts to happen to us that we don't want to happen, our first impulse is to run away. If we are not able to run away, our next impulse is to make it stop. If we are not able to run away or make it stop, we tend to disassociate and endure whatever is happening. This state of disassociation is the trauma state. It is a vital mechanism in our systems. If something bad is happening to you, this disassociated state is frequently preferable to being present with what is happening and can help you survive the experience. If you are being badly injured in an accident, disconnecting from the pain can help you survive.

Although this trauma state can be useful while the traumatic event is happening to us and for a period of time thereafter, we tend to hold on to our traumas and integrate them into our sense of self, which is not so useful. Trauma can be obvious physically, but we can also experience trauma emotionally, and even mentally, when we are confronted with feelings or ideas that overwhelm us. My experience is that trauma usually has some combination of physical, emotional, and mental components.

Trauma is about time. It happens in a particular moment, and then keeps us connected to the moment it happened. It is as if that moment becomes stored within us, like the trauma is frozen in time. The moment we went into the trauma state becomes a fixed point in our system, and the rest of our system has to organize itself around that fixed point. We store our traumas in our physical, emotional, and mental systems, and we can identify our traumas through the reactivity that arises when we approach them. Trauma feels a very specific way. You can learn what trauma feels like so you can identify it when you experience it in yourself and in others.

Trauma appears in many different ways and at many different intensities. You may have a small, purely physical trauma from spraining your ankle, or a huge trauma from a violent sexual assault that has physical, emotional, and mental aspects. The sprained ankle may be purely physical, or it may include emotional aspects if it happened in front of many people and you felt clumsy and embarrassed, or mental aspects if you had high expectations of your performance and think that this failure has ruined your chances at success. I would like to point out that we all have many traumas, they affect our behavior, and that trauma has a very particular feeling. The feeling of trauma is reactivity that increases in intensity very quickly. You can get a sense of how affecting the trauma is by how quickly it arises and by how powerful the feeling is.

We have all experienced trauma in our lives, and a large part of our reactivity is caused by these traumas. Something starts happening that triggers the memory of this trauma state, we begin to feel the feelings we had then, and want to either run away, make it stop happening, or, if neither of those options are possible, disassociate. This is the basis of much human behavior. It has little to do with what is actually happening and is rarely a very effective response to the moment. I recommend you look for and identify reactivity in your life to get a sense of the effect your traumas are having on you. This is one of the purposes of our practice of self-inquiry.

The effect of trauma in our lives is huge, but it does not have to stay that way. The Deep Living Practice incorporates aspects of trauma resolution as a way to help you learn to resolve your traumas. If you have intense trauma in your life you may need help to do this, and I highly encourage you to get it. But even if you need such professional help you will resolve your traumas much more quickly and easily by doing the Deep Living Practice. I had a very traumatic childhood, and the extreme reactivity it caused in my life was a prime motivation to develop this Practice. I had help resolving some of the deep traumas of my past, but I was also able to resolve at least 80 percent of the trauma I experienced in my life on my own using the Deep Living Practice.

Let's get back to resourcing. When we go into this reactive trauma state it can feel as if we are being hijacked. Circumstantial triggers can make our feelings change very suddenly. We feel threatened and feel that we have to defend ourselves, or we feel that what is happening is too much to bear. We may go into avoidance strategies, collapse into tears, or even panic. The first step to resourcing is to notice when these things happen to us. We can do this through developing our witness and reviewing our behavior in self-inquiry. Later, we will discuss how to resolve trauma, but the first step is how to get out of the trauma state.

One of the first things you learn when you study how to resolve traumas in other people as a practitioner of trauma resolution is how to resource someone—how to get him or her out of his or her trauma-induced illusion and present with what is actually happening in the moment. You need to be out of the trauma state to resolve it. It is great to have someone available to do this for you. At the same time, it is extremely valuable to learn to resource yourself.

Actually we have already begun. One of the most effective ways to re-source yourself is to be able to put your consciousness in your pelvis and perineum. This is the first thing I suggest people do. Using your senses to pay attention to what is actually happening around you is also good for resourcing. Train yourself to pay attention to the specific details you are experiencing through your senses. Getting good at these two practices will help you learn to resource yourself and are what I use when I am in intense situations. Here is an interim practice to play with.

Practice: Finding and Using a Resource

Feeling safe is the key to feeling resourced. Very different things give a sense of security to different people. In that I am not with you to help you, you need to find it for yourself, but my experience is that if we look for something we will find it, so the first step is to start looking.

Remember some time in your past when you were feeling very safe and secure. As you explore the memory, see if you can identify details of what was happening. Maybe the posture you were in, or a song that was playing, or something you were wearing, or an object that was present. What we are looking for is a posture, a memory, or an object that will help you get back into the state of feeling safe and secure. I encourage you to explore different memories and different ways to recall the memory. When you find the right one it can be a very effective tool.

The next challenge is to use this tool. When you start to feel the reactivity of trauma coming on, or you feel you are already lost in it, stop whatever you are doing and do whatever it takes to get into your resourced state. This may mean sitting in a corner and singing a song to yourself, or closing your eyes and imagining feeling the warmth of a fire on the front of your body. I used lying down, closing my eyes and remembering a children's story that I heard on a particularly good night in my childhood. It may seem impossible to do this, but it is not. Think of the alternative. You can continue to act out in your reactive traumatized state, or you can start to do something about it. Again, this is an interim measure. Once you feel resourced by whatever method you have created, you can start to bring attention to your pelvis and pay attention to what is actually happening around you.

I would like to say a few words about collapsing. When we collapse, we lose touch with what is going on around us and become lost in a reactive state. The classic collapse is to feel overwhelmed and start to cry. It usually includes feelings of helplessness and frequently self-pity. Most people who have a tendency to collapse feel it is something that happens to them and that they do not have a choice in. But you do have a choice. Collapsing is a very ineffective strategy that develops when we are young. Collapsing is irresponsible. By being irresponsible we give up our power, and by giving up our power we create a feeling of helplessness. This feeling of helplessness tends to make us feel overwhelmed, which, in turn, supports the choice to collapse. Like so many other behavioral patterns it creates a loop that is very hard to break out of. Many people who collapse are addicted to collapsing.

If you are prone to collapse, I encourage you to consider the idea that you can choose not to do it. I also encourage you to focus on the resourcing practices so you have an alternative when the tendency to collapse arises. When you feel a collapse coming on, choose to resource yourself instead.

Next we will talk about anger. It can be useful to get a little angry with yourself for choosing to collapse, and using the strength of the anger to support the choice to resource instead of collapse. I've worked with many people who went from feeling totally weak, helpless and who collapsed frequently, to feeling powerful, stable, and free. Their turning points were the moments they felt the collapse coming and then made the choice not to collapse. Even if they collapsed five seconds later, they had found the choice, and with practice they learned to exercise that choice at any time, until the choice to collapse became a distant memory. Let's explore how we can use anger in a constructive way to support our Practice.

-Chapter 20-

Anger

As you begin to feel your feelings you will probably experience anger. Anger is a powerful and misunderstood feeling. Anger has a bad reputation. This is because most people are irresponsible with their anger. Some examples of how people are irresponsible with anger are blaming others for what makes them angry, acting out unconsciously in anger by losing their tempers or becoming violent, and using anger to justify their actions. We will begin our discussion of anger by talking about how to be responsible when feeling your feelings.

If you are practicing self-responsibility, you will realize that you are responsible for whatever you are feeling. There is frequently a great temptation, particularly with anger, to blame someone else for what you are feeling. By doing this you are not taking advantage of the opportunity the feeling is giving you.

I have already mentioned that our conditioning judges and classifies our feelings, which is what I call emotions. If you ignore these classifications, and just feel what you are feeling, you can experience your feelings as energy moving through you. This energy has different qualities at different times. The different qualities of the energy you are experiencing are information that you can learn to interpret. As I also mentioned, I use the names of emotions to refer to these different qualities of energy, because we are familiar with them. I encourage you to let go of the classifications and judgments of your conditioning and start looking at your feelings from this different perspective.

Look at whatever you are feeling as a flow of energy coming from your truth that guides you to the most appropriate response for whatever situation you are in. Through doing this, your feelings will support you to live your truth. Reaching this state is one of the goals of the Deep Living Practice. Your feelings may be in response to what is going on around you, but they are not caused by what is going on around you.

Most people tend to not want to feel what they are feeling and blame something or someone for making them uncomfortable. What is actually making them uncomfortable is the choice not to feel the feeling, which is usually derived from their conditioning, and they are experiencing their resistance to their feeling as discomfort. If we can realize that whatever we are feeling is extremely valuable, and focus on allowing and interpreting our feelings, we can shift our feeling about the person we might be blaming to one of gratitude, for they are helping us find ourselves. This is a big jump and we will break it down into much smaller steps. A great way to start this process is by looking at anger.

Anger is an alarm that goes off in your system when your behavior is not aligned with your truth. If you look at it this way, anger becomes one of the most valuable tools to help you find your truth. The incredible power of anger can give you the strength to change your behavior and come closer to your truth.

When you feel angry, resist the temptation to waste the opportunity that anger presents you with by blaming someone else, and consider how you might adjust your behavior to align with your truth. It can take a while to learn to do this. If you miss the opportunity in the moment, use self-inquiry to explore it after the fact. This will also expand your imagination, for frequently the truth that your anger is guiding you to is something that your conditioning has told you is not even a possibility. Anger is very often the key to shifting patterns and behavior.

Angers' bad reputation is well earned by people being irresponsible with it. When we are irresponsible and unconscious with anger, it can cause great damage. It is an extremely powerful energy. If we can direct this energy toward supporting ourselves and others, it will become the strength that sets us free.

If you notice a pattern within yourself—let's use stubbornness as an example—you will frequently feel anger when you are experiencing it. If you can allow your anger and take responsibility for it, you will see that instead of being angry at the person whom you are being stubborn with, you are angry at yourself for indulging in a childish strategy that is not really getting you what you want. Then you can use the power of the anger to support the choice to override the stubbornness. When we use anger this way, it transforms to determination and this determination can get us through the many challenges of the Deep Living Practice. If we continue to allow our anger responsibly, it becomes our passion.

We are heavily conditioned to repress our anger or to be unconscious with it. Most of us are unaware of any other options. This is another function of how our conditioning has developed to keep us powerless and obedient and to guide us away from the tools that will help us find our truth. Because of this, it is frequently very challenging to get in touch with our anger. There are many situations where we can't even imagine being angry, in which anger is the key to transformation but we've been conditioned to not feel it. Open up to the possibility of finding anger, look for it, and you will begin to find it in many unexpected places. Frequently it is masked by resignation. We will take a deeper look at resignation later.

Sometimes we are so lost in a feeling we don't even consider that it may be anger that we are truly feeling. Helplessness is a feeling many people get lost in. Feeling angry that you are feeling helpless is frequently the way to move through helplessness, but in the state of helplessness it is rare that you will find your anger unless you actively look for it. Looking a level deeper you will notice that the choice to look for your anger is the beginning of the choice to stop feeling helpless.

Our conditioning has created many places for our anger to hide. Frequently guilt is a motivating factor in behavior. Guilt is anger that your conditioning says you have no right to feel. If you are experiencing guilt, look for the anger and let it guide you to your truth. This will usually include confronting some aspect of your conditioning, but this is exactly how you become free of it.

Boredom is another feeling that masks anger. Boredom is what we feel if we are angry and our conditioning is telling us that this is an inappropriate situation to allow anger. We disassociate to avoid the anger and experience what we call boredom. When boredom occurs you usually don't want to be doing what you are doing, but your conditioning has made you think you have to. Look for the anger, do what you want to do, and in most cases the boredom will immediately disappear.

Another feeling where anger hides, sadness, is even more deceptive. For many children there is no room for anger. If they express anger they are punished or rejected. Because of this, many children learn to transform their anger into sadness, because sadness frequently gets them a better response than anger. Many times when people are experiencing sadness, they are not really sad, but are actually angry. They are unconsciously transforming their anger into sadness. This is not to say that there is not actual sadness. There absolutely is, but it feels very different than the sadness that is masking anger. It is useful to learn to tell the difference. If you are with someone and he or she actually feels sad, you will probably be able to feel it. If her sadness does not touch you, it is quite possible that she is actually angry. This is hard to feel within oneself as the sadness feels genuine until you learn to tell the difference. Start by considering the possibility that anger might be behind your sadness, and look for it. As you get better at self-inquiry, this will become easier. As you get better at feeling your feelings you will begin to experience that if you deeply feel a feeling, it will pass. Actual sadness will pass, but anger transformed to sadness will not. This is another way you can tell the difference.

We've talked quite a bit about how to feel your feelings. Now it is time to look at a method to do it. This is something else that I learned in my practice of trauma resolution. The way I was taught to help people resolve trauma was to support them to carefully approach the feeling they were feeling when the trauma happened, and then allow the feeling without going unconscious. When I use "going unconscious" in this context I mean when someone loses the ability to be aware of what he or she is doing and becomes lost in his or her behavior. Supporting people this way works incredibly well. It may take a while, using the Rhythm and resourcing, to get them to the point where they are ready to feel the feeling. But once they do, they only have to feel the feeling for a short time, usually less than a minute, for the trauma to resolve. It is frequently a very intense minute, but when the person has really felt the feeling, the trauma is gone, and the transformation is almost magical. Often the person feels that reality has radically altered. Things that used to feel threatening no longer feel that way. Relationships to others change and perception of the world and the people in it shifts.

Over my years of practicing and experimenting, I found that this process of feeling repressed feelings also supported healing and transformation in non-traumatic situations. Then in my personal process of learning to allow my repressed anger, I saw that I was doing the same thing I was supporting people to do in my trauma resolution sessions, and it was having an incredibly transformative effect on my life. I found that this narrow zone between suppressing your feelings and going over the top of them by acting out was a very powerful place where amazing things happened. As I continued to experiment, I found that when I was in this zone I felt so much more present, clear, happy and fulfilled than when I was in any other state. I began to see that it was possible to live in this state. It was more than just a therapeutic possibility. When I refer to "Deep Living" I am talking about this state and the entire Deep Living Practice has been developed to help you get there.

I bring this up during our discussion of anger because anger is a good feeling to use to learn to feel your feelings. There are several reasons for this—anger is a strong and easily identifiable feeling, the effects of allowing your anger are great, so it gives you more confidence in the process, and we tend to be particularly resistant to anger, so if you can overcome the resistance to allowing your anger it will be easier to overcome your resistance to other feelings. Let's take a look at how to do this.

> *Practice: Feeling Your Anger*
>
> *It can be useful to have help to start this practice, and even more useful to have skilled help, but whether you are doing it alone, or with assistance, the process is the same.*
>
> *It starts with you looking at what makes you angry and making a list. This self-inquiry is an important part of the process. From this list choose one of the things that makes you the angriest. You may need to try the process with several different subjects to find the one that works.*

In life it is irresponsible to direct your anger toward someone else, but in this process it can be useful to direct your anger outward to help you get in touch with it. With whatever you have decided as your subject, remember a time that it happened to you or imagine it happening to you now, and allow yourself to get angry. If you have help you may want to create a situation that makes you angry, and have your helper play the role of the person making you angry. We do this with great effect in our groups and sessions.

Approach your anger with the Rhythm. Don't rush toward it. Move slowly, pull back a bit as you begin to feel it, and wait a bit before moving forward. Allow yourself to feel it building slowly. If you feel it is too much and that you will be overwhelmed with it, take a bigger break and rest a bit before going on, or maybe it is enough for the moment and you can come back to it later.

It is important that you stay conscious for this process to be effective. If you have help, have the person sit in front of you and support you by keeping eye contact with him or her. If you are alone, work in front of a mirror and keep eye contact with yourself.

Remember, we are allowing the energy to move outward, so direct it toward your partner or your image in the mirror. If you feel like you want to yell or hit, allow the feeling, but do not do it. We are looking for this narrow zone where you are fully allowing the feeling without going over the top of it by acting out. It can sometimes help to physically push a bit. Your partner can offer resistance or you can push against a wall.

If you do go over the top and yell, hit, or go unconscious some other way, just consider it part of the learning process. You might need to go over the top to become familiar with the point where it happens. Learn from your experience and be more aware of using the Rhythm next time. If you do go over the top, or come close without quite making it, take a break and come back to it later. Your repressed anger feels like pressure inside you. If you release the pressure, you may need to take some time to let it build up again.

Keep coming back to it until you are able to do it.

Don't get impatient. It will probably take you a while to learn to do this. It took me about six weeks from the time I decided to do it until I could actually do it. Then it took a few more months until I could do it easily. I can't stress enough how valuable it is to learn to feel your anger, both for how effective it is in changing patterns, and what a relief it is to stop living with repressed anger, as well as how important it is to learn to feel you feelings in general, for once you get in touch with your feelings they will support you to make life choices that will guide you to your truth, not to mention how vibrant, alive, and connected you feel when you are in this state of fully allowing your feelings to pour through you.

The key to allowing yourself to feel your feelings is to make the choice to feel your feelings. When you are not actively in the process of trying to feel your feelings, play with the idea of making the choice to feel your feelings and imagine what it might be like. After a brief discussion on the nature of power and force, we will turn our focus on how to refine the Deep Living Practice to support making these kinds of challenging choices that will change your life.

–Chapter 21–

Power and Force

Now that we are starting to experiment with allowing anger, let's look at the difference between power and force. Most of us are much more familiar with force than with power. Most everything, in our conditioned culture, is done with force.

Force is like a bulldozer. It gets things done, but it requires fuel and maintenance, makes noise, creates pollution, and will eventually wear out. It has the quality of being invasive. Power is like the ocean. It is huge by comparison; effortless, limitless, and is deeply connected to its surroundings.

One of the goals of the Deep Living Practice is to get you in touch with your power. The first step is to realize that there is a difference between power and force, and that they feel totally different. If you want to experience your power, you need to be conscious of when you choose to use force and choose not to. This will probably be challenging, because most of us feel our force is our strength and without it we will be defenseless.

In our conditioning, force has a distinctively male feel to it. Many people equate force with masculinity. Because of this, men tend to use force more frequently than women, and have a harder time letting it go, though many women have been conditioned to emulate male models of behavior, and have challenges letting go of force as well.

When we use force, there is frequently the quality of coming up into it. Think of someone getting up out of a chair saying, "Let's do it!" and you will get a feeling of the quality of force. The feeling of power is one of coming down. You settle into it. It feels expansive, vast, and effortless. Effortlessness is the quality that identifies power. If there is effort, it is force.

Force can be effective. We are living in a world created by force. But remember, force creates many consequences. This is why there is pollution, poverty, conflict, and a damaged environment. Force requires vast amounts of energy to sustain it. In that it gets things done, it is very seductive, but if we want to find effortless joy, we need to come down into our power, where we will be in harmony with our environment. If in your practice of consciousness, which includes paying attention to the effects of your actions, you notice there are many adverse consequences to what you do, you are probably using force.

I highly encourage you to make the choice to stop supporting force in your life. It is exhausting and keeps you from reaching your maximum potential. Force is how we bring our conditioning into reality. Doing this is not living responsibly.

This leads us to the secret of finding your power. You will find your power in your vulnerability. Your vulnerability is your willingness to be totally honest and expose yourself completely. I know this may be hard to believe, as our conditioning tells us that vulnerability is weak and dangerous, but my experience is that the exact opposite is true, and this is yet another example of how our conditioning has developed to keep us away from our power.

When you are in your vulnerability, you are not hiding anything. You see the world much more clearly through the transparency of your vulnerability. You can feel when people are lying to you. When you are totally exposed it becomes very hard to manipulate you, because manipulation frequently involves the threat of exposure. There is nothing to argue about when you are being vulnerable, because you are presenting yourself as you truly are.

When you have the courage to drop into your vulnerability you experience a rock solid sense of power and confidence that comes from knowing exactly who you are and not having to hide it. There is also a feeling of directness and simplicity in knowing who you are in relation to the world, knowing that everyone around you knows who you are and needs to interact with you just as you are. Again, there is nothing to gain by arguing with vulnerability.

Coming into your vulnerability is a major part of the Deep Living Practice. Your vulnerability is your truth. Your vulnerability is your power. Coming into your vulnerability is practicing courage. As you sink into your vulnerability you realize you *are* your vulnerability. There is nothing weak about it, but you will not know this until you experience it. This experience is exactly where we are heading.

–Chapter 22–

Developing Your Practice

When you start the Deep Living Practice, it is beneficial to focus on fundamental skills like connecting with your pelvis, getting in touch with your feelings, creating your witness, self-inquiry, and the pursuit of honesty, courage, consciousness, and self-responsibility. As your Practice develops, it is useful to continue working with these things, as they will make your life easier and more fun. But another part of their purpose is to develop the skills for the real heart of the Practice, which is disconnecting from your conditioning and moving toward your truth. Once you have developed your fundamental skills, I suggest you shift your priority and make moving toward your truth the focus of your Practice.

I am very concerned in helping you create an effective, practical Practice; one you can actually do and experience tangible and permanent results within a short amount of time. Many practices I explored sounded great, but didn't produce lasting results, had some aspect I was never able to accomplish, or were presented as taking a very long time to achieve results. One of the ways you can make the Deep Living Practice work is by breaking it down into parts you can actually manage. If something seems too difficult, break it down into smaller, more achievable, steps. It doesn't matter if you are taking big steps or small steps, as long as you are moving. As long as you are taking steps, you will continue to feel better, become clearer, and enjoy your life more.

Occasionally stop and look at what you have accomplished. In the midst of the Practice, you can often feel overwhelmed, and sometimes you may get stuck in resistance for a while, but take a moment to look at how your life is now compared to how it was several weeks ago, or several months ago, and this will help you continue.

Most people start the Deep Living Practice before they understand what it is really about. Your understanding of the Practice deepens and continues to develop with experience, and there is frequently a point of realization that supports a higher level of dedication. This comes through a combination of beginning to experience the benefits of the Practice, and becoming clearer about the consequences of continuing to allow your conditioning to control you.

Your truth wants to come out. Your truth is your purpose in this life, and a deep part of you wants to fulfill it. Our deepest motivation is to live our truth. If a feeling we are repressing is keeping us from living our truth, this deep part of us will guide us into situations that will bring up this feeling. We are telling ourselves one story that aligns with our conditioning and explains why we are doing what we are doing, while this deeper motivation to live our truth, which most people are unconscious of, is actually driving us. It is usually driving us into situations that our conditioning doesn't want to experience. We experience these drives as attractions and repulsions. These attractions and repulsions are the motivations behind most people's behavior.

When I realized this, I was furious. I felt like I was a hamster on a wheel. I understood that whatever choices I made, and whatever story I told myself, had nothing to do with what was actually happening. I understood that a deeper part of my unconscious mind was making me do the exact things my conscious mind was trying to avoid. The women I was attracted to, the job I thought I wanted, the place I chose to live, were all choices being made by an aspect of myself that I was unconscious of. That aspect knew I needed to have certain experiences. I was just a puppet with an illusion of self-determination that was being guided down a path, and I was using my illusion of self-determination to fight that path every step of the way. I thought, "What a ridiculous way to waste my life," and in my fury I stopped everything else in my life and put my full focus on supporting the path of my truth instead of fighting it. I realized that the fight was the source of my unhappiness and suffering, and that the deeper force driving me was where I truly wanted to go. Once you have experienced enough of the Deep Living Practice to really feel this dynamic, you will probably shift your Practice into high gear.

At a practical level this means focusing on the next step and taking it, or if the step is too big, breaking it down into smaller parts and taking those steps. Keep your focus on what is next. Looking too far into the future gets in the way. With a little experience, you will learn that what you think is going to happen in the future is coming from your conditioning, and it is very rarely what actually happens. Your conditioning protects itself by projecting an outcome that will discourage you from proceeding. Stay focused on achievable goals.

This brings us to making a master list of what steps you need to take in your Practice in order to find your truth. This list comes out of your practices of consciousness and self-inquiry. This list is fluid and flowing. At first I suggest you order your list from easiest to hardest, but in time you will start to get a sense of what is next. It will float to the surface. This will become clearer when we look at developing intuition.

Keep your Practice focused. Work on one thing at a time, do what you need to do to clear it, cross it off your list, and then look at what is next. People frequently try to do several things at once, and then tend to feel overwhelmed and not accomplish much. I suggest you split your practice time between general attention to fundamental skills, and focused attention on clearing your list, while staying conscious of finding the balance between pushing too hard and avoidance.

Another thing to be aware of is the common tendency to follow the path of least resistance. The path of least resistance does not support growth. In the Deep Living Practice the path of least resistance is actually the path of most resistance, as it is allowing your resistance to your truth to guide you. If you are doing the Deep Living Practice as intended, it will bring up intense feelings. If it does not, you are being unconscious that your conditioning is actually determining your Practice.

Let's look at how to clear items off of your list. This is the heart of the Deep Living Practice and a bit of an art. There are no fixed ways or rules about how to do it. I will share my experience, but feel free to invent and develop your own practices.

The first answer to how to clear items from your list is "whatever works". The second, and more important, but not particularly satisfying answer is, "it is the choice to clear the item from your list". As we get deeper into our process of self-responsibility and consciousness, we will see that we are making the choices that create our experience, and that we can learn to become conscious of them and make other choices. Once we have learned to do this, life becomes very easy.

Let's look at the items on your list as choices that are not serving you, and that you are unconscious of, and the Deep Living Practice as what we can do to support the process of becoming conscious of these choices and making other ones. One of the first things I suggest is being as light about your Practice as possible. It doesn't help to get serious, and getting too serious can actually get in your way. I think of the things I create to help clear items off of lists as games, and I encourage you to do the same.

Frequently, what you need to do to clear an item off your list is to feel a feeling you have been repressing. You can create a game that will support you to feel the feeling you have been avoiding. There are countless ways of doing this. Here are a few basic and effective ones, but remember, it is not about the game. It is about feeling the feeling.

The first method is to choose to pay attention to the aspect of yourself you want to change. I spoke about this in the practice of consciousness, and this is a very powerful application of it. Look at something on your list and make the choice to bring your consciousness to it. Pay attention to how you feel when you are doing whatever it is. An example from my personal practice was my desire to be special. It was huge in me, and therefore became one of the first things I addressed. I decided to pay attention to any time I had a thought that had to do with my desire to feel special. It was shocking. It happened every few seconds. At first, this felt like a giant weight, and I felt it was too big for me to change, but I stayed with it anyway. After several days I had a sudden shift where I started to feel the absurdity of my desire to feel special, and I began to find it funny. It was happening so often and in such strange situations. I would see a couple that I didn't even know and find myself thinking that she should be with me instead of him, or I would see a list of names about something I had no involvement in and have the thought that I should be included. This is when I learned the value of not taking things too seriously, as finding the humor in the process allowed me to stay with it. As I stayed with the process, and really paid attention to what I was feeling as these thoughts arose, I noticed that actually I didn't feel special at all. I felt the exact opposite. I felt worthless, and I noticed that I felt I had to do things in order to be loved because I felt I was unlovable. As I allowed these feelings, my tendency to want to be special disappeared. I crossed it off my list and added "feeling worthless" and "feeling I had to do things in order to be accepted".

Choosing not to support a pattern, and feeling how it feels not to support it, is another way to clear something off your list. This is what I did with my pattern of doing things in order to be accepted or loved. This was a very deep pattern and took a couple of months to clear. I started to carefully watch all of my impulses to see if they were to make people like me. Again, it was almost all of them. I spent some very uncomfortable time just sitting and feeling that I should be doing things, and then not doing them. Again, it brought up feelings of being worthless and unlovable. After several weeks of sitting, I began to have impulses that felt entirely different. These new impulses were for things I either had to do, like eat or use the toilet, or things I wanted to do, like go for a walk, but had nothing to do with anyone else. Feeling this difference made it possible for me to take the next step in this practice.

It is frequently useful to start practicing in a controlled situation with limited input, and once you can do it there, try it in more challenging situations. It was hard enough to choose not to follow the impulses to do things to get people to like me when I was alone, but much harder when I was with other people. It was only through doing this that I was able to start feeling how I actually felt around people, instead of trying to avoid the feelings by doing things to get them to like me. These feelings were not very pleasant as, at a deep level, I had a very low opinion of myself, but it was only through feeling this lack of self esteem that I became aware of how low my opinion of myself was, which allowed me, in time, to explore and address the reasons for it, and eventually, through staying with the Deep Living Practice, come to accept and love myself.

Another practice in clearing your list is "flipping" the item. This comes back to the practice of self-responsibility, where you realize it is impossible to do something you don't want to do. This is particularly useful for items on your list that you tell yourself are things that you don't want to do. For example, you notice that you frequently argue, and you have put "arguing" on your list of things you want to change in your life. As opposed to saying, "I don't want to argue", flip it and say, "I want to argue". Then look for the benefit you get out of arguing. This may be the attention you get, or the feeling of being right. Remember, when we enter the world of feelings, things don't make sense. Be open to reasons for your behavior that may seem strange or ridiculous. An example of this would be if arguing made you feel sexually attractive. Frequently, finding the deeper motivation for the behavior is enough to let the behavior go, and clear the item from your list.

If you don't get clarity about what the deeper motivation is, make a conscious choice to do the thing that you tell yourself you don't want to do. In our example you might choose to argue with everybody, whether you agree with the argument or not. You don't have to do this in life; you can set it up as a game. The trick is to be conscious as you do it. Pay attention to how you feel as you give yourself permission to argue as much as you want, and see if you can find the part of yourself that wants to argue. This is a time where you will frequently be surprised, and feel great joy while you are arguing. When you find the part of yourself that wants to argue, and see what benefit you are getting that is causing the joy you are feeling, you will find your deeper motivation for arguing.

If, in our example, you find that your deeper motivation was the attention you get when you are arguing, you can put your desire to get attention on your list. Then you can shift your focus to this new aspect—your desire to get attention—which is your deeper motivation for arguing. If you argue in the future, you will see that it is a strategy for getting attention. Frequently this will be enough to support your choice to stop arguing. Then you can create a game to explore your desire for attention.

A similarly effective game is exaggerating patterns. If you find yourself doing something that you want to change, do it in a hugely exaggerated way. If you tend to be judgmental, be the most judgmental person you can possibly be. Get a robe and a gavel and gather some friends and pass judgment on them. Maybe even sentence them to some punishment for their misdeeds. Again, the trick is to pay attention to your feelings as you play these games and learn from them. Sometimes you will learn something that will make your Practice more honest, and therefore more effective, and sometimes exaggerating the pattern will support you to have a feeling that will transform the pattern. If you find it challenging to exaggerate the pattern, doing it will help you break free of the conditioning that tells you that this is something you are not allowed to do.

Remember, in all of these games, it is not about what you do, it is about having the feeling that is the result of what you do. When the feeling starts to come up, let go of the game and allow the feeling. As you learn to feel your feelings you will see that when you can allow the feeling that lies beneath the pattern for about a minute, frequently even less, the pattern will change and you will transform.

I want to remind you that although it may seem like there is a massive amount to do, and that particularly at first, clearing one thing might bring your attention to several others, as you make even a few steps, your experience of life will begin to change and become more open, free, exciting, and clear. At first the unfamiliarity of this may be uncomfortable, but I encourage you to stay with it. In time you will begin to feel more wonderful and alive than you could have ever imagined feeling, and come to see that the fact that there is so much to clear in your system is not a huge burden, but instead an incredible opportunity to keep feeling better and better.

-Chapter 23-

Your Relationship to Yourself

Now let's look at relationship. This is a huge topic, and we will address several different aspects of it. We will start with your relationship to yourself, because this is the template for all the other relationships in your life.

Your relationship to yourself will change and develop as you continue the Deep Living Practice. We will begin with the concept of identifying with your witness and paying attention to the other things that are happening within you, as if they were another person that you are in relationship with. We will be considering your relationship with your body, with your feelings or emotions, and with your mental construction.

To have a successful relationship with yourself, it is essential to pay attention to and listen to yourself. At a physical level this means paying attention to what your body is telling you. Physical pain is one of the ways your body communicates with you. How people relate to physical pain is very telling of their relationships to themselves. Having a high resistance to pain, disliking showing pain, ignoring pain, and medicating pain so you can get things done are all ways of relating to yourself that are not very attentive or caring. If you treated another person in one of these ways—ignoring him, hiding him from others, bullying him, or drugging him when there is a problem—you wouldn't have a very successful relationship. If on the other hand, you listen to him, consider what he is saying, and base your choices on what would be most beneficial for all concerned, you will probably have a much better relationship.

Practice: Make Dates with Yourself

Set aside some time in a quiet place. Either sit comfortably or lie down, and listen to yourself. Listen to your body. Listen to your feelings. Listen to your mind. Just pay attention. The same way you might invite someone you care about to go out on a date, do this with yourself, ask yourself how you are doing, and really listen to your answer. If you find this hard to do, look at the reasons why. This will give you useful information about your relationship with yourself.

This may seem similar to the self-inquiry practice, but at first, particularly if you don't have a good relationship with yourself, do this as a separate practice. Many people who do not have good relationships with themselves have lost trust in themselves. This practice can begin to restore it.

Make a commitment to yourself about doing this practice. It is very important that you keep this commitment. It is much better to make a smaller commitment that you actually keep, than a larger one that you do not keep, although the greater the commitment you make, and keep, the more quickly you will improve your relationship to yourself.

Allow the relationship to grow. At first I suggest having your date sitting or lying in a quiet place, but over time you might want to take a hot bath, or take a walk, or do something else you want to do. Listen to yourself and do nice things for yourself. Eventually you can make this practice part of your self-inquiry, but also occasionally have a date with yourself and give yourself a special treat.

Outside of this practice, bring consciousness to how you treat yourself in day-to-day life. Do you push yourself too hard? Do you have a low opinion of yourself? Do you insult yourself in your mind? These are things to notice and put on your list. How you feel about yourself has a major effect on your perception of reality.

Spend time looking at yourself in the mirror and feel what feelings come up. The way you groom yourself is very telling about your relationship to yourself. I suggest you look at the deeper motivations behind why you groom yourself the way you do. If you have a low opinion of yourself you might not groom yourself well, or you may overcompensate and be overly fastidious. Your sexual strategies or conditioning about gender may be reflected in your grooming. Playing with how you groom yourself can be an effective way to both explore your relationship to yourself, and also to your conditioning, because frequently your sense of grooming and style come out of your conditioning, and might not be a true expression of yourself.

As you explore your relationship with yourself more deeply, make lists about the things you like and dislike about yourself. Self-acceptance becomes a major concern as the Deep Living Practice develops. What are the things you judge about yourself? This is an area where it becomes particularly obvious how your relationship with yourself is the basis for your relationship with others. Things you judge other people for are actually things you judge in yourself. When you notice you are judging someone for something, put it on your list of things you judge in yourself. With self-inquiry you will find how this judgment applies to you. A wonderful effect of the Deep Living Practice is that you will become less judgmental.

As you look at your relationship to your emotions and feelings, we come again to self-acceptance. Most people have a hard time feeling their feelings, because they don't think they should be feeling them. Start paying attention to what feelings you accept and what feelings you don't accept, and put the ones you don't accept on your list. This is a very fruitful place to work because the choice to not accept what you are feeling comes from your conditioning. If you notice the feelings you do not accept, you will have the opportunity to not allow the choice to not accept them to control you. When you realize this, you will see that feeling these feelings you are not accepting is the path to finding your truth.

Your relationship to your mental construction is the one having the greatest effect and is the most challenging to work with. I mentioned your internal dialogue and not letting it guide you. Our Maniac on the Corner Practice is an excellent place to start. A useful way to continue to work with your relationship to your unconscious mind is to connect with its childlike nature by using the metaphor of an inner child.

Practice: Inner Child Work

Set two chairs facing each other. Sit on one, close your eyes, and take a few moments to Balance and Center. As much as you can, feel yourself as an adult—strong, capable, and able to take care of yourself. Then imagine yourself as you were when you were four years old. Imagine the child you were sitting on the other seat facing you. Then feel how you feel as an adult in relation to yourself as a child. When you are ready, open your eyes and, speaking out loud, ask your inner child how it is feeling, or if anything is bothering it. Then get up and sit on the other seat. Close your eyes and feel yourself as you were when you were a child. Assume the posture of this child. Let yourself go into feeling like a child as deeply as possible. Open your eyes, and imagine your adult self sitting in front of you. Respond to your adult self. Don't hold back. Say everything that comes to your mind. Feel any feelings that arise. Go as deeply into your experience of yourself as a child as you possibly can. When you feel done, return to the other seat. Take a few moments to come back to your adult self, then tell the child how you feel about what it said. Ask the child any questions you may have, and respond to everything the child asked. Go back and forth between adult and child several times until you feel it is time to stop.

In the adult role, remember that you are leading the process and are the responsible one. The purpose of the exercise is coming into a better relationship with your inner child. When in the child role, go into it as deeply as possible. Be a child. It is important to always end in the adult role, telling your child how you will respond to the things you've talked about. It is also important to remember that the entire exercise is to be spoken out loud.

Frequently your child self will not want to respond. Often this is because the child is angry with you. How you are as an adult with yourself as a child is telling about the state of your relationship with yourself. This is an excellent time to practice patience and your listening skills.

If the child does not want to talk, don't press it. Let it know you are available whenever it is ready. Come back to the exercise later. Tell it when you are coming back, and keep your word. This is another opportunity to rebuild trust in yourself. If you remember our discussion about aspects of the unconscious mind, you will recall that one of its primary functions is keeping you safe and healthy. If your adult self behaves in self-destructive ways, it creates mistrust within you, that is evident in your relationship with your child self.

Keep coming back to this practice until your child communicates with you. After it has communicated, consider what it has to say, and see if you want to make any behavioral adjustments based on how this childish aspect of yourself feels. This is a balancing act. On the one hand, you want to listen to what your child wants and consider it. On the other, you don't want to let the childish aspect of yourself run your life. The goal of the practice is to start communication and rebuild trust. Over time a goal of the Deep Living Practice is to convince your unconscious mind that it is safer to make your choices based on what is actually happening, as opposed to memories and past strategies. Connecting with your unconscious mind through the metaphor of the inner child is a great way to start this process.

Don't get too carried away with the metaphor of the inner child. I suggest you do this practice actively, but only for a few weeks. I have seen people take their inner child too seriously and allow it to control them. Watch out for this. Ideally you will start communication over the period of a few sessions. Once you are communicating, you can build relationship and trust. This can include going for walks or doing things you liked to do as a child. As you do this, you can stop speaking out loud and carry on the dialogue in your head. Over the next few times you play with your inner child, begin to integrate its voice as an aspect of yourself. Include it as part of your internal dialogue as opposed to continuing the practice of connecting with the child individually.

As the Deep Living Practice develops, your relationship with yourself and others will be a major focus and we will continue to discuss various aspects of your relationships. In the short term, pay attention to how you treat yourself. Treat yourself well. Be excellent with yourself, both in relation to your Practice and in life in general. If you notice yourself not treating yourself extremely well, put it on your list, because this is something you will definitely want to explore, address, and clear.

–Chapter 24–

Physical Practice

Now that we are considering your relationship to yourself, let's look at your relationship to your body and some of the physical aspects of the Deep Living Practice. As I mentioned, I started my professional practice working with people physically.

Our bodies are amazing gifts that give us the opportunity for incredible experiences. Our capacity for pleasure and the joy of movement are two examples of this. At the same time, many people's experience of pain and discomfort make their lives very challenging. My years of exploration of what our bodies can do, and how they heal, has given me valuable insights into ways you can be with your body that will support you to find comfort, balance, and functionality.

The first step in the physical part of the Deep Living Practice is the Date with Yourself Practice. There are many different ways you can learn to relate to your body, but I feel spending time listening to it and learning to let it guide you is the most beneficial. One of the greatest lessons I learned in my years of working with bodies is that we know how to heal ourselves. Through our conditioning and giving up self-responsibility, this ability has become impaired in most people. After years of experimenting with many different philosophies and techniques, I found the best support I could give my clients was to help them get more in touch with their ability to self-heal. Working on your relationship to yourself is the most effective way to begin this process.

It was when working with bodies I first began to experience the effects of fixed points. Eventually my style of bodywork focused on identifying fixed points in people's bodies and supporting movement. I found one of the most useful ways of doing this was simply bringing attention to the fixed point. Often we are not aware of what is holding us back and, until we are aware, the chance of changing it is very small. Frequently awareness is all it takes to start the process of transformation. Start to look for fixed points in your body, feel how they are affecting you, and do what you can to support them to move. If you like to receive bodywork, I suggest you find people who will help you with this process through conscious touch and gentle manipulation.

Most people have a huge amount of holding in their bodies. We experience holding in our bodies as tension or discomfort. This tension or discomfort can be caused by stress, repressed feelings, physical misalignments or adhesions, trauma, muscular contractions, and many other possible causes. The reason I use the term "holding" is that I have seen that, whatever the cause for the tension or discomfort, it is frequently related to a choice the person has made, usually unconsciously, and is "holding" onto. Part of the Deep Living Practice is to become aware of these choices and stop holding onto them. Here is a straightforward way to locate some of them and let them go.

Practice: Progressive Relaxation

This is a very effective practice that seems simple, but I found very challenging to master.

Close your eyes and focus on your body. Feel some area in your body where you are feeling tension or discomfort. Take a deep inhalation, and with your exhalation try to relax that part of your body, playing with the idea that you are letting go of whatever it is you are holding onto. As you do this, remain aware of the possibility that you may be holding onto something, and consider what it might be. Repeat. Repeat. Repeat until you are able to let go of what you are holding onto that is causing your pain or discomfort. In some cases it will become obvious what you are holding onto, and you may have to do some other process in order to let it go. Other times you will be able to let it go with just this process, and sometimes without even knowing what your holding was about.

This is something many people told me to do many times. For years I tried this to no effect. After years of working on myself I finally learned to do it. It may be easy for you, it may not be. Either way, I highly suggest you practice and learn to do it. Being able to relax is a wonderful skill to develop, and something I use frequently whenever I notice I am holding onto something in my body.

Realize that, while you are relaxing, whatever holding you are addressing may have emotional or mental components. Allow feelings, memories, or ideas to come up. Once you become more in touch with yourself and learn to allow your feelings, this is all you need to do to clear your system.

If you find this practice challenging, the Exploring Tight Muscles Exercise is a more dynamic and initially easier way of exploring the same principles. Stay with the Progressive Relaxation Practice, though, as you will ultimately find it the simpler and more direct way to become aware of the things that you are holding onto, let them go, and relax your body.

Now I would like to suggest a practice that may be challenging to accomplish on your own, but I highly encourage you to try. As my skill as a bodyworker developed, I began to feel more and more information coming from the person I was working with. Part of my way of working was to touch people very consciously and listen to what their bodies were telling me. I started to get a feeling of what their bodies wanted to do to heal. It was as if the body knew exactly what it needed to do, but the person I was working with was not aware of it. I let the body guide me, and I moved it the way I felt it wanted to move. When I did this, the body frequently seemed to understand what I was doing. It would start to move by itself, exactly the way I was moving it. It was as if by starting the movement, I created a sense of permission in the body, and after feeling this permission, the body took over. Then I started to teach the person I was working with to do these movements without me touching them, and eventually to initiate these movements without any outside help. Working this way was incredibly effective and became the focus of my professional practice.

Many good bodyworkers are able to help people reach this state. It is referred to as "unwinding". I find unwinding more beneficial than any other physical practice I know. It is as if we are getting our minds out of the way and letting our bodies heal themselves. Once you have experienced unwinding, it is not hard to learn to induce it on your own. I'm not sure how effective this will be if you have never experienced unwinding, but here is how I teach people to induce it in themselves. If you are not able to begin unwinding through this practice, find a bodyworker who works with unwinding to help you get started.

Practice: Unwinding

This is best done on a firm mattress or a thick mat on the floor. The movement can get very large and fast. It is important that you set up your practice space in a way that you feel sure you will not hurt yourself. If you are next to a wall, put pillows or cushions against the wall. Part of being able to reach the state where unwinding happens is giving your system a sense of permission that it is allowed to move any way that it wants. Your system will only feel this sense of permission if it feels safe.

Lie down. Close your eyes. Feel your body. Inhale deeply. With your exhalation relax into the mat you are lying on. Focus on the mat supporting you. Feel it beneath you and how it is holding you. Take a few breaths like this.

Feel if a movement wants to start in your body and allow it. The first few times you may want to start the movement yourself if you feel even the faintest impulse to move. It can help to give your system a little nudge. This is also a way of giving your body permission to move. Eventually though, we are looking for spontaneous movement that comes directly from your body and is outside your conscious choice to move.

Frequently some part of your body will start to shake. Allow it. Sometimes it is more like squirming or stretching. Whatever movement comes up, encourage it, and allow it to grow. Many people are surprised how easy it is and how quickly the movements become very large. Let yourself go with it. Give your body some time to do whatever it wants to do.

As I mentioned, frequently your body will shake. This is great. Trauma frequently leaves the body with a shaking movement, and you can do quite a bit of trauma resolution on your own this way. As you get better at allowing your body to unwind, feelings or memories can arise with your movements. Allow them. This can become a very deep process, through which you can clear many things out of your system.

As you are doing this process, pay attention to what is happening, but don't control it. You will probably experience an incredible intelligence behind the movements. One area will work for a while, then another, flowing around your body in quite an amazing way. One thing I recommend is that you look for repetitive patterns. Sometimes you might notice the movements repeating themselves as if they are stuck in a loop. If you feel this, consciously add a sudden movement. Then watch what happens. Frequently this will break the loop. If not, tune into what you are feeling, because you are probably resisting a feeling that wants to arise.

Once you are able to start unwinding on your own, you will see that you can also stop unwinding whenever you want. Practice starting and stopping a few times to make it clear to yourself that you can control the process. Lay down. Take a few breaths and start unwinding. Choose to stop. Get up. Walk around a little. Lay down. Take a few breaths and start again. Once you learn how to get in and out of this state, it is very easy.

I recommend you spend time unwinding every day. If the mattress on your bed is firm enough to allow movement, you might want to do it for a few minutes before you go to sleep at night. It is a great way to move through the backed up things in your system.

I had a very traumatic childhood, and had a lot of backed up issues to work through. I also had many physical problems and was frequently going to professionals for help. When I discovered the ability to unwind on my own, everything changed for me. After learning to unwind, I was able to move through many of my issues without professional help. This was a great step toward self-responsibility.

I noticed something very interesting while doing this practice. When I went into unwinding, I was a quivering, shaking mess rolling around on the floor. I was spending several hours most days in this state, and I began to feel that this state was a much more honest state than the state I was in when I was out in the world interacting with people. I began to see, that this quivering, shaking mess was much closer to who I really was, and that I was having to compose myself in order to function in the world. I stayed with doing this practice for about nine months, until eventually the movement stopped. Then I could get up and be in the world without having to compose myself and hold back all the time. This was a scary process in itself, but I can't begin to tell you how wonderful it felt to be out in the world and feel relaxed at the same time. I saw that the tension that I had always felt, and thought was part of who I was, was really just me hiding my scared and damaged body. It is hard to describe how liberating it was to be out in the world without holding back. It was one of those things that was beyond my imagination of how wonderful life might be.

Although I received amazing support from many people, I feel I did at least 80 percent of the work behind my transformation on my own. A significant part of that 80 percent was done with the practices in this chapter.

-Chapter 25-

Sensitivity

Through your practice of feeling your feelings and your focus on conscious-ness, you will begin to become more sensitive. Sensitivity is frequently discouraged by our conditioning, but your sensitivity is a wonderful gift. Our world, and the people in it, have become quite harsh, which makes being sensitive a challenge. Don't let this stop you. Your sensitivity is part of your power. To choose to dull or deny your sensitivity is a choice against yourself.

We can start to explore our sensitivity by looking at our five senses; sight, hearing, touch, smell, and taste. These are the ways we are taught that information comes to us. Very shortly after I began my search, I came to realize that this is a very limited view of what is actually happening. I've already used the term "energy" several times. I realize this is an ambiguous term and would like to discuss what I mean when I use it.

As I began my practice of consciousness and started to pay attention to what was happening around me, I became aware of various feelings I was experiencing in different situations. I noticed that when I was around someone who was angry, I would feel differently than when I was around a calm person. I started to notice that I had different feelings when I was in a busy city than when I was in the country; each city, in fact, evoked another feeling. When I use the term "energy" in this context, I am talking about this phenomenon that seems to emanate from people and things that creates these feelings in us.

As I continued to explore and develop my sensitivity toward these varied energies, I started to feel subtler experiences of these kinds of phenomenon. I had a friend who collected semi-precious stones, and I noticed my feelings shifted when I held different stones in my hand. I started to notice how I felt different when I changed the colors of the clothing I was wearing. I experienced that different energies were everywhere and that they were having an effect on me.

This became even more obvious in my study of bodywork. I started to feel things going on in the bodies I was touching. With the help of my teachers, and over time with experience, I learned to interpret what I was feeling. I found all these energetic experiences very hard to talk about, and realized that our language doesn't have adequate words to discuss these kinds of energetic phenomenon. Over time I realized that this was, again, how our conditioning has developed our culture to keep us away from our sources of power, and that the way language has developed is a major part of our conditioning.

Frequently when I am touching a body, I get information with my hands. This information is nothing like the information I get from simple touch. It is like I am hearing with my hands. I noticed when I was working with trauma, that I would experience something in my mouth that was not really like taste, but over time I found was an accurate indicator of how old the trauma was. I began to see that the information available to us is not limited to our five traditional senses, and I opened up for other streams of information from other sources.

I also noticed how heavily we rely on sight, and that by doing this we often ignore other streams of information that are coming to us. In the first years of my bodywork practice I frequently worked with my eyes closed. I found this made it easier to perceive these other forms of information. With practice, I learned to keep my eyes open while choosing which streams of information to pay attention to at any given time. As your practice of sensitivity develops, experiment with closing your eyes to help you become aware of the more subtle sensations you are experiencing.

Over time, I have come to experience that there is so much more available, again far beyond imagination, of what is possible. Many find the clarity with which I perceive people magical, but there is nothing special about it.

I have just spent time developing my sensitivity and learning to interpret it. The things I perceive from these other streams of information are as clear to me as the information coming from my traditional senses, and just as reliable. My experience is that anyone who wants to can learn to do this. As you continue the Deep Living Practice, your awareness and sensitivity will increase. Open up to these streams of information and pay attention to them. They have the potential to greatly enrich your life.

Some people become quite uncomfortable as their sensitivity develops. The primary reason for this is resistance. If your conditioning is telling you not to be sensitive, you may experience discomfort as your sensitivity is developing. Self-acceptance and embracing what is happening, instead of fighting it, will help you ease through this transition.

Some people become disturbed because they don't understand what is happening to them. They start to perceive things outside of their sensory perception and think there is something wrong with them, or that they are going insane. From your conditioning's point of view, your true self probably won't fit into the reality your conditioning has taught you to believe in. Allowing this process can feel like going insane. I know this may be challenging, but to find your truth you may need to go insane from your conditioning's point of view; so go. Allowing your sensitivity is much easier if you don't fight it. Actually, the discomfort is caused by the fight.

Many people who knew me 15 years ago think I went insane. I am so happy I did. I love my life, I have great relationships, I function easily in the world, I have no stress, I don't argue or complain, and I feel I am living my purpose. This is the insanity I am trying to guide you to. What helps the most in this situation is community. Find other people who are exploring similar things. Discussions I had with peers who were also working with sensitivity and energy were instrumental in my learning to trust and interpret what I was feeling. Many people are interested in exploring these kinds of things, and I encourage you to find them.

Another challenge your developing sensitivity may present you with is the feeling of becoming overwhelmed. If this happens, bring your attention to your pelvis. It really helps, and as you become better at it, it helps even more. I found that sometimes my sensitivity increased in sudden big steps, and I would spend a few days limiting how much stimulation I exposed myself to until I got used to it. You may want to try this. Also, realize your life is changing, and some situations may no longer be appropriate for you. I no longer enjoy being around very loud music or people who are drinking alcohol. Also remember that you already know how to block your sensitivity. You've probably been doing it most of your life, and you can choose to do it if you want. As your practice of consciousness develops, you can learn to pay more or less attention to these streams of information, depending on what is appropriate in the moment, but the first step is to learn to allow them.

Sensitivity is a skill that I highly suggest you develop. It will make your life much richer and ultimately much easier. There are several other life skills I find very useful, and we will look at them in the next few chapters.

–Chapter 26–

Empathy

Another extremely valuable skill to develop is empathy. Empathy is our ability to feel what someone else is feeling. It is one of the most wonderful states available to us.

I was in my forties before I discovered the value of empathy and, though I had heard the word before, I really didn't understand what it meant, nor could I remember ever having experienced it. As I began to explore empathy, I found that the vast majority of information about it was on how to prevent it, and was written for people who had a natural affinity for empathy and found that it caused problems in their lives. Relatively little information was available on how to develop empathy.

I found several reasons why people feel they need to avoid empathy. The primary one is that if you sense someone else feeling something you don't accept in yourself, it will make you uncomfortable. This is an issue that frequently comes up for bodyworkers, and many bodywork instructors teach ways of blocking the clients' energy or clearing it out of your system. My experience is that it is a much more effective practice to learn to accept the feelings within yourself. Then you never experience feeling uncomfortable, or that you are taking on any feelings or energy from the other person. You experience what the other person is feeling, which is extremely useful information if you are working with him or her, and then the feeling moves right through you. Feelings only get stuck in your system if you are resisting them in yourself. This is not only a consideration if and when you work with people professionally, but also applies to all the relations you have in life.

Another challenge with empathy is to not become too heavily affected by the intensity of feelings either in a person, or if you are in a crowd, the intensity of the group. You can remain present and at ease by connecting to your pelvis, and by not fighting what is happening. One of my favorite metaphors for how to be with the intense energies and feelings that comprise our experience of life, is surfing. Life is like the ocean. It is massively powerful and many different forces are moving in many different directions. It is extremely exhausting and quite futile to try to stop life, or fight it. What works is to pay attention to what is happening and move with it. Learn to identify the direction life is headed and ride it. Learn to surf life.

What is so wonderful about empathy is that it gives you the opportunity to experience things beyond your own experience. In my years of exploring reality, and what life is about, I came to see that what we are experiencing in each moment is the only thing that truly feels real and trustable. Billions of people are on the planet. Each one is having an experience, and all of these experiences are joining together to create a collective experience to which we are all contributing. Through empathy you get to feel someone else's experience, and thereby expand your own. It's such a simple and immediate way to expand your experience, and we are literally surrounded by countless opportunities to do just that.

Another metaphor I am fond of is looking at life on earth as a trip to a magnificent amusement park. Empathy is one of the ways to go on a ride, and since we are here, I highly suggest you go on the rides.

> *Practice: Beginning Empathy*
>
> *My experience is we are all naturally empathic, but most of us have learned to block it. The way to support the choice to allow your empathy is to choose to stop blocking it. This may sound ridiculously simple, but the way to increase your empathy is to try to be empathic.*
>
> *You need other people to practice empathy. You can do it with friends, but you can also do it with strangers. In my studies of the*

interactions of our physical, emotional, and mental systems, it is clear that the physical system is largely a manifestation of what is going on emotionally and mentally, and we can use this to help us develop our empathy.

Look at someone and imagine how he or she is feeling. Look at the expression on her face and mimic it. Feel how this feels. Exaggerate her expression and feel how it feels. Now take on the person's posture, feel, then exaggerate, then feel again. You can also do this with the way people walk or move. Try it at a dance, and feel how it feels to dance the way other people are dancing. Your willingness to mimic people and to allow their feelings is the first step to learning empathy.

This is a good place to start, and we will explore other practices of empathy in our discussions of intimacy and relationship. A key aspect of allowing empathy is your willingness to feel the feelings the other person is feeling. To do this you need to be willing to accept the same feelings within yourself, therefore self-acceptance is a major component in the practice of empathy.

Empathy is a skill, and though I find it a quite amazing skill, it is not inherently beneficial. You can also use empathy against someone. Most people who want to manipulate or control use empathy. Good salespeople use empathy to sell things, and some criminals use it to choose their victims. On the other hand, it can be incredibly beneficial. Most effective healers are using it in their practices. By developing your own empathy and consciousness you will always be aware of what is going on around you, which will make it difficult for people to use empathy against you.

It can feel wonderful when someone is being empathic with you. It is a feeling of being truly seen and understood. Empathy is at the heart of compassion. Compassion is feeling empathy and acceptance at the same time, and is a wonderful gift to give someone. Be careful with compassion though, because sometimes pity will sneak in. If there is pity, or any sense of being better than the other person, it is not really compassion, and neither the other person nor you will feel good.

Also do not mistake empathy with sympathy. Sympathy is when you feel what someone else is feeling and it triggers a memory of when you had a similar feeling. It's surprising that sympathy has such a good reputation, because my experience is that it doesn't feel good at all. The person feeling the sympathy goes into their memory and leaves you alone with your feeling, which is very empty compared to the connection you feel through empathy.

I find empathy one of our most valuable life skills. The time you spend developing empathy is definitely worthwhile. Next we will look at another extremely valuable life skill, intuition.

-Chapter 27-

Intuition

The Deep Living Practice's goal is to support you in finding your deepest truth. Your intuition is the voice of your truth. Part of the Deep Living Practice is to learn to be in touch with your inner voice and follow its guidance. We all have this inner voice, but most of us have been taught to ignore or disregard it. We are taught to be analytical and rational. There is nothing wrong with being analytical and rational, but it is not all there is. Relying exclusively on these aspects keeps us from reaching our maximum potential.

Let's consider the right and left sides of the brain. The left brain is the analytical, logical, linear, detail-oriented, language-based part of our brain, and the right brain is the intuitive, multi-tasking, imaginative, big picture, symbol part of our brain. The left brain is where our conditioning thrives. Most of us are taught to develop left-brain skills and to rely on our left brain to make our choices. Our left brain is wonderful, but so is our right brain, and most of us have been taught to disregard much of its input. I have found that the right brain is actually better at making life choices, and also at perceiving what is happening around us, without the bias of our memories. Ultimately each side of our brain has its place and function. Our maximum potential is to learn to use them both in the most appropriate way for any given situation. For most people the first step in this process is to relearn to pay attention to their right brains. I say relearn, because we are all primarily right-brained as children, since our right brain develops before our left. Through the Deep Living Practice we can learn to re-experience the joy and wonder we felt as children with the added benefit of consciousness.

One thing that keeps us from accessing our right brains is our heavy reliance on our left brains. Most people spend a lot of time, and use a lot of brain activity, trying to figure things out. Early in my process I noticed that my brain was doing this almost constantly. Here is a practice that was very successful in helping me break this pattern.

> *Practice: Stop Figuring Things Out*
>
> *Choose to focus your consciousness on the act of figuring things out in your brain. When you notice yourself doing this, say to yourself, "I don't know, you figure it out and get back to me," to stop the process of figuring the thing out. Let the "you" you are referring to be your inner voice. Keep doing this every time you find yourself trying to figure something out. It may be several times a minute at first, but stay with it. It may sound stupidly simple, I know that many of these practices do, but I also know that they work if you actually do them, and not let your conditioned mind convince you to not even try.*
>
> *The second part of this practice is to spend five minutes each morning before you start your day lying on your back with your eyes closed practicing Progressive Relaxation. Focus on some part of your body with each inhalation and relax it with each exhalation. After five minutes sit up, with your eyes still closed, be quiet for a minute, and listen for your inner voice.*
>
> *My experience was that after a few days I began to hear my inner voice just as I sat up. I got very clear messages about what I needed to do. This practice completely changed my life. I have been following the guidance of my inner voice ever since.*
>
> *After practicing this for a few weeks, I had both broken the pattern of constantly trying to figure things out with my brain, which was an incredible relief, and I learned what my inner voice sounded like. It has a very different sound and feel than the internal dialogue. Once you learn this difference, you know which voice to follow, and which voices to disregard. Once you are able to do this, you can let this practice go.*

While working on this practice, I noticed that I did not feel very good when I was paying attention to my internal dialogue. I noticed that most of what was going on in my head was an argument. As I became aware of my inner voice, I noticed that it spoke immediately, clearly, and with no doubt whatsoever. Then afterwards, my internal dialogue would begin to argue with whatever it said. I also noticed that when I paid attention to my inner voice I felt calm, clear and happy. I made the choice to learn to access my inner voice and intuition, and follow them to the best of my ability.

I began to actively look for my inner voice and how to access my intuition. During this time I was deeply into my practice of consciousness, and was particularly focused on experimenting with the size and shape of my consciousness. Through this I discovered a practice that helped me get in touch with my intuition.

> *Practice: Accessing Intuition*
>
> *If you remember, in the Capacity for Consciousness / Shape of Consciousness Practice we brought our attention to what the shape of our consciousness is at any given moment by focusing on where we are more or less conscious. By doing this we become aware of our consciousness having an edge at the outer limit of where we are more conscious. Focus your attention on the edge of your consciousness. It doesn't matter what shape it is in. It will always have an edge.*
>
> *As you focus your attention on the edge of your consciousness, open up for intuitive flashes. I experience them rising up out of the edge of my consciousness. The best way I can describe how I perceive these intuitive flashes is that they pop up like time-lapsed films of mushrooms growing.*
>
> *Watch for the tendency to discount them or brush them aside. Thoughts like, "It couldn't be that," or "Oh no, not that!" are the ways we block our intuition. Focus on the act of blocking, and actively choose to allow and explore any thought or image that arises.*

I found this way of connecting with my intuition very effective, particularly in my professional practice where I was experimenting with using intuition instead of technique to guide my sessions. Any time I did not know what to do next, I would stop, put my attention on the edge of my consciousness, and wait until my intuition told me what to do next. My intuition always spoke to me, but I did have to avoid the temptation to do something out of my mind or my training, to make space for my intuition to speak. This is the main obstacle for most people. They don't give their intuition a chance. They feel insecure, and instead of staying with their insecurity for a moment and allowing their intuition to arise, they feel like they have to do something, and by doing something, they miss their intuition. Give your intuition a chance.

Our ideas of what we should do can also get in the way. We think we know what is supposed to happen, and our intuition tells us something else, then we ignore our intuition even though it is trying to guide us to our truth. In my training courses, where I am helping people get in touch with their intuition, I frequently experience people clearly knowing what their intuition is telling them, but busily looking for another answer, because their mind is telling them that their intuition could not possibly be right. Frequently when I point this out they will say, "I thought of that, but it couldn't be so simple." Your truth is frequently simple and obvious, and our complicated conditioning refuses to accept it.

Something that surprises many people about intuition is how immediate it is. My experience is that it comes in a flash. Many people miss it, because it comes and goes before they notice. The trick here is to pay attention so you don't miss it, as well as to be careful not to brush it aside when it comes. Once you look for the answer in your mind, your chance of finding your intuitive response becomes much less likely. Here is an exercise where you can have an experience of the immediacy of your intuition.

Exercise: Answering Another Person's Questions

This exercise is similar to the What Are You Afraid Of? / What Do You Want? Exercise and will require a partner. This is also an exercise that will help you develop empathy.

Sit opposite your partner and take a moment with eyes closed to feel yourself. Then direct your attention to your partner and feel how that feels. Open your eyes, and then ask your partner "What are you afraid of?" Answer the question for him with the first thing that comes to your mind. Repeat this again and again for five to ten minutes. He will be sitting and saying nothing, while you are both asking the question and answering for him.

When you have finished the exercise, get feedback from your partner about how accurate your answers were. You will probably both be surprised by the accuracy of your answers. It is interesting to do this exercise after you have done the regular What Are You Afraid Of? Exercise and see how your answers differ from your

*partner's answers. Frequently you will say things he did not say,
but that he feels are true.*

Try this again with the "What do you want?" question.

Another way to tap into your intuition, and begin the practice of allowing
it to guide you, is to follow your impulses. We all have impulses to do and
say things. Most people repress most of their impulses most of the time.
Our conditioning teaches us that impulse control is a good thing. My experience is that often our impulses are our truth, and that by repressing
them we are denying our true selves.

Experiment with allowing your impulses. The trick here is consciousness.
It is vital that you remain conscious of the effects of your actions as you
allow your impulses. It is through the consequences of your impulses that
you can tell if your impulse originated in your conditioning, or in your
truth. If your impulse originated in your conditioning it will probably
create an unpleasant situation. If it originated in your truth it will have,
frequently surprisingly, wonderful results. The challenge here is that you
can't rely on your ideas about what the consequences of your impulses will
be, because they are most likely coming from your conditioning, hence
the need to experiment with allowing them while being conscious of the
results. As you will see, once you have become proficient in the basics,
consciousness becomes the primary thrust of the Deep Living Practice.

Impulses come very quickly and often have a small window of opportunity.
Learn to take advantage of those opportunities. If you do, it has a magical effect where you start living your truth and obtain this deep sense of
happiness and fulfillment I am guiding you toward. Your impulses can
show you the way. If you miss an opportunity, don't waste time and energy
getting angry at yourself for missing it. Notice that you missed it, resolve
to catch it next time, and start looking for your next impulse.

As we are seeing, our truth feels a certain way, and our conditioning feels
very different. It is by paying attention to, and learning this difference,
that we find our way. Following impulses is another practice where we
rely on our feelings to guide us. Impulses coming from, and leading you
to, your truth, feel one way, and impulses rooted in your conditioning and
fear feel very different. This brings us to our next chapter, which will be
a discussion of reactivity versus responsiveness.

–Chapter 28–

Reactivity and Responsiveness

When we start to follow our impulses, we need to become aware of our reactivity. A reaction and an impulse are very different, and feel that way. To help you understand this difference, let's explore reactivity and responsiveness.

A reaction is when our behavior in a situation is out of proportion to what is actually happening. Conversely, a response is when our behavior in a situation is appropriate to what is happening. Self-responsibility includes behaving responsibly instead of reactively.

Reactions are frequently connected with trauma and can be used as a way to identify trauma's presence. If you remember, trauma appears as a fixed point frozen in time in our physical, emotional, or mental system. When something is happening, and we begin to approach this fixed point, the trauma activates, part of our consciousness is transported back in time to where the trauma resides, and our behavior is affected by the conditions of when the trauma occurred.

Reactivity is frequently tied to trauma, but not always. Reactivity is usually related to fixed points, but there are also non-traumatic causes for fixed points. One of the main non-traumatic sources for fixed points is belief. This is one reason belief is so dangerous. It is the source of much reactive behavior. When we identify with our beliefs, we feel threatened when they are threatened, and we tend to go into reaction. Fear-triggering unconscious behavior is what distinguishes a reaction from an impulse or a response.

Reactivity can happen at a wide variety of levels. When our reactions are large and acute, they are very easy to recognize, but frequently reactivity is happening quietly, chronically, and unconsciously. It can affect our behavior without us even noticing. We may think we are in a particular mood, or the effects of the reactivity on our behavior may be so frequent we think it is who we are. Self-inquiry is a valuable way to explore why we behave the way we do, and what our motivations for behaving that way are.

I like to use the following metaphor as a practical example of how responsiveness compares to reactivity. Imagine a brick flying at your face. A response would be to move out of the way and let the brick fly by. But if as you are moving out of the way, you bump into a fixed point that keeps you from moving, the tendency is to go into reaction, which in this case may be putting your hands up in front of your face, letting the brick hit your arms. Notice the difference in feeling between calmly stepping aside and watching the brick fly by, which would be a response, and the reaction, which is the sudden intake of breath, accompanied by fear and tension, of putting your hands up and waiting for the brick to hit. The training of athletes, soldiers, and policemen includes practices to help them stay calm and responsive in intense situations. One of the goals of the Deep Living Practice is to support you to remain calm and responsive in all of life's situations.

I encourage you to pay attention to when you become reactive, and explore what is happening in your system that is causing your reactivity. Here is a fairly complicated but very effective practice that can help you find the roots of specific reactive behavior.

Practice: Exploring Reactivity with a Pendulum

Frequently when we are in a reactive state, it is because whatever is happening has triggered a past experience, and we are reacting to that past experience instead of responding to what is actually happening. These past experiences are stored in your unconscious mind, and you can access them by using a pendulum. I recommend that you do the Inner Child Work Exercise until you are able to communicate easily with your unconscious mind through the inner child metaphor before you do this practice. If you have a problem getting clear messages from your pendulum, the Inner Child Work Exercise is where you can solve the problem.

The first step is to make a small pendulum. This can be done easily with a short length of thread with a light weight tied to one end. The thread only needs to be long enough to swing easily when held in one hand, and the weight only needs to be heavy enough to not be affected by wind or drafts.

After you make the pendulum, practice using it to communicate with yourself. The pendulum can make four simple movements; swinging side-to-side, swinging forward-and-back, making clockwise circles, and making counter-clockwise circles. We want to equate these four directions with four answers; "yes", "no", "I don't have that information", and "I don't want to talk about it." You can do this by holding the pendulum in your dominant hand with your upper arm relaxed by your side, closing your eyes, and taking a moment to tune in with yourself. Then ask yourself aloud, "Which direction is yes?" The pendulum will move in one of these four directions. Open your eyes and make a note of it. If the pendulum does not move, go back to the Inner Child Work Exercise and ask your inner child why it doesn't want to use the pendulum. When you resolve whatever the issue is with your inner child, you should get a response from your pendulum. After getting a direction for "yes", repeat the process until you have directions for the other three answers. Make notes of them all, then come back the next day and repeat the exercise. If the answers are the same, you are ready to continue. If they change, keep repeating the process until you get consistent answers.

Once you are getting consistent answers, practice using the pendulum for a few days until you get comfortable using it. You can do this by asking all sorts of "yes" or "no" questions. Start by asking, "Do you want to answer some questions now?" If the answer is "no", let it go and try again later. If the answer is always "no", check in with your inner child to find out why.

You can ask any question you want, but at this point we are primarily focused on opening the lines of communication, so have fun with it and don't take it too seriously. Record your questions and answers in your notebook. This becomes necessary as the practice develops.

It's interesting to ask questions that give you the answers in situations where you are tempted to say, "I don't know." By this time in your Practice you must have questions about why you are doing the things you do, so practice by asking them. The only constraint at this point is that you are restricted to "yes" or "no" answers. You will see if you ask a question that you cannot possibly know the answer to, the answer will probably be "I don't have that information." If the answer is "I don't want to talk about it", make a note, as this will be something you will want to get back to later.

The teacher who taught me this practice felt that everything we had ever experienced was stored in our unconscious mind, and could be accessed through the use of the pendulum. This may or may not be true. My experience is that it doesn't matter if it is true or not. Memory is extremely unreliable, and I find it does not help to get very focused on what actually happened. What does matter is to understand that a process in your mind is affecting your present experience of reality, and that this practice offers an opportunity to shift that. I find this an extremely effective practice whether the information you find is true or not.

That said, let's get to the next step in this practice. Create a half circle on a sheet of paper with the round part facing up. Write a zero on the left side bottom and the number 100 on the right side bottom. Draw nine lines radiating out from the center point of the bottom line that are equally spaced as they intersect the circle's circumference. Label these lines 10-90 in increments of 10 from left to right. This will create a scale that looks like this.

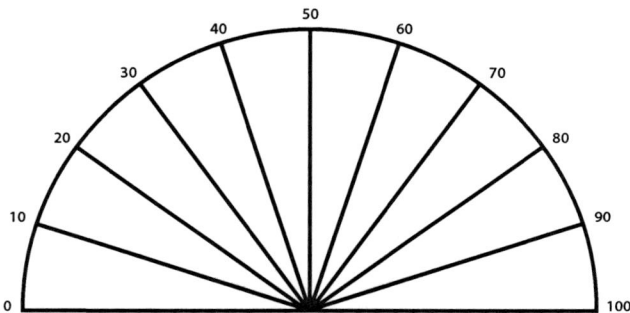

With this figure we have the ability to use our pendulum to get numeric values and to also indicate matters of degree. The answers to our questions are not always absolutely "yes" or absolutely "no", particularly when we delve into the world of memory.

For our next step, recall a recent time when you had a particularly intense reaction to something. We will use this as an example of how to use the pendulum to locate the memory at the root of the reaction.

Hold your pendulum directly over the point of your scale where the radial lines converge. Close your eyes and remember yourself having whatever reaction you have chosen to explore. With your eyes closed, ask yourself, "To what degree was I in memory at that moment?" Keep your eyes closed as the pendulum starts to swing, and then open your eyes and see what number your pendulum is indicating. If you have picked an intense reaction, the result will probably be more than 90 percent. Now that you know that you weren't being present, and were actually in memory, it is time to determine exactly what that memory was.

Now we have a mystery to solve. There is no set way to flesh out the details. Ask questions that help you define the event that is affecting your behavior. You can do it any way that you want. Here are some first questions to get you started.

"How old was I when this happened?" In your mind turn the numbers on the scale into years—10 equals 1, 20 equals 2, and so on. If your pendulum shows less than 1, ask "How many months old was I when this happened?" and in your mind turn the numbers into months. If the pendulum shows 10, you can ask if it is 11 or 12 with "yes" or "no" answers. If it is under 1, you can ask for weeks, days, hours, minutes, or seconds. Just keep adjusting the scale in your mind to make it work. The event may even be before you were born, in which case you can use the scale to go backwards in time.

Next, I would find the location of the event by asking the likely places—home, relatives' home, hospital—whatever might be a possibility. Once you find the building, find the room. You can also use the scale on these kinds of questions. If you ask, "To what degree did this thing happen at home?" and the answer is 100 percent, it was at home. If it comes in at 80 percent, it was probably close to home, maybe in the yard. With less percentage it will be further from your home.

As you continue to do this process, your mind will open up to this information and you will begin to intuitively know which questions to ask. Later you may also begin to know what the answers will be. After doing this process for a while, you might even be able to achieve the same results without the pendulum. It becomes an advanced form of your self-inquiry practice.

Other things to find will be, "Who was present in the room?" "What were the emotional states of the people involved?" "What did the people do?" Again, open your intuition to what questions to ask. You will learn to reconstruct the events more quickly with practice.

Also, get details that may not seem related, like what time it was, what people were wearing, or the décor of the room you were in. This kind of detail will help in the next step of the process.

Make notes in your notebook of the questions and answers. Keep asking questions and exploring the memory until you have an idea of what happened and have enough information to recount the event. Frequently you will have an "a-ha" moment when you realize the exact thing that happened that triggered you.

When I did this process, I found it amazing how every question had an answer. I enjoyed solving the mystery and found it fun to go into great detail. Again, it doesn't matter if the memories you recover are true or not. Through doing this, I got reasons that explained why I did the things I did. I went back through all of my questionable and bad behavior, and found a story to explain why I behaved the way I did. This gave me such a feeling of relief and empowerment. I went from feeling that there was something wrong with me, and that I was inherently broken, into seeing that, in this strange world of behavior, everything made sense in a certain way, and that I had been doing the best I could, considering these events. Through this I felt empowered to make changes.

If you remember our discussion of the subconscious, we talked about how our memories are like photographs. Through this practice we can identify the memories—whether they are accurate or not—that affect our current behavior. Once we recognize these memories, we can shift our relationship to them. Remind yourself that a tiger can hurt you, but a photograph of a tiger cannot hurt you. Use your practice of consciousness to pay attention to the feeling of reaction, and realize that when you are having that feeling, you believe that the photograph is dangerous. This can be challenging, as frequently reactions come very quickly, and you feel like you have been hijacked. If you focus your practice of consciousness on disconnecting from believing in your memories, your relationship to your reactions will change over time.

This process is greatly supported by the very choice to do something about your reactivity. That you have decided to not accept your reactivity as part of who you are by doing this process, is a major part of what makes the process work. Once you have found the memory, we can do another practice to take away its power over you, by transforming it.

Practice: Transforming Memories

Lie down comfortably in a quiet room with your eyes closed. Imagine a giant bookcase filled with photo albums of your memories. Imagine taking an album, opening it, and taking out a photo that represents the memory you want to transform.

Raise your right hand from the elbow and imagine holding the photo in your hand. Speaking out loud, tell the story of the memory you want to transform in great detail. This information will come from the results of your pendulum practice, so before you start, review your notes. As you are telling the story, feel free to add details to flesh out the story. Also, as you are telling the story, allow the feelings you felt as the event was happening, and tell the story with these feelings.

When you are finished telling the story, lower your right hand. Then raise your left hand and imagine the photo in it. Tell the story of the memory again, but this time, make it how you would have wanted it to be. It is very important to really stretch your imagination here. Let the story get as wonderful and magical as you can. Don't hold back. Make it fantastic. Many people find it challenging to make the story wonderful enough, and the ability to do this is the ability to break free of the memory. Keep practicing until you can tell the story in such a way that you feel happy and excited while telling the story. Let this feeling come through in the telling.

When you have finished the story, lower your left hand. Then raise both hands and imagine putting the transformed photo back in the album, and the album back in the bookcase. Lower your hands, then lie still for a few moments.

Frequently our practices are focused on an easier and more superficial level, to support transformation at a much deeper level. As you go further into the Deep Living Practice, you will come to see that it is all about choice. It is about becoming conscious of the choices you make, seeing the effect that they are having, and making different choices. Your choice to do the practice in the first place, and then your willingness and ability to make the second story truly fantastic, are the keys to success in eliminating reactivity from your life. After you do the practice, examine the second story in your self-inquiry and see if there are even more wonderful possibilities that you did not allow. This is a crucial part of transforming your memory. It may take practice to learn to let your imagination go and create a wonderful and powerful new memory for yourself.

These two practices, when done together, are incredibly effective. Using these practices I went from being extremely reactive, to being mostly responsive. When I started this practice, I reacted to most situations, as well as to my memories of those situations. Even when nothing was triggering me, I would remember things that had triggered me and get upset.

I really enjoyed doing this practice, particularly the first part where I was reconstructing memories. I like puzzles and detective stories, so I had fun figuring out which questions to ask, finding the answers and, as I've already mentioned, I found it an incredible relief to have some explanation of why I behaved the way I did. I started with remembering things that I had reacted to strongly, finding the memory behind the reaction, then transforming it.

After a while I switched to doing the process on the events and memories I was reacting to in day-to-day life. This is where I really began to notice the practice's benefits. Whenever I reacted, I would make a note, put it on my list, and then in the evening before I went to bed, I would take care of at least one thing from my list. After doing this for a couple of months, I went from being reactive several times a minute to several times an hour. I can't describe how different this made my experience of life. I stayed with a daily practice until I was only being reactive several times a day. Then I would just do the practice occasionally. Now, many months go by without me feeling any reactivity at all.

This practice is a technique, and I am wary of techniques, as they frequently block intuition and limit possibilities. But I recommend doing this one anyway, as it has had such a wonderful effect on my life.

-Chapter 29-

Deeper Motivations

As part of our self-inquiry, we explore our mental and emotional processes to find what is motivating and controlling our behavior. When we do this, we will find that fear is the motivation behind most of our behavior.

Fear is what drives most people, most of the time. It is a primary goal of the Deep Living Practice to change this, which is why courage plays such a central role. When people look at their fear, they often do not look at it very closely. They say, "I'm afraid", and don't consider what they are afraid of. If we do not examine our fears, we are powerless to stop their effect on us.

Working with our list of fears in the Courage Practice is an effective way to change this. In this practice we break our fears down into specific parts and confront them individually. As you progress with the Courage Practice, you will find the deeper roots of the fears you are working with. Eventually you will see that the fear of death is beneath your more superficial fears. One of my teachers said that the root of all fear was the fear of death. Most people's conditioning teaches them to be afraid of death. This creates a loop in which they never really live, because they are afraid to die. Sadly, this is true for most people.

What happens when we die? We don't know. If everything stops, it stops. If it transforms, it transforms. Whatever will happen, will happen. Being afraid of what is going to happen isn't going to change it. Degrading your life, because you are afraid of death, is an unwise choice.

Many people's conditioning tells them to be afraid of retribution after death. My experience is that retribution exists in life. Whatever choices you make have consequences that affect your experience. I see people creating their heaven or hell right here on earth. If those conditions extend beyond life here, so be it, but if you live here honestly, courageously, responsibly and consciously, you will have a wonderful experience here, and as good a chance as any to have a wonderful experience beyond.

Your relationship to death is a huge issue, and one in which your conditioning affects you deeply. I encourage you to explore your relationship to death. Not addressing this relationship is at the core of how most people's relationship to death develops in a way that does not support them. Most of us accept our conditioning about death blindly. Think about death, examine your feelings about it, discuss it and explore it until you come into a relationship with death that supports you to take advantage of life for as long as possible, then accept death gracefully.

The fear of loneliness is another factor that frequently motivates our behavior. At the root of loneliness is the lack of self-acceptance and self-love. Developing self-love is a primary objective of the Deep Living Practice. When you fully accept and love yourself, loneliness disappears. Not accepting and loving ourselves is a function of our conditioning. As we let go of our conditioning, self-acceptance and self-love result naturally.

That we don't accept ourselves as we are is at the root of what is not working in our culture. It is considered punishment to make someone be alone. Once you accept yourself, you stop fearing this. You enjoy being alone. We will explore this in great depth in upcoming chapters, but for the moment, in your self-inquiry, look how often the fear of loneliness is what is motivating your behavior.

Here is an exercise to help you look deeper into yourself and identify the major facets of your behavioral makeup.

Exercise: The Trap Door Game

This exercise is best done with a partner. One partner lies down with eyes closed. The other sits by his or her side and guides the process.

First you help the person lying down identify a desire, something he wants in his life. Then ask him his earliest memory of having this desire. Once he remembers, encourage him to relate the memory as a story. After he has told the story, tell him to imagine that a wizard appears and changes reality, so that his desire is fulfilled.

Now have him create a detailed fantasy of life with the desire fulfilled. When he has done that, ask him what he has now (in the fantasy) that he didn't have before. Get several answers. Look at the answers, pick the thing that feels most significant, and repeat the exercise from the point where he remembered the first time he wanted this new thing. It will usually be earlier in his life than the previous memory.

Go deeper and deeper until you've reached the earliest memory he can access. Repeat the game several times with different desires. You will find, no matter what superficial desire you start with, you will always come to a point at which the same series of desires and memories arise. These are some of your behavioral makeup's core aspects.

In my years of working with people, I have found that a few key elements are usually the basis of a person's behavioral makeup. This exercise can help you identify some of them. These are very powerful and effective things to transform. When you start working with these fundamental aspects, be careful. When we work at these very deep levels, we are deconstructing our senses of self. On the one hand, this is exactly what we are here to do, but at the same time, it can be challenging to adjust to the changes. Don't push yourself too hard, and take plenty of time to resource yourself. If strong resistance to the process comes up, allow it. Feel how it feels. We always want to accept whatever we are feeling and be ready for whatever is next.

In the short term, it is very effective to discover the deeper motivations for our behaviors and work with them, but eventually our goal is to find the deepest motivation of all, which is to live our truth. To do this, we need to feel the feelings we are repressing and break away from the control of our conditioning. At the same time, most of us continue to repress our feelings and follow our conditioning. This conflict is what is behind unhappiness and suffering. It is important to decide which side you are on—the side of your conditioning, or that of your truth. This choice will be tested over and over again. Remaining conscious of this choice, and continuing to make it, becomes our focus as the Deep Living Practice develops.

–Chapter 30–

Attachment

The feelings of attachment we develop for our parents and caregivers when we are children have a huge effect on us. It is a natural part of our development. As infants we are unable to take care of ourselves and are dependent upon others. The attachment between parent and child is part of our biological process. Most people accept the role of attachment in their lives, and don't question it. By not questioning its role in our lives, we allow attachment to affect us much longer than is appropriate.

I constantly see attachment issues behind people's suffering and unhappiness. What is appropriate for a five-month-old or five-year-old child does not work for a thirty-year-old adult, but I constantly see people extremely attached to trying to make attachment work, and suffering in the process. I would like to go into the effects these feelings of attachment have on our lives and some things we can do to address them.

At the core of attachment is the belief that you need someone, or something, else to survive. One of the reasons why the feelings of attachment are so strong is that they are driven by these existential fears. As long as it is true that you are unable to survive without support, these feelings of attachment are beneficial. They are mutual, as the parent also has a strong tendency to get attached to the child. This works wonderfully while the attachment is appropriate, as it motivates the parent to give the child the support it needs, but also makes the separation process challenging, as the parent is frequently attached to the attachment as well.

Many of our behavioral strategies develop to keep us from feeling things we don't want to feel, and a strong attachment bond will keep you from feeling helpless. If you have the feeling that someone is there to take care of you, you can relax knowing everything will be okay. The feeling that Mommy and Daddy are there for you is very seductive, and many people make the quest for this feeling one of their primary goals in life.

Another way to look at this is that part of us does not want to grow up. This is one reason I put such a strong focus on self-responsibility. Becoming an adult and behaving maturely is taking responsibility for yourself. Most people do it to some degree, but very few take complete responsibility for themselves. We live in a society with lots of old children and very few responsible adults.

One of the reasons for this is that few of us were well nurtured as children. Not many of us got the feeling that we were loved and accepted exactly as we were. We are so focused on trying to get this feeling, that we don't even consider other possibilities. This longing for nurturance and acceptance is a deep motivation for many people and drives a huge amount of superficial behavior.

This becomes very confusing, because attachment is frequently mistaken for love. Attachment and love are two totally different things. Attachment is a feeling of wanting to be taken care of that is based in helplessness, or conversely the feeling of wanting to take care of someone or something that is helpless.

Love is a very ambiguous term. In the Point of View, the definition of love is the feeling of wanting the best for someone, and the feeling you feel when you experience someone's happiness. We will discuss love, and other interpretations of love, in future chapters, but for the moment, accept this definition as part of the Point of View. If you do, you will see that one of the most frequent uses of the word love is as a replacement for the word attachment.

Our conditioning about attachment and love runs very deep. In that our conditioning has developed to keep us weak and controllable, it only makes sense that it would substitute attachment, which is rooted in helplessness, for love, which is very powerful.

So much of our conditioning about love and romance is designed to encourage the desire and quest for an attached relationship. "My soul mate", "my other half", "someday my prince will come", all of it, and so much more, carries the underlying message that you are not enough by yourself, and you need someone else to be complete. This feeling is at the root of most human unhappiness, and most people have been conditioned so successfully to believe that they are not enough within themselves, that they will choose the attached state over empowerment, self-fulfillment, freedom, and joy.

Remember that these attached relationships are developed with the people who are taking care of us when we are very young. How these relationships play out has a major effect on your relationships in the future. As an adult, when you continue to look for the kinds of attached relationships you had as a child, you tend to project your memories of the person you had your original relationship with, on the person you are currently in relationship with. This tendency is one of the major causes of difficulties in people's relationships. In a future chapter we will look further into attachment's role in relationships with other people, but for the moment I would like you to consider the possibility of letting attachment go.

This is challenging, because we have a tendency to be so attached to attachment, and also because life without attachment is beyond most people's imagination. In the next chapter we will discuss choice, and as you will see, this relates directly to how to let go of attachment. The choice to let go of attachment begins with imagining what life would be like without attachment.

Attachment affects our experience in many ways outside relationships with other people. We get attached to ideas, objects, memories, goals, and all variety of things including attachment itself. These attachments have their root in the attachment bond between child and caregiver and are compensations, strategies, sublimations, and similar complications driven by this original desire.

Practice: Looking for Attachment

Attachment causes a very definite feeling. It is the feeling of neediness. Become familiar with this feeling and watch for it.

If you feel you need something, check and see if it is something you actually need, like some oxygen every five or ten seconds, or some food from time to time. If it is not something you really need, even though you will feel like you really need it, you are probably feeling attachment. People become attached to all kinds of things—routines, foods, clothing, anything can be an object of attachment. The thing to understand is that it has nothing to do with whatever it is you are attached to. It is all about the choice to be attached, which is based on the feeling that you are not enough within yourself to survive.

Imagine life without attachment. Our conditioning tends to look at life in terms of black and white, with thoughts like, "If I can't have what I want, I don't want anything." Just because you don't feel you need things, doesn't mean you can't enjoy things. Once you let go of attachment, you will see that neediness actually gets in the way of you enjoying so many of the possibilities available for you, both because you are so focused on your object of attachment you are not aware of other possibilities, and also that frequently the intensity of your neediness itself gets in the way of you getting what you think you want.

The secret to happiness is accepting and enjoying what is happening. When you look at life this way, you see that desire is actually the choice to be unhappy. Desire is you wanting things to be different, instead of enjoying things as they are. Why you want them to be different is most frequently an effect of your conditioning. Attachment fuels this process and makes you feel that your life will be threatened if you do not receive the things you desire. My experience is that the brief feelings of joy you get when you get your object of desire are not worth all of the pain involved in wanting and not getting. As well, you will see that desire is a choice and it is not about the object. If you are in the state of desire, you will just shift your desire to some other object, because at the deeper level you have chosen to be unhappy and not want things to be the way they are.

Many people think that suffering is part of life. "No pain, no gain." That to struggle and achieve is what life is all about. This is conditioning. When you let go of attachment, life is wonderful beyond description. There is no wanting, disappointment, comparison, jealousy. All of these things just become memories and seem rather silly when you see people indulging in them.

In the last chapter I mentioned how the fear of death is the root of many fears, and that fear is one of the most frequent motivators of behavior. It works like this. Say you are afraid to approach someone you are attracted to. Underneath might be the fear of rejection. If you allow this feeling of rejection, you may be afraid that you will feel like nobody likes you. If you allow this feeling that nobody likes you, you may feel like you will always be alone. If you allow this feeling of loneliness you may feel like you need other people to survive. This is where attachment comes into the process. If you are still in a state of attachment, being alone means no one is there to take care of you. If there is no one to take care of you, and you feel you need someone else to survive, you will feel like you will die. Attachment is fueling the fear and making it seem life threatening to go up and talk to someone.

I mentioned fear of loneliness as a powerful motivator, and that the key to letting go of loneliness is self-acceptance. In that the root of attachment is that you feel you need someone else to survive, it includes the idea that you are not enough by yourself. This leads most people to feel that something is wrong with them that will be fixed by their connection with another. Part of the process of letting go of attachment is realizing that you are perfect exactly the way you are and totally capable of interacting with the world on your own. Self-acceptance is the entrance to self-love.

Attachment keeps us connected to this helpless state when we were not yet able to take care of ourselves. It prevents presence. I said that I did not find it effective to try to be present. One reason for this is that while you are supporting attachment in your system, you are not present with what is actually happening, as you are staying connected to motivations from your past. As you are doing your Looking For Attachment Practice, pay attention to your internal dialogue and notice how many of your thoughts have attachment at their root. I find it much more effective to choose against being attached, and through this, it becomes much easier to be present. Everything becomes easier. Life is so much more wonderful when you choose to let go of attachment, but there is no way you can know this until you decide to try. This begins with considering the possibility, and imagining your life without attachment.

Letting go of attachment is one of the most challenging aspects of the Deep Living Practice. One of my teachers used to say that attachment is the last thing to go before you are truly free. But don't get attached to letting go of attachment. It is really quite a tricky thing to let go of, so don't rush the process. I mentioned earlier that it is all about choice, so let's take a deeper look at choice next.

-Chapter 31-

Making a Choice

As I work with people, I frequently suggest that the person I'm working with do something, such as allow his or her anger. She will tell me that she wants to, but doesn't know how.

The way to do it is to choose to do it. I know this answer may not be the clear instructions you are looking for, but once you find the ability within yourself to make these kinds of choices, you will understand what I mean and see that it is really very simple. Actually, most everything I am talking about—allowing your feelings, being in touch with your empathy and intuition, presence—are utterly simple, in one sense, because they are all natural aspects of ourselves, but, because of our conditioning, we are choosing not to allow them, so they can seem extremely difficult, or even impossible. Becoming conscious of the choices we are making that create our experience and learning to make the choices that guide us to our truth is at the core of the Deep Living Practice. In this chapter we will explore making these difficult choices.

I've found that making a hard choice is a process, and that it is very useful to track your progress as you are making the choice. To do this I use a scale of 1 to 10, with 1 being an absolute "no", and 10 being a total "yes". When you are at 1, there is no chance of you doing the thing you are considering doing. When you are at 10, you have already made the choice to do it. Frequently, when we first consider doing something, we are at 1, but even starting to consider the possibility of doing it moves us to 2 or 3. If you won't even consider the possibility, you stay at 1, and the issue becomes a fixed point, which as we have seen, locks us into certain aspects of experience.

If you have fixed points, consider softening them, unless you want your life to remain as it is. Most often it is the exact fixed point that you feel you absolutely do not want to change that is causing the experience you want to change. If we want to find our truth, we have to be ready to let go of everything. We might not need to, but we have to be willing to. If we make conditions, they define us, and these conditions, by definition, come from our conditioning. A goal of the Deep Living Practice is to live unconditionally, which, of course, our conditioning will tell us is not possible. But my experience has shown me that living this way is unimaginably wonderful.

The next step in making a choice is to imagine what would happen if you made the choice. This will move you further up the scale toward the number 5. Five is the magic number on the scale, because this is where the balance shifts towards "yes" instead of "no". Once you can allow yourself to imagine doing the thing, you are in the 3 to 4 range. If you imagine a favorable outcome, you will be around 4. If you imagine something terrible happening, you will be closer to 3.

At this point remember that your imagination is dominated by your conditioning and that it is unlikely that what you imagine will happen is what will actually happen. This gets easier with experience, as over and over again, while you are experimenting with making these unfamiliar choices, you will see that things very rarely turn out the way your conditioning tells you they will. When you decide you will try to make the choice, even though part of you might not want to, you get up to 4 on the scale.

Now we come to courage. As we approach 5, where we are actually going to start doing whatever it is we are considering doing, we will very likely begin to feel fear. As you feel the fear, look at it, and find exactly what you are afraid of. You may be afraid of more than one thing. Identify each of your fears, and address them individually.

Sometimes it is more effective to let go of the choice you are playing with at the moment, put your full attention on what you are afraid of, and clear that out of your system, before you get back to working on the choice. Continue to do this with your fears until you reach the point where you are ready to do the thing, even though you are afraid. Now you are at 4.9.

This is when you will start to have feelings. Your goal is to stay conscious and present as your feelings arise. This is frequently one of the most challenging moments of the process, and it can be supportive to have someone to help you stay present, focused, and to point out when you are using avoidance strategies.

At this moment, part of you will probably want to avoid the process and run away. If you choose against running away, it is very likely that you will want to stop the process or destroy whatever it is that you are focused on. Choose against this as well. Our goal is to feel what happens if we don't fight, and we don't run, but we just stay and allow ourselves to feel what we are feeling without doing anything about it. This is how to get to the point where you are truly feeling your feelings.

When you are just over 5, you may feel overwhelmed. If you feel it is too much, back off for a bit and rest. Remember to use the Rhythm. For the process to be transformative, it is essential that you allow your feelings with consciousness. This may include some shaking, sweating, or maybe some tears, but stay aware and avoid yelling or hitting. Sometimes physically pushing against resistance can help, but it is not about the fight, it is about allowing the feeling. Sometimes at this point you will start to breathe quickly and deeply. This kind of breathing is an effective way to *avoid* feelings. It moves them through you. We don't want to do that. We want to have the feeling. So if you notice you are breathing heavily, settle down, and breathe normally.

Let the pressure of the feeling build up. Let it keep building until you think you will explode. Then don't explode. The pressure you are experiencing is the feeling pushing against the resistance that still remains to your allowing the feeling. This is the 5.1 to 7 range of our scale. It can be quite exhausting. If you start to get too tired, take a break and come back to it later. Also, if you make a big jump where you allow a big portion of the feeling, but you don't allow it completely, you will probably want to take a break to give time for the pressure of the feeling to build up again.

Don't push yourself too hard, and remember that patience is a very important part of the process. If you keep coming back to it, you will reach the point where you can fully allow the feeling. Once you learn to make the choice to fully allow a feeling, it gets easier. You feel the mechanism of making the choice within yourself and learn to access it at will. You still may have some challenges as you approach harder choices and deeper fears, but as you continue the Practice you will be able to allow anything.

Our 7 to 10 range is about accepting whatever you are feeling and relaxing into it. Frequently at this point you will feel joy. You will smile and your eyes will shine. This is the range in which the transformation takes place. Sometimes it is not a rush of joy, but a sense of peace and calm. What seemed so important a moment ago will suddenly seem totally inconsequential, and you almost can't even remember why you were so upset. There is a wide variety of feelings that accompany these transformations, but no matter which feeling it is, it will bring you closer to what is real for you.

There is no set amount of time for this process. If you have no resistance at all it can happen in a flash. This happens more and more frequently as you become experienced in the Deep Living Practice. If you continue to resist your feelings, it can take hours, days, weeks, months, years, or might not ever happen. The choice is up to you. If you find yourself fighting, use your self-inquiry, and look at why you want to fight the feeling.

Be aware of avoidance patterns. Many of these are strategies that create states where change is not possible. Self-pity is one of these. I see the path from who you think you are, to who you really are, as a straight line. Self-pity is an exit off this path that takes you to a very unpleasant place. It reminds me of the rest stops on limited access highways where the food is bad, everything is expensive, you have to pay to use the toilet, and there is nowhere else to go except to get back on the freeway. Self-pity is an uncomfortable state that never changes until you decide to leave it.

If you have a tendency to go into self-pity, I suggest you exaggerate the pattern. Remember, we are allowing whatever is there. I had a friend who used to decorate her closet in black and throw herself a pity party. As you allow your self-pity, stay with the feeling. Avoid doing anything to distract yourself. Dive into your self-pity and feel the pain and futility of it, until you feel ready to try something else. Self-pity is the result of allowing fear to control you. The antidote to self-pity is the practice of courage.

As you proceed with the Deep Living Practice, you will frequently feel two, or more, feelings at the same time. You may be thinking about a specific instance and feel both anger and sadness. When this happens, choose one of the two. Think of it as a fork in the road, where one path is going to keep you on the straight line to your truth, while the other will take you off into your conditioning. Imagine allowing each of the two feelings. Whichever one is more exciting, frightening, or causes the more intense feeling, is probably the way to go. If you make a choice, and it feels off, you can go back, and try the other.

The ability to make the choice of which feeling to support is one of the skills you will develop as you continue the Deep Living Practice. As you develop this skill, you will need to learn to distinguish between choosing to support a choice, as opposed to getting attached to a choice. We are looking for the quality of, "Let's try this and see what happens," as opposed to, "It has to be this way," or, "I'll never do that!" Realize that the way you do things, has as much effect, and often more, as the things themselves. Our goal is to find a more relaxed and expanded way to be in the world. If we become tight and driven in our Practice, we are defeating our purpose.

Becoming aware of the quality of the way we do the things we do leads us to the most important choice of all. This is the choice between saying "yes" or "no" to your true self. When we get to the core of the Deep Living Practice we shift from saying "no" to our conditioning, to saying "yes" to our truth. We want to focus on the "yes" and let the "no" fall away. This "yes" or "no" happens at many different levels, and we will continue to discuss various aspects of this for the remainder of the book, but at the moment we want to focus our sensitivity on learning to feel the difference between the choices of "yes" and "no" and starting to support the "yes".

It is very important that we don't repress anything. We want to say "yes" to whatever we are feeling, even if we are feeling "No, I don't want to feel this." Saying "yes" to your "no" is an essential part of allowing your truth. Your resistance is what you are feeling in the moment, and by not allowing it, you create separation and mistrust within yourself. By accepting yourself exactly as you are, you connect with your power.

We don't want to repress our resistance, we want to allow it, feel how it feels, then make our next choice. At the same time, as we come to these forks in the road, where we have the opportunity to make a choice of what to support, we need some basis for this choice. We want to make this choice based on the feeling of "yes". We will look at this more deeply in the next chapter.

The primary level at which you look at your "yes" is in your choice to support your truth over your conditioning. The entire book, up to this point, has been about helping you make this choice. The process of this choice is just like any other choice, and we can apply our 1 to 10 scale to it. It is a huge and challenging choice. I encourage you to be aware of it, and track your progress as you proceed with your Practice.

Much of what we have talked about in the book has been addressing your mind to get you to make the choice to experiment with the Deep Living Practice and see what happens. For most people I work with, it doesn't take very long for them to start to understand the Point of View, and decide to dive in. Actually and actively choosing your truth over your conditioning, though, is far more challenging and tends to bring up much resistance and many feelings.

I see this as a mountain where the number 5 on our scale is the peak. Reaching the peak is an uphill climb and you may feel frustrated as you are learning to do things you are not used to doing. When you get close to the top, it becomes particularly challenging as your conditioning will fight for supremacy using fear, doubt, and resistance to stay in control. It frequently takes a push to get over the top. The good news is that once you really choose to say "yes" to your truth, which requires that you actually start doing the things that I am suggesting, as opposed to thinking that you will do them, everything gets much easier.

After you get over the peak, you start to get a sense of your truth and realize that it was always there. All you have to do is stop doing all the things your conditioning is telling you to do to suppress it. You just need to relax into yourself. Say "yes" to yourself.

Even though at this stage you might get quite uncomfortable, because without your conditioning you don't know who you are, or how you are supposed to behave. You now have the opportunity to answer these questions from your truth.

As you are doing your self-inquiry, you may want to ask yourself which side you are on in relationship to whatever it is that you are looking at. Are you supporting your truth, or your conditioning? You may sometimes find yourself supporting your conditioning out of habit. It has a very strong hold on us. Here is another way to apply your vigilance to break that hold.

> *Practice: Checking the Status of Your Yes*
>
> *When you are considering making a challenging step, ask yourself, or have someone ask you, if you are going to do it or not. Pay attention to what happens directly after the question. Did you immediately say "yes", or did you hesitate or equivocate? If you did say, "yes", what was the quality of your "yes"? Was it strong and bold, or was it meek and half-hearted? Whatever your answer was, rate it on a scale of 1 to 10 and keep track of how your choice develops as you work on it.*

The choices you are making, both consciously and unconsciously, are directly creating your experience of reality. We use our practice of self-inquiry to become aware of what these choices are, and our practices of consciousness and courage to learn to make the choices that will bring us to our truth and allow our deepest experiences to unfold.

–Chapter 32–

Letting Your Feelings Guide You

Once we develop our sensitivity and the ability to feel our feelings, we can start to let our feelings guide us. This is a wonderful part of the Deep Living Practice. When you become adept at this, your life becomes very simple and clear. You will leave doubt and confusion behind.

Your feelings are the voice of your truth. Your thoughts are the voice of your mind, which contains your conditioning. I'll repeat here that your thoughts are not bad. We just want to learn to stop allowing our conditioning, which expresses itself through our thoughts, to control our life choices. Instead, we want to make our life choices by listening to our truth through our feelings.

I have encouraged you to pay attention to your feelings while you are thinking about things. You will notice that you feel different feelings while having different thoughts. When you do this, you will start to see that feelings have different qualities. Pay attention to the different qualities of different feelings. We can get much information from them.

How do your feelings feel? I don't mean if they feel good or bad. Good and bad aren't feelings, they are judgments about feelings, and are frequently rooted in conditioning. I am referring to the way that some feelings are more pleasurable than others. We want to bring our awareness to how different feelings make us feel differently and start to examine the variations of these feelings.

When I am making choices, I move toward some qualities of feelings and away from others. There is no right or wrong about this, it is just that some qualities of feelings feel better to me than others, and I have found that if I make the choice that elicits the feeling I enjoy more, the choice creates an experience I enjoy more.

Here I'll illustrate the qualities of feelings I prefer. I encourage you to experiment with what qualities of feelings you prefer; the ones that will create the life that is most in line with your truth. You can tell this by the feeling of, "this is exactly what I want to be doing in this moment." If you are not feeling this feeling, do something else, and keep doing something else until you are feeling this feeling.

One of the qualities of feelings I look for when making decisions is expansion. Here is how I use this in life.

Practice: Making a Decision

Break the decision you want to make into clear parts and create separate statements to clearly describe what the options are. Close your eyes and inhale. With your inhalation, bring your attention to your pelvic floor and perineum. As you exhale, relax into yourself.

Make one of the statements to yourself, and imagine you have made the decision to do the thing. Pay attention to the quality of how you feel. As I said, I like the feeling of expansiveness, so I notice if my feeling centers feel expansive or contracted while I am imagining that I have decided to do this thing. Then try the other choice. Make the statement that you are not going to do the thing, or that you are going to do another alternative, imagining that you have made the choice, and feel how that feels. Compare the two feelings. Whichever feels more like the feeling you prefer, in my case expansiveness, is the one you choose. If you don't have much of a preference, you might have to do it a few times in order to feel which one is the choice more in line with your truth. At first the difference may feel subtle, but once you become practiced at this, the answers are usually very clear.

I have made my decisions this way for many years. Once you get good at it, you only need to do this for challenging decisions. Most of the time you just pay attention to how you are feeling. If I feel expanded, I keep doing whatever I am doing. As soon as I feel a contraction, I stop, and look at what I need to do to return to my expanded feeling.

Contraction/expansion is not the only guide I use. I am drawn toward many feelings. I sat down once and made a list along with their counterparts. Here it is:

I move toward feeling:	I move away from feeling:
Expansion	Contraction
Inclusion	Exclusion
Simplicity	Complication
Support	Opposition
Cooperation	Competition
Balance	Imbalance
Generosity	Greed
Vulnerability	Resistance
Abundance	Neediness
Flexibility	Stiffness
Movement	Fixed points
Presence	Disassociation
Excitement	Fear
Soft	Hard
Free	Attached
Powerful	Dependent
Appropriate	Inappropriate
Honest	Dishonest
Courage	Cowardice
Consciousness	Unawareness
Responsibility	Irresponsibility
Yes	No

This is not a list of hard and fixed ideas, but more an indication of tendencies that guide me toward an experience I deeply enjoy. My aim is the feeling of supporting something without being attached to what happens. I find using the concepts of "appropriate" and "inappropriate" an effective way to look at life without judgment, while exercising my ability to make choices and staying conscious of the consequences of those choices.

Once you make a choice, it is important to not become attached to it. Things change. If whatever you are doing starts to feel contracted, or inappropriate in some way, check in again and see if the choice is still appropriate.

Most people interpret perfection as something to strive for. This is an example of how language has developed to support our conditioning. I have come to see that there *is only* perfection, and it is awe-inspiring how incredible the perfection we live in is. Our choices have consequences, and they perfectly create the experience to guide us toward our truth, if we pay attention to, and are guided by, the feelings they create. I frequently entertain myself by watching perfection unfold around me. I have learned that things are perfect, whether I want them to be or not, and if I am unhappy, it is just because I am incapable of seeing the perfection of what is happening. The choice to look for perfection, instead of becoming involved in disliking what is happening, is an example of a choice that keeps me in an expanded state. Often I am incapable of understanding perfection, and I choose to accept this.

I often see people making choices when they don't have to. I suggest you wait to make a choice until the choice needs to be made. Take advantage of the changes that may have taken place, or the information that might be obtained by waiting.

Most people make choices before they need to because they are worrying. Worrying is allowing your past fears to project onto the future. Not only does worrying feel bad, it also affects how you perceive the world, and through that, it affects your reality. As the old saying goes: "Worrying is praying for what you don't want". In my experience, this is true. By worrying about something, you greatly increase the probability that what you are worrying about will happen. If you don't allow worrying to affect you, you will see that often you don't have to make the choice at all, or by the time it needs to be made, it ends up being a different choice.

Something that you need to learn before you are able to make your decisions based on your feelings, is the difference between fear and what is inappropriate. Most people make most of their decisions based on fear. An important part of our Practice is courage, which is not allowing fear to control your behavior. When we tune into our feelings about making a decision, and feel fear, we want to do the thing we are afraid of in order to stop allowing fear to control our behavior. This will not be an issue for long, if you actively do the Courage Practice I mentioned earlier. If you make that practice a priority, your relationship to fear will change in a matter of weeks, and then you can do these advanced practices more easily. The feeling that something is inappropriate for you is a very neutral feeling. It doesn't have a charge like fear has. If there is no charge, it is not fear. The lack of an intense feeling is a sign that it is something you don't need to concern yourself with.

This brings us to attraction and repulsion. Let these feelings guide you, for as you well know, they definitely have a charge. Attraction and repulsion are life's way of telling us that something is there for us, and yes, I mean both attraction *and* repulsion. They are two aspects of the same thing. It is just that your conditioning approves of attraction and disapproves of repulsion. I find them equally valuable, and I encourage you to actively pursue both.

When it comes to attraction, many people let their minds get in the way. They think the attraction is about something specific like relationship, sex, social standing, or any variety of things. If the aspect they think the attraction is about does not happen, they stop pursuing the attraction, and miss the real opportunity.

Approach attraction with an open mind. Attraction can be about anything. It is life's way of guiding you. Maybe the person you are attracted to will introduce you to someone else, maybe you will have a different kind of connection with this person than you thought you would have, or maybe you are just there to make another person jealous, so that person does something he or she wouldn't have done without you there. As we go on in the book, I will be talking about giving of yourself and participating in life. Attraction is your invitation to participate. I encourage you to follow your attractions and be available for anything that feels exciting.

Repulsion is attraction that you judge. Very often, if people repulse you, it is because you do something that they do that you judge yourself for, or they are doing something you would really like to be doing, but you don't allow yourself to do. The information you can get from exploring repulsion can be very useful. Take advantage of it.

> *Practice: Exploring Repulsion*
>
> *Invite people you don't like to lunch. This practice had a huge effect on my life. At lunch, I would tell the person that there was something about him or her I found challenging, and that I realized that it was something about me and had nothing to do with him or her. I would ask if we could talk about it, and through talking about it, I would come to understand what it was in myself that bothered me. The person I invited always enjoyed the experience as well. I did not end up having friendships with any of these people, but I also stopped being annoyed or repulsed by them. I also found that over time, I was no longer annoyed or repulsed by anyone.*

If, when approached by a practice like this, you find yourself saying, "No way. I would never do that," realize that this is your conditioning speaking. This response is an example of you creating a fixed point that will keep you from finding your truth.

I want to end this chapter with one more practice. This is a strange one, and illustrates a way of being that I find very attractive. I love the idea of looking at life as an experiment, not taking things too seriously, and playing with different things. This is a practice I did with my partner that proved helpful in getting us out of the habit of letting our thoughts guide our actions.

> *Practice: Let Muscle Testing Guide You*
>
> *I have learned a variety of muscle testing techniques from a variety of sources, and every one of them told me not to use muscle testing to make major life decisions. My partner and I decided to experiment with this, by using muscle testing to make all of our life choices. This kind of experimenting with your life can help you break old habits. If you would like to try this, here is what to do.*

Focus your practice of consciousness on all the choices you are making. You will see that you are making choices all the time. Start using muscle testing to make the choices.

If you are unfamiliar with muscle testing, here is an easy way to do it. Touch the tips of your thumb and middle finger of each hand together, forming two circles, and let the point where the thumb and finger are touching be in the center of the circle formed by the other hand, so the two circles are interlocked. Say, "My name is (say your name)", and then try to pull your hands apart while keeping your thumbs and middle fingers pressed firmly together. It should be rather hard to pull your hands apart. Then say, "My name is (say a name other than yours and from the opposite gender)", and try to pull your hands apart while keeping your thumbs and middle fingers pressed together. It should be much easier to pull them apart. We will interpret when your hands are strong and you are able to hold the circles, as "Yes, I will do that." We will interpret when your hands are weak and you cannot hold the circles as "No, I will not do that."

Now use this to make all of your choices. Choices about where you will go, what you will do, what you eat. Every choice you can catch. We did this for about six weeks, catching every choice we could and doing whatever the muscle testing told us to do.

Doing this practice will bring awareness to how many choices you make and how you usually make your choices. Most people are either making their choices without paying much, or any, attention to the process of making them, or they are relying on their mind, and therefore their conditioning, to make their choices. This practice is useful as a step to change the way you make your choices, but ultimately, not the way to make your choices, as the choices you make by muscle testing are also heavily affected by your conditioning. Ultimately you want to make your choices based on your feelings.

If you choose to experiment with letting muscle testing guide you, don't take it too seriously. The main thing we got out of this practice was breaking our habit of making decisions based on what we thought we wanted. Another interesting thing we learned was that it really didn't matter what we did. We approached the practice in a light way and had fun no matter where it led us. We saw that how we felt about what was happening was more important than what was actually happening. It really didn't matter what we were doing as long as we didn't think it mattered. The core of freedom is the understanding that nothing really matters. There is no benefit to taking life too seriously.

-Chapter 33-

Pelvis Exercises

Next I would like to bring your attention back to your pelvis. The pelvis is a very powerful and neglected part of the body. By now you have probably experienced how supportive it is to be able to bring your attention to your pelvis and perineum. There is more about the pelvis to explore.

Our posture, the way we hold ourselves in the world, is largely affected by how we think and feel about ourselves. If you look at the body's structure, you will see that the pelvis is the part of the body around which all the other parts organize. In learning to work with people's posture and structure, I was taught to make adjustments in the pelvis, and then see how these adjustments affected the rest of the body. I was also taught that, as you do this, you must support the person through the emotional and mental changes such readjustments create, or they will return to their previous postural state.

Through my years of working deeply with people's pelvises, I came to see that the way the person held their pelvis, or the "set" of their pelvis, was a direct expression of who they thought they were and how they felt about themselves. Frequently I would find their pelvis a fixed point that was a major factor in what they were experiencing as reality. I found that by supporting people to allow movement in their pelvises, I could support their transformation. Another way of saying this, is that the set of your pelvis is largely a product of your conditioning, and to allow movement in your pelvis is extremely beneficial in the quest to find your truth. After learning this, I developed a series of exercises my clients could do on their own that support pelvic movement.

Before I explain these exercises, I would like to present some information about the structure of the pelvis. The pelvis is made of three bones. One is called the sacrum. This is the triangular bone at the base of the spine. The other two bones include your hips, your sitting bones, half of your pubic bone, and are referred to as your hip bones. They are mirror images of each other, which connect to the sides of the sacrum at joints called the sacroiliac joints. They join in the front of the body, at a joint in the middle of the pubic bone, called the pubic symphysis. The pubic bone is the horizontal bone just above your genitals. Together with the sacrum, the hip bones form a bottomless bowl-like structure that make up your pelvis.

These exercises promote movement between the three different bones of your pelvis. Most people don't realize they have a joint in the middle of the pubic bone and that movement is possible there. This is a cartilage joint, which means that there is a softer ligament connecting the harder bones together. This ligament can get harder or softer. The softer it is, the more movement is possible, and the harder it is, the less movement is possible. At the same time, the more it moves, the softer it gets, and the less it moves, the harder it gets.

The point of these exercises is to learn to move your two hipbones and your sacrum independently of each other, by creating movement between the sacroiliac joint and the pubic symphysis. These are very small movements that can take a while to learn.

Exercise: Pelvis Exercises

These exercises are in three parts. To learn these exercises, we will do them while lying on our backs.

Part 1: Moving the Pubic Symphysis

Place the fingertips of both hands on your pubic bone. Find the joint in the center of the bone. You will probably experience it as a slight depression running vertically through the center of the horizontal bone just above your genitals. When you have located it, place the fingertips of your hands on either side of it, with your fingers pointing toward your feet. This is the starting position for this part of the exercise.

Part 1-1: From the starting position, let the fingers of both hands slide along the pubic bone away from the pubic symphysis until you feel them curve towards your body. Stop just after the curve and adjust your fingers so you can put pressure in toward the joint. Apply equal pressure from both sides. Keep the pressure up for about 20 seconds.

Many people are very tender in this area, and adding pressure may be painful. If so, lessen the pressure until there is no pain. This will change over time. Keep adjusting how hard you press so you are giving strong pressure without pain or excessive effort. This also applies to the next two sections of part one.

Part 1-2: Return to the starting position. Alternating between hands, press the pubic bone straight down toward the floor. Do this several times and feel which side moves more, or hurts less, as you press down. Choose whichever side moves more, or hurts less, and apply steady pressure for about 20 seconds. If one side moves more, but hurts more, choose the side that hurts less.

Part 1-3: Return to the starting position. Slide your hands slightly toward your head until your fingertips reach the top edge of your pubic bone. Press toward the floor into your abdomen until your fingertips are on the top side of your pubic bone. Alternating between hands, press either side of the pubic bone in the direction of your feet. Choose whichever side moves more, or hurts less, and apply steady pressure for about 20 seconds. If one side moves more, but hurts more, choose the side that hurts less.

Part 2: Isolating Movements in Your Hip Bones

I will describe this exercise for the right hip bone. You will also do it for the left hip bone. You can choose to do all four parts on the right, then all four parts on the left, or do each part right and left before moving on.

Feel your sacrum on the floor. You will only be moving your right hip bone. These will be small movements. Make these movements using the muscles in your pelvis instead of the muscles in your legs or abdomen. Do not move your sacrum or your left hip bone. If you are moving your sacrum or other hip bone, the movement is too big. For some, or all, of these exercises, you may not be able to make these movements at first. This is common. If you cannot make a movement, try to make it, and imagine you are making it. If you stay with this exercise, and practice it frequently, you will be able to make these movements in a relatively short period of time.

Part 2-1: Swinging. Although you are lying down, imagine the motion your hip bone would be making if you were standing up and swinging your leg back and forth. Doing this lying down, the bottom of your sitting bone will be moving toward the ceiling, then the floor. When you have made the movement four to five times, you can move on.

Part 2-2: Shearing. Put your attention to the top of your right hip bone on the side of your body, where your hand would be if you put your hands on your hips. Keeping your focus here, move the right hip bone alternately between the directions of your head and your feet. When you have made the movement four to five times, you can move on.

Part 2-3: Rotating. Put your attention on the two points where your hip bones create bumps on the front of your body. Imagine if these points, on both sides, were to rotate towards each other in an arc, where they would meet in front of your body. Make the small movement that would be the beginning of this arc. When you have made the movement four to five times, you can move on.

Part 2-4: Flaring. Focus on your right sitting bone and imagine it making an arc, side-to-side, parallel to the floor. When you have made the movement four to five times, you can move on.

Part 3: Combining the Movements

Part 3-1: Keeping your sacrum and left hip bone still, move your right hip bone in random combinations of the movements from part 2 of the exercise. Do this for about 20 seconds.

Part 3-2: Keeping your sacrum and right hip bone still, move your left hip bone in random combinations of the movements from part 2 of the exercise. Do this for about 20 seconds.

Part 3-3: Keeping your sacrum still, move your right and left hip bones in asymmetrical random combinations of the movements from part 2 of the exercise. This will probably be very challenging at first, and you may not be able to do it for more then a few seconds, but over time you will be able to do it longer. Do it as long as it feels appropriate.

It can take a while to learn these exercises, but once you do, you can do them in a very short time. As with many things, I find doing frequent short practices instead of long less frequent practices more effective. I teach these exercises lying down, but you can do them anytime, in any position. You can do them when you are standing in line, or sitting and waiting. Do all three parts twice a day, and part two frequently all day long, whenever you have a minute or two between things.

These are very powerful exercises. Since our idea of who we are is held in the set of our pelvis, and we are shifting the set of our pelvis, these exercises can be extremely destabilizing, so be careful with them. This feeling of destabilization just shows that these exercises are working. It is important for you to regulate your process in a way that is nurturing for you. If you feel you are getting too unstable, take a break from the exercises until you feel you are ready to continue with them.

That said, I encourage you to do these exercises frequently. They are very effective in supporting major transformation. Frequently feelings can arise as you are doing these exercises. Allow them. Don't suppress a feeling in order to finish the exercise. Also, don't stop the exercise to avoid a feeling. If it is challenging, you can approach doing the exercise with the Rhythm to support you to be able to fully allow the feeling being brought up by the movement.

Also start allowing movement between the different bones of your pelvis while walking. Most people in North American, European, and some Asian cultures tend to walk from their hips, just moving their legs while keeping their pelvises fixed. Try walking by allowing your step to originate in your spine at your waist and letting your hipbones sway and move in relationship to each other. It is much healthier, and much more fun. You will see women and men who are allowing their sexuality doing this, as well as many people from Latin and African cultures. This is an example of how our conditioning manifests physically.

Addressing the fixed points, and supporting movement, in the pelvis is a valuable part of the Deep Living Practice. Doing these exercises will support transformation, letting go of your sense of self, and helping your body find its natural alignment.

-Chapter 34-

Language

We create our experience of reality through the choices we make. One of the ways we do this is through the things we say and the way we use language. This is a powerful part of our conditioning and has a very deep effect on us. Our relationship to words, and language, is extremely ingrained into our systems.

We need some level of conditioning to learn how to be in the world, but so much of this conditioning has developed to keep us controlled, powerless, and disconnected from our truth. In this chapter we look at how language and the way we speak, contributes to these aspects of our conditioning. Many words represent things we think of as desirable and good, but they actually support our choices to give up our power, freedom and self-determination. Let's look at a few of them.

Most people think hope is a positive word and attribute, but when we examine hope more deeply we see that it directs your attention into the future. Many people have been taught they can't find the strength to live without hope, but upon further exploration you will see that hope is a tool for control. It takes you out of the present, which is where you can actually be effective, and puts your focus on the future, which does not exist in this moment. If you make your choices based on what is happening in the moment, you have the possibility of creating a much more wonderful reality than if you are basing your choices on what you want to happen, or have been told might happen.

Faith is similar. If you don't take responsibility for yourself, you may choose to believe in something to avoid feelings of insecurity, but if you want to find your truth, you will see that belief and faith will only get in your way.

We are told it is good to be respectful, but when you examine what respect really means, you see that it is treating people the way they want you to treat them. There is nothing wrong with treating people the way they want to be treated, but you have no obligation to. You get to choose how you want to treat people. I suggest you make conscious choices on how you treat people based on what feels appropriate to you in the moment, instead of how they feel, or society feels, they are supposed to be treated.

The same is true for duty. Duty is doing something because your conditioning tells you to. Again, it is great if you truly want to do whatever it is, but you have no obligation to, and the way our culture glorifies duty, is how we collectively coerce each other into following our conditioning.

Most of the time, when someone is being nice, he or she is being dishonest. It usually means that the person is behaving the way she thinks the person she is being nice to wants her to behave. If you look a little deeper, being nice is being both dishonest and manipulative, as you are trying to get the other person to behave in a certain way toward you. This may create a superficial sense of everything being pleasant, but I have found that people who do this build up resentment over time that starts to show up in unconscious behavior. Being nice is something we are taught is good, but it ends up creating a lot of trouble. A friend of mine says, "Less nice, more happy." This is my experience too. In the long run, honesty is the only thing that really works, and as I said, nice is rarely honest.

The pursuit of perfection is one of the leading causes of unhappiness. Most of us have the idea that perfection is a distant thing we must always strive to attain. This is an idea put into our culture to keep us constantly dissatisfied with what is, and wanting things to be better. The basis of this is the religious idea that there is a heaven. If you work hard and obey the rules now, you will be rewarded with the perfection of heaven in the future. This is nothing but a mechanism to control people.

As I have become more conscious and present with what is happening in the moment, my relationship to the concept of perfection has shifted dramatically. Now I perceive the absolute perfection of everything that is happening, and how through this, people are creating their personal heavens and hells moment to moment. The more present I am, the more obvious this is. I am in complete awe of how incredibly perfect everything is. I get the sense that perfection is the only thing possible. I've come to see that everything is perfect, whether we want it to be or not.

I had a teacher who used to say, "Forgiveness is an act of cowardice." When we forgive, we are becoming codependent and are encouraging the person to continue whatever behavior we found inappropriate. The most loving thing to do is to support the person to be aware of the consequences of his or her behavior, to see the real motivation behind the behavior, and to be responsible for the choice to behave that way. If the person chooses to continue the behavior you find inappropriate, the most loving response is to withdraw support for anything having to do with the behavior. The most caring thing to do is to support the people around you to live their highest potential in each moment.

My point here is to encourage you to look at what the words you are using really mean, instead of letting your unconscious acceptance of their meaning affect your reality. Use language to define your experience, instead of letting language define you.

We are taught that some things are inherently bad, but I find that many of them can actually be quite useful. Anger is a great example of this. We are seeing that if you can learn to be responsible with your anger, it is an incredible power available for you. When you line your anger up with your truth, it is your power, and when it is out of line with your truth, it will help guide you toward your truth through the process of allowing it, letting it become the resolve to make the changes necessary to align with your truth, then living your truth and letting your anger become the fuel of your passion.

Most of us are doing everything we can to avoid our insecurities, but insecurity is honest. We live in an unpredictable world. We don't know what is going to happen. What keeps most people disconnected from honesty are the things they do to avoid insecurity. I have found insecurity is the beginning of the path to your truth. I find it refreshing and delightful when people approach me with insecurity, instead of indulging in one of the acts most people affect in order to make themselves and those around them think they are secure.

Vulnerability is your willingness to feel what you are experiencing, and share it with others. It has a bad reputation. It is considered weak and dangerous. This is because we live in a culture that has developed to keep us weak and controllable. My experience is that when we are the most vulnerable, we are the most powerful. This is it. This is what we are and what we feel. There is nothing to argue with, there is nothing to discuss. What makes us controllable is our fear of being found out for who we really are. When we accept ourselves fully, and show ourselves courageously, we can no longer be manipulated, and it becomes quite easy to see if someone is trying. I know there is a huge amount of fear about vulnerability, but I encourage you to experiment with it. Vulnerability is wonderful. It is where you will find your power.

If you are being deeply honest and conscious of your feelings, while you are tuned in to whatever situation you are in, and have made the choice to participate fully (which are all parts of the Deep Living Practice), you will find that being selfish is the most wonderful thing you can do. Each of us is a gift. We have come here to contribute our part into this joint creation of reality. When we find our deepest truth, and start to give of ourselves, we feel incredibly wonderful. It is a feeling beyond anything I can describe. A sense that you are in exactly the perfect place, doing exactly what you want to be doing, and everything around you is falling perfectly into place to support you to continue. When you reach this state, you will feel so incredibly supported, and so much energy, and abundance, coming to you, that all doubt and insecurity wash away. In this state you will find that if you do even more of what you really want, if you participate even more fully, if you selfishly go for an even more wonderful experience, you will be giving even more to the people around you, and receive even more back from them. You will see that being selfish is a wonderful thing, and being more selfish will be even more wonderful. Obviously, if you are in a contracted, fear-based, self-involved state, selfishness usually has consequences that do not create a very pleasant reality. It all depends on the way you are doing the things you are doing, but it is interesting to see how with consciousness, many things that we consider bad can become wonderful.

The more we look at language, and explore it, we see how the disempowering aspects of our conditioning are so deeply embedded in the words we use, and how what we have been told is a distorted mirror image of what would support us to find our true selves. We are taught to be dishonest with ourselves, and others, and frequently have no idea that we are doing it. There are many things we fully believe when we say them, but if we look at them in our self-inquiry, we will find they are not really true.

"I can't…" is one of these. Occasionally it is true, but more often it is not. What is usually true is that you don't want to. By saying, "I can't…", you create a reality where it is impossible. Saying "I don't want to…", creates an opportunity to look at why you don't want to do the thing, and through this, consider the possibilities available for you. You cut yourself off from your power by saying, "I can't…"

"I don't know," is also very rarely true. More frequently you do not want to know, and are saying this to avoid something that you are uncomfortable with. Our practice of self-inquiry is the antidote for, "I don't know."

"I don't want to," is another thing people tend to say that I often find to be untrue. When you say, "I don't want to," it is almost always your conditioning speaking, so pay attention. Frequently people truly want exactly what they are saying they don't want, but their conditioning is telling them it is wrong or bad. This isn't always the case, but it often is, and when it isn't, your conditioning is still almost always behind your not wanting to do the thing.

Another tendency people have when talking is to be indirect about what they are saying. It is not always dishonest, but it keeps you from experiencing the full effect of what you are saying, and getting the greatest potential from the moment. One way people do this is to distance themselves from what they are saying. When I ask someone how he or she feels, I frequently hear, "There is a feeling of sadness," instead of "I feel sad." People tend to diminish things, like saying, "I'm a little angry," when they are very angry. They will add phrases like, "sort of," or "kind of" to buffer themselves from their content. All of these things are based in the fear of showing ourselves completely. It is through showing ourselves boldly, and clearly, that we will experience the consequence of our actions, and through that get the feedback to guide us towards our truth.

Many people fall into automatic behavior in many ways. One of the most popular is giving automatic responses. Look for this in yourself, and others, as you are speaking. When you hear something, do you always say the same thing? Do you frequently tell the same stories in the same situations? One of my teachers initiated a huge process in me by encouraging me to pay attention to how I answered the telephone, and to stop doing it automatically. We indulge in automatic behavior to avoid presence and intimacy. If you would like a deeper experience of life, become conscious of automatic behavior, and choose not to support it.

Although it is not language, nervous laughter is another popular strategy to avoid feelings. It is quite prevalent and has a good reputation, because most people find laughter non-threatening. I love real laughter, but the vast majority of laughter that I hear is nervous laughter, and I don't find this attractive at all. The most obvious way to identify nervous laughter is that you will notice that nothing is funny. Many people who use this strategy do it all the time, and are frequently perceived to be happy people. It is a relatively effective strategy, but it is usually a mask for deep fear and unhappiness. By indulging in the strategy, people keep the contact superficial and dishonest. Nervous laughter is also quite contagious. Many people who don't use it as a regular strategy will resort to it when exposed to something that makes them particularly uncomfortable, instead of allowing their honest response. Frequently when something is overtly sexual, people will laugh, as opposed to allowing their sexual response.

As the Deep Living Practice develops, I will continue to encourage you to integrate it into your day-to-day life. Working with language, and how you speak, is a powerful way to do this. Paying attention to what you say, how you are saying it, what it really means, how honest and direct it is, how appropriate and vulnerable it is, is a wonderful way to practice consciousness.

You will see that some of your habits with language, and how you express yourself, are very challenging to change, because they are so deeply ingrained in your system. You will also see how radically your experience can shift when you change the way you communicate. I've come to see the words we say are magic spells that weave the fabric of our reality.

-Chapter 35-

Some Things to Consider

Almost everyone I meet is holding back. People don't feel they have permission to be who they are.

There is no one to give you permission. You are responsible for yourself. Watch for the feeling that you aren't allowed to do something. It is frequently a voice in your mind from the past. More often than not, it is a voice you are attached to, so you will have existential fear of doing the thing you feel is forbidden. This is the time to practice courage.

When I point out where people are holding back, they frequently tell me that if they were to stop holding back they would be too much for other people. I hear this all the time. Everybody is holding back because they are afraid of being too much for everybody else. It's crazy when you think about it. Be one of those who are not holding back, giving a feeling of permission for others to be bigger and more powerful. Again, it is the practice of courage.

We are amazingly powerful. Our conditioning has developed to keep us unaware of how powerful we are. If you don't hold back, you will have a much greater effect on the world around you. This is wonderful. We are here to participate in life. Go for it. As you go for it, though, pay attention to what effect you are having. This is the core of our practice of consciousness. As children, we don't hold back, and we are usually not very conscious of the effects of our actions. Most of us are taught to hold back and repress our impulses. We learn to live that way, and it is the source of much of our unhappiness.

My experience is that holding back is usually the cause of depression. The person wants to be doing something that he or she is not doing. In deep and chronic depression, it is frequently something very different than what the person is doing in her life, often beyond her imagination, and that would require a huge amount of courage to allow. If you suffer depression, or know someone who does, consider this possibility. I have seen changes in people's lives that can only be described as miraculous.

Holding back is exhausting. Your deeper truth is motivating you, and your conditioning is saying "no". It is as if you have one foot on the accelerator and the other on the brake. Most people go through life fighting themselves this way. This fight causes self-doubt and confusion, while using a huge amount of energy. When people feel lazy, the conflict between their truth and their conditioning is frequently the cause. The fight between truth and conditioning is exhausting and obscures our purpose. It is the reason many people always feel tired, and it makes us more susceptible to disease.

Part of the Deep Living Practice is to stop holding back, but also to be conscious of the effects of your actions, and be empathetic to the people around you. As you do this, a process of regulation begins, and you will feel what is appropriate for the situation. If you are being conscious, it doesn't feel good to do things that feel inappropriate. This state of conscious regulation is very different from the state of holding back because you are afraid of how people will react. It feels open and expansive. You feel capable and ready to respond to whatever comes. When you are holding back you feel tight, contracted, and are prone to go into reaction.

Once you are able to reach this state of conscious regulation, the goal is to allow as much of your energy as you are capable of being conscious of. As you hold back less and allow more, you will reach a point where you may become overwhelmed with excitement, and it will become more and more challenging to stay present. Through working on your practice of consciousness, you will continually be able to allow more of your true power while staying conscious. For several years, the bulk of my Practice was spent alternating between becoming more conscious and allowing more energy. This is an exciting time where your possibilities in life really begin to expand, and you can return to the childlike wonder and joy that lie underneath your holding back.

◊◊◊   ◊◊◊   ◊◊◊

When I ask people what they want, one of the most frequent answers I hear is freedom. Unless you are being physically restrained, you are already free. You can go anywhere and do anything. It is the choices that we have made that take away our feeling of freedom. Usually we are selling our freedom in exchange for a feeling of safety and predictability. You may have made some agreements that support this, and there may be some consequence to breaking those agreements, but the truth is that you are free. If you can accept this, and be honest with yourself about it, you can start the process of making the choices that will lead you to your experience of freedom.

At the heart of a feeling of personal freedom is the realization that nothing matters. This is a challenging concept for many people. In our conditioning, we tend to think that if nothing matters there is no point in doing anything. If you consider it though, you will see that it is in that nothing matters where there is permission to do anything.

The universe is vast, and we are comparatively insignificant. In the scheme of the history of the universe, whatever you are concerned with has very little meaning, so lighten up. Take some risks. Have some fun. Create some incredible experiences. By doing this you will probably be making a more positive insignificant contribution anyway, so enjoy your freedom, and take advantage of the opportunities in your life.

◊◊◊   ◊◊◊   ◊◊◊

Pay attention to how you define yourself. It is invariably coming from your conditioning, but frequently it is so deep that you think it is who you are. Anytime you use the words "I am...", whatever comes next is very likely a statement of limitation.

◊◊◊   ◊◊◊   ◊◊◊

Speaking of limitations, let's talk about boundaries for a few moments. Many people are very attached to their boundaries and consider them extremely important. Boundaries are hard limits, or fixed points, around which your reality needs to organize, and are usually generated from fear. They are an attempt to create a feeling of safety and predictability, but they are unnatural and the deep motivation of your truth to arise will probably guide you to unconscious acts that will frequently put you in situations where your boundaries are confronted or crossed.

Boundaries are a poor substitute for consciousness. If you are incapable of being conscious in a situation, some artificial boundaries can be a useful solution. But if you would rather experience all that life has to offer, it is far more exciting, and actually safer, to be aware of what is happening around you, and to make decisions, moment to moment, about what is appropriate and inappropriate for you.

Identify your boundaries, then explore them. Frequently you will find that the things you have boundaries to protect you from are actually the things you want. Your conditioning is just telling you these things are not allowed, so you are afraid. As you develop your ability to be more conscious, it is a wonderful feeling to let your boundaries go. You will realize that what you thought was protecting you was actually imprisoning you.

◇◇◇   ◇◇◇   ◇◇◇

People frequently tell me about things that annoy them. I find being annoyed quite irresponsible and a waste of energy. If you find yourself feeling annoyed, choose to use that energy doing something about it, instead of wasting the energy by not liking the thing that is annoying you.

Not liking something isn't very much fun. Frequently stopping being annoyed only requires doing something differently or saying something to someone, but usually you are afraid to do it, or say it, so instead you choose to be annoyed by it.

At times attachment can be involved, so check and see what role your attachment is playing. Sometimes the cause of your being annoyed goes deeper than the mere source of annoyance, where what is annoying you is reminding you of some aspect of yourself that you do not like. Use the opportunity to identify the aspect, and then choose to do something about it. Remember, it is probably about doing something you want to be doing but don't allow yourself to do, or something you do, and judge yourself for.

◇◇◇　　　◇◇◇　　　◇◇◇

Complaint is a similar irresponsible waste of energy. When you take responsibility for creating your reality, you will see that complaining is ridiculous. Often you are doing something, and saying you don't want to be doing it. Put the energy into addressing the issue, instead of complaining about it. Complaint is rampant in our culture and has a very toxic feeling. Not only do I encourage you not to complain, but also I would suggest that you choose not to have it happen around you. It feels quite bad, although the person complaining sometimes feels better after complaining. Make the choice not to listen to complaint, and either ask the person to stop, or you can go somewhere else. You will feel much better when you choose to create a reality that does not include complaint.

◇◇◇　　　◇◇◇　　　◇◇◇

Arguing is another thing that makes absolutely no sense. One person is telling another person what he or she is supposed to do or think, and usually that person is doing the same thing back.

Everybody gets to do exactly what he or she wants. It is only through attachment that we get invested in other people's behavior. It doesn't do any good to try to change people who don't want to change. It is a very unpleasant thing to do. It doesn't feel good. Once you ascertain that this person does not want to fulfill whatever it is you need, let go of trying to make him do it, and find someone who wants to do whatever it is. Don't waste your life arguing.

◇◇◇　　　◇◇◇　　　◇◇◇

Speaking of wasting life, we come to waiting. What are you waiting for? If there is a good reason, great, but more often than not, you are avoiding something because of fear. It is not a very good use of your time. Whenever you decide to do whatever it is you are waiting for, it will always be now. It can be now, now, or it can be now a week from now, or now a month from now, or now a year from now, but whenever you finally decide to do it, it will always be now, so you might as well just do it now.

◇◇◇　　　◇◇◇　　　◇◇◇

Stress, like everything else, is a choice, and not a very good one. Stress comes from having expectations. Our expectations are often rooted in our conditioning, and when they are not, our relationship to our expectations usually are. Many people feel stress is inevitable. Some even feel that if they are not feeling stress, they are not really doing something worthwhile.

Stress actually makes you much less efficient and effective, even though many people who experience stress feel that the stress is what makes them good at what they are doing, or is what keeps them going. This is conditioning. Let go of all of these thoughts. Examine your expectations and how you feel about them, and find what your motivations actually are. The only reason anyone experiences stress is that, at some level, they feel they are supposed to. If you can let go of your expectations of yourself, everything will be easier, and you can experience a much more enjoyable life.

◇◇◇　　　◇◇◇　　　◇◇◇

Something else to look at is resignation. It will probably get in your way as you continue with the Deep Living Practice. Most people have many different levels of resignation in their system. Because of past experience, they have decided they will never get something that they want, and out of frustration, they have given up even trying to get it. Resignation becomes a fixed point and frequently blocks the path to your deeper truth.

The way to get around resignation is to choose to allow the longing for the things that you have given up any chance of ever getting. Frequently the longings are for relatively simple things, like being held, or being accepted as you are. It can be very challenging to allow these longings, as there was frequently so much pain involved in not getting these things you felt you needed.

Choosing to allow these longings is frequently a process involving many different feelings such as helplessness, anger, hatred, and desperation. As the process continues, allow everything that comes up, but keep moving toward the longing. To clear the resignation, you need to return to the depth of the longing before you chose to give up.

It can help this process to get other people to give you the things you wanted as a child. Don't give yourself the object of your longing too soon, though. What works the best is to really get into the depth of your longing, and *then* receive the thing you were longing for.

What frequently happens is that we choose resignation, and then develop our behavioral patterns based on that resignation. If we can return to the longing, and receive what it is that we want, we can let go of the structure based on the resignation.

Usually attachment is involved, in that the longing is to get the thing from a specific person. We need to let go of the idea that we need it from that specific person, and see that we can get the thing we want from someone else. If we can allow ourselves to do this, it really feels just as good, and by doing this, we make a step towards letting go of our attachment.

It is never too late to have a good childhood. I have found great value in creating situations for my clients that give them the things that they felt they needed as children. So often, their focus on wanting these things from their past becomes a fixed point. By fulfilling the longing, their systems relax, the fixed point softens, and they are able to focus on the present, which is where their lives are actually happening. Give yourself a happy childhood.

◇◇◇   ◇◇◇   ◇◇◇

I want to remind you that you are not your behavior. When I use the word "behavior", I am referring to all the things you do, driven by your conditioning, instead of being guided by your truth. Your behavior is an expression of all the choices you have made. You made those choices largely by a combination of being told to make those choices and reacting to the things that happened to you. By exploring and deconstructing your behavior, we can identify those choices that are keeping you from living your truth, and make other choices that will guide you to an experience of happiness and fulfillment that is beyond your imagination. When you look at your behavior this way, from the perspective of your witness, it can make it much easier to see it for what it is, and disconnect from it.

Remember that you are in an animal body that has instincts, hormones, processes, and all variety of things going on. It is important to learn to accept and love this part of yourself, but also to realize that you don't need to be driven by it. We have this amazing consciousness, that we are still learning to use, that allows us to make choices. We no longer need to be driven by these instincts. At the same time, they are there, and it does not work to ignore them. Allow them, accept them, and make choices about how to be with them in a way that brings you the most joy.

Finally, remember this is true for everyone else as well. Other people are also amazing beings who think they are their behaviors. Don't take their behavior too seriously. Try to see their deeper motivations and the truth underneath. This becomes much easier as you become clearer within yourself. Interactions and relationships work much better when you have a sense of what is really going on.

–Chapter 36–

States and State Shifting

I have been encouraging you to pay attention to how you are feeling. You will have certainly noticed that you feel different ways at different times. I refer to how you are feeling in the moment as your "state". Start to pay attention to what state you are in, and realize that the state you are in is not fixed and can be shifted.

We are always experiencing one state or another. The state you are in is frequently affected by the relationship between your conditioning and what is happening. If you shift that relationship, you shift your state. Some states are more desirable than others. We want to use our practice of consciousness to look at the choices behind the states we create for ourselves. Most people are not aware of these choices, and feel helpless in relation to the state they are in. We can learn to choose our state through state shifting.

The first step is to identify your current state. If you are frequently in a certain state it can be hard to notice, because then you tend to think the state you are in is who you are. Life outside the state can be outside your imagination.

Remember, your truth, and natural state, is one of deep happiness and fulfillment. If that is not what you are feeling, identify how you are feeling as whatever state it is, and start looking for ways to shift your state into one that brings you closer to your truth. If you are in the same state most of the time, watch for other states to develop as you continue your Practice. If you experience many different states, start to pay attention to when they come and when they go. Become aware of what triggers a state and what knocks you out of a state.

Once you start to look at states from the perspective of your witness, you will see that, even though they are frequently triggered by certain events and circumstances, they really are arbitrary. Nothing makes you choose a certain state at a certain time, besides your unconscious patterns. These patterns, of course, can be very deep and challenging to break. Trauma is also frequently involved in triggering states. None of these things are fixed, though, unless you choose them to be. If you focus on state shifting, you can learn to get out of any state, no matter how deeply entrenched it may be.

If you want to shift a state, look at the deeper motivations behind why you are in that state using your self-inquiry. In that you are sometimes in that state, realize that part of you wants to be, and look at what benefit you get out of being in the state. This can bring clarity, and frequently show you a path to let it go. Resignation can also be involved, so look for the possibility of this and find what you are longing for underneath. Most particularly, you want to look at what triggers the state, and do a process to shift the effect of whatever this stimulus is, using the tools of the Deep Living Practice.

The trick is to not focus on getting out of a state, but to focus on getting into another state. As I said, some states are more desirable than others. Pick states that you enjoy, and learn how to get yourself into them. There is a wide variety of ways to do this, and it can be very simple. Sometimes all it takes is a memory or a simple act like singing a song or making a gesture. Objects can also be useful. My partner used a silly doll on a keychain to shift her state when she found herself taking things too seriously. Our sense of smell is very powerful, and I've known people who carry a bottle of a particular essential oil with them to support state shifting. Look for a simple trigger, and you will likely find one.

I find gratitude a wonderful state. It is fairly easy to get into the state of gratitude. Here is a practice that will help.

Practice: Gratitude

Ask yourself what you are grateful for, and then answer. Do this over and over again for several minutes. Include big things, but also little things. Shift your attention to all there is to be grateful for. Take some time to notice. Stay with it until you shift your state.

States can be addictive. If you keep getting sucked into a state, obviously you need to address it, but even the choice to focus on the more preferable state is part of the bigger choice to take responsibility for yourself and consciously create your reality.

Another way to shift your state is to find physical markers of the state you want to be in.

Practice: State Shifting with Physical Markers

I've mentioned how our body is a manifestation of our mental and emotional states, and you can use this in reverse to generate a state. When you are in the state you want to be able to return to, notice small and specific things that you are feeling physically. How do the palms of your hands feel? How does your tongue feel? How are you holding your mouth? How do your genitals feel? These are just a few examples. It can be anything your attention is drawn to. When you want to come into the state, you close your eyes and remember these things. With a little practice you will be able to bring yourself into the state whenever you want.

As you proceed with the Deep Living Practice, you will probably experience moments of greater clarity and joy than you have previously known. Pay attention to the physical markers you experience when you achieve these states, and use them to return to those states at will.

Most people are lost in their behavior, and think their behavior is who they are. In this state they are saying "yes" to their conditioning and "no" to their truth. As you find the point within yourself where you are choosing more "yes" to your truth than to your conditioning, you will experience a major state shift. You will no longer have the lost and confusing or forceful and rigid feelings of your conditioning, and you will begin to find your truth. As you get a sense of your true self, shift your focus into moving toward it. Stop fighting against resistance and begin to relax into yourself. There will still be many things to clear from your system, but the fight is over, and your state will be much easier and lighter.

Once you've reached this point and begun the process of relaxing into yourself, you will see that you will occasionally fall back into your conditioning and behavioral patterns. The difference will be that you will notice it, and know that you have a choice whether you will continue to allow your conditioning to control you or not. You will come to see that there is a "switch" within you that allows you to make this choice. You will see when you have made a choice to go into the pattern, and you will be able to choose to not go into the pattern. Once you have found this switch within yourself, it is as obvious as the light switch on the wall and as easy to operate.

It is an amazing moment when you find your switch. I remember the exact moment I found mine for the first time with extreme clarity. I felt such a rush of excitement and gratitude, because all the energy I had put into my Practice had paid off. I finally knew that I was going to make it. All the doubt and uncertainty of my previous life was behind me, and all of my potential was waiting for me to find it. A new phase of my journey had begun.

–Chapter 37–

Self-Acceptance and Self-Love

One of the primary goals of the Deep Living Practice is to help you come into a state of self-love. Self-love begins with self-acceptance. Much of the lack of self-acceptance revolves around not accepting what you are feeling. We make many of the choices that drive our behavior based on trying to avoid feelings we don't want to feel. In order to come into a state of self-love, we need to accept all of our feelings.

This is challenging for most people, and our feelings of attachment are part of what makes it so difficult. At the core of attachment is the feeling that you need someone else to survive. Implicit in this is that you are not enough by yourself. Most people feel this way deep down inside, but are trying not to feel this way. It is this *trying* that constitutes a big portion of their behavior.

The way out of feeling as if you are not enough is to dive into it. Allow your feelings of neediness and unworthiness. For many people this feels like a bottomless pit, but my experience is that it is not. If you go into it 100 percent, you will get to the bottom. Frequently at the bottom, the shift is extremely unspectacular. Suddenly the negative feelings are gone and you perceive a calmness that some people mistake for disassociation. But it is not. It is the open and expanded feeling of self-acceptance.

Approaching this process is very different for different people. Many of the people I have worked with have developed deep feelings of self-hatred.

This makes this process very difficult. If you have these feelings, I suggest you move in this direction very slowly. It is important to develop good resourcing in yourself and with the people around you. Most importantly, keep reminding yourself that this is not who you really are. It is a creation of your reactions to the things that happened to you as a child.

When we go deeper into feelings of self-hatred, feelings that one deserves to be hurt, humiliated, and sometimes even destroyed can frequently emerge. Obviously you want to be careful when exploring such dangerous feelings, and it may be appropriate to get professional help. Even this can be difficult, though, because many professionals are not comfortable with such powerful feelings. Be conscious of this as you line up the support you need, and find someone who is emotionally prepared to support you. Know though, that as difficult as the process may be, it is doable. I had deep self-hatred that I have let go of, and I have seen many others work their way through it. It just takes determination.

In one sense it is an advantage to have such strong self-hatred. If the feelings you have are extremely unpleasant, it will motivate you to start and continue your process even though it is quite challenging. I talk about the importance of courage, but in my case it was desperation instead of courage that motivated me to change. I had reached a point in my life where I really didn't want to continue living feeling the way I felt, and this motivated me to do things I never would have done otherwise. Courage is wonderful, but desperation works just as well.

Children who were victims of physical, emotional, or sexual abuse frequently develop these feelings of self-hatred. Many of my clients were abused as children, and I know from personal experience that we can leave the effects of this behind. I also know that it can be a challenging path, and I suggest a slow approach with lots of resourcing and regulation of the pace of the process.

A particularly challenging part of this process is the desire to die. Many people have this desire, including those who are not victims of abuse. Although it can be very frightening, I find it is only through feeling this feeling fully that you can transform it. As I mentioned, it is impossible to do something that you do not want to do, and since you are living, at least 51 percent of you wants to be alive.

I have found you need to truly allow your desire to die, and deeply consider the possibility of killing yourself, if you are going to get firmly in touch with your choice to live. Finding a deep connection to this choice to live is essential to finding self-love. Through our conditioning, many of us are conflicted about whether we really want to be here or not. This conflict is the source of much of the doubt and indecision we experience. Once you find the choice to live and are 100 percent behind it, everything is different. You stop undermining and fighting yourself. Your life becomes so much easier.

If you look at it with perspective, it is not easy to be alive. There are more miscarriages than full-term births. Many people do not survive. You did. Part of you absolutely wants to be here. Part of you has chosen to be here. We want to find that choice, get you to identify with it, and constantly choose to reinforce it. If in the process of considering whether you want to live or not, you fear you may actually kill yourself, get professional help to support you through this process.

One of the most gratifying parts of working with people has been helping them find their deep desire to live and watching how their lives change as a result. In this respect, some of the most damaged people I have worked with have had some of the most spectacular results, because they were so motivated to change.

The process is frequently more challenging for people who have developed strategies and behaviors that work well. They are usually successful and popular. They have lives and relationships they enjoy, but they still feel something is not quite right. They like their lives, but they don't love them, and they feel something is missing. It is frequently harder for these people to motivate themselves to change, because they feel they have more to lose.

If you are one of these people, and you get to a challenging step, you will probably feel, "What would I want to do *that* for?" I know it is hard to see in the moment, but the reason to do it is to lose that unsettled feeling.

This feeling gets stronger in people when they reach their late thirties or early forties. It is what is behind mid-life crises. You have reached your peak, and your true self knows that if it is going to express itself in this lifetime, it is time to start, or you might miss the opportunity.

Most people act out a bit, make some superficial changes, and then drop into resignation. Some actually change their lives, and move closer to their truths. Whether you confront these challenging feelings or not, depends on what you want to get out of life. It is your choice, but my experience is that nothing is more important than you living your life as fully and deeply as possible while realizing your greatest potential.

One thing to keep in mind is that we are following the path of your joy. No matter where you end up, or what you have to give up, you are going to feel joy. Your life may be unlike anything you ever imagined your life would be, but however it is, you are going to be feeling joy, loving your life, and loving yourself for making the choices you have made.

I mentioned before how the fear of loneliness is one of the major motivations of behavior. The core of loneliness is feeling uncomfortable when you are by yourself, or with the idea of being by yourself. Self-acceptance and self-love are the antidotes for loneliness. I've shared this with many people and they frequently tell me they can't imagine it, but when you love yourself, you are totally happy when you are by yourself.

It may seem strange in a culture that puts people in a room by themselves for punishment, but once you reach this state of self-love, it is wonderful to spend time with yourself. It is also wonderful to spend time with other people. Actually it is even more wonderful than you may have experienced spending time with other people before, because when you reach a state of self-love, you can let go of the sense of needing the other. This may be beyond your imagination, but the feeling of neediness actually gets in the way of deep connection. Attachment prevents true intimacy, and as wonderful as you may think it feels to have the one you feel you need be there for you, it feels so much better to connect with another when you are both radiating self-love. We will go into this more deeply in a future chapter.

A key aspect of self-love is surrender. It is about surrendering to yourself. Allowing yourself to be exactly who you are moment by moment. Allowing yourself to feel exactly what you are feeling moment to moment. Most of us are fighting ourselves. Many of the thoughts in our heads are the results of the argument between who you think you are and who you really are. When you have judgments, they are driven by judgments of yourself. If you follow the Deep Living Practice and surrender to who you really are, it will lead you to self-love.

It is important to note here that many of the feelings you will have as you proceed with your Practice are not your deepest truth. They are the result of your conditioning in relationship to your truth. I've talked about the path between who you think you are and who you really are. These feelings are the journey. They probably won't make sense, there will be surprising, sometimes shocking, developments, but if you can just say "yes" to whatever arises, and allow it fully and deeply, these feelings will deliver you to your truth.

One of the challenges to self-acceptance is comparison. Through our being taught to be someone other than ourselves, we get ideas of what we are supposed to be like. We compare ourselves to these ideas and feel bad about ourselves when we are not like them. Most of us get caught up in making these comparisons. It is something to watch for, and choose not to support.

Can you imagine a rose bush feeling bad because it is not an oak tree? We all have our places and our purposes. The challenge is that most of us have been taught not to live them and are trying to live a life that is not our truth. We are constantly looking for something else. Unfortunately we look outside and compare ourselves to things that we think we are supposed to be. The answers are all within us. If each of us can find our truth, and live it, we will feel joy and fulfillment far beyond anything we will feel by being like the things we are comparing ourselves to.

One of the challenges of this is that we live in a culture that defines what is good, right, beautiful, or successful in certain ways. Letting go of these social directives and expectations takes a lot of consciousness and courage, but it is the people who do this that change the world. Regardless, the point here is your happiness. If you come into a state of self-love and live your truth, your experience will be wonderful. By doing this, we come closer to the rock-solid feeling of perfection that is life, and our lives unfold in ways that are outside our imaginations, but simultaneously wonderful and fulfilling beyond description. Stop trying to be like others, find yourself by allowing and accepting your feelings, surrender to the perfection of who you really are so you can find your greatest potential, and let it radiate out into the world.

−Chapter 38−

Giving, Taking, and Receiving

Now that you are paying attention to your state, direct your consciousness to whether you are giving or taking energy. As we become more sensitive and aware, we can get a sense of how, at a deeper level, giving and taking are energetic phenomena. The states of giving energy or taking energy feel very different from each other. To reach this level of awareness, we focus on our underlying feelings, while experimenting with more superficial examples of giving and taking.

An effective place to start is to focus on your choice to participate. How engaged are you in any given situation? Offering to help, getting involved in what is happening, and joining the conversation, are simple ways to move toward a state of giving. When you walk into a room, do you affect what is going on in the room, or does what is going on in the room affect you?

Many people spend most of their time taking. One way people do this is by separating themselves from what is happening around them, and then relating to the world from this state of separation. Another way is by becoming extremely self-involved. Some people get very uncomfortable if they are not the center of attention. In all of these cases, the primary focus of the person in this state of taking, is concern over how whatever is happening will affect him or her. This usually generates a lot of busy internal dialogue that creates many unpleasant feelings. Besides not feeling good, this state also makes change very difficult. If you are sucking energy into yourself, your system becomes compacted, and it becomes much more challenging to allow movement. Transformation is all about movement. If you notice you are in this state of taking, I suggest you actively do something to support a state shift.

The simple truth is that giving feels better than taking. It is why many people enjoy doing charity work. Find ways in your life to support you to come into a state of giving, though I also suggest you not overdo it. Some people use the good feelings they get from giving to avoid other feelings they don't want to feel. It is about finding a balance.

We are looking for balance, but it is not a balance between giving and taking. It is a balance between giving and receiving. Taking and receiving are two very different things. Taking has the quality of neediness and is frequently driven by attachment. Receiving has the much more expansive quality of us allowing ourselves to be nourished. We need nourishment, and it is essential we strike a balance between giving and receiving. We want to allow ourselves to be nourished, but move away from the needy and aggressive feeling of taking.

Many people also have a hard time receiving. Here is an exercise that may help if you are challenged in this area.

Exercise: Letting Someone Hold You

If you have difficulties receiving love and nourishment, it is probably because of a lack of self-love or the fear of appearing needy. In our chapter on self-love we talked about the importance of resourcing and that letting this kind of love and support in is necessary to feel resourced.

You start this process by finding someone available to hold you and care about you. This may seem challenging, but it is not. Remember, it feels great to give, and many people are looking for opportunities to do so. You don't even need to know this person well, although it is fine if you do. It feels good to hold someone, and care about him or her. I do this exercise in groups, where people take turns holding each other. Most people really enjoy the holding part of the exercise, yet feel uncomfortable being held. I know in the state of taking, it is outside the imagination that someone would want to support you, but you will be surprised. If you are afraid to ask for this kind of physical support, put it on your list of things you are afraid of, and work up to it.

Once you find someone to hold you, have her sit comfortably on the floor leaning against the wall with enough pillows so she is comfortable. Approach her slowly, using the Rhythm, and allow all the feelings that arise as you get closer. Give yourself plenty of time. For some people this process takes quite a while. You may not even make it all the way the first time. Even if it takes several sessions, stay with it until you can lie in her arms.

Some people feel awkward when holding or being held. Here is a simple way to approach it. The person holding sits comfortably against a wall with a pillow supporting her back, her right leg straight out in front of her, and her left leg bent with her foot flat on the floor. The person to be held kneels facing the wall directly on the holder's right side. Then he leans over to his right side as the person holding him takes him into her arms and supports him with her body, arms, and bent leg. The person being held puts his right arm around the person holding him. Keep adjusting until both people are comfortable. Use pillows for additional support if necessary. It is important that the head of the person being held is supported and that there is solid contact between the chests.

Once you can lie in someone's arms, see if you can relax while you are being held. Experience what you feel as you try to relax. For some people it can take a while to reach a point where they can comfortably lie in someone's arms, and many different, and surprising, feelings may come up in the process. You may need to come back to this process several times. You will also see that the process is different with different people, and you may want to explore what it is like, and what comes up, as different people hold you.

This practice is very challenging for some, and quite easy for others. No matter how it is for you, pay attention to your ability to let love and support in. Most people resist at some level. This is something you need to address because, as I mentioned, your capacity to allow love and support are directly connected to your feelings of self-acceptance and self-love, and these are states we need to achieve on our path to our true selves.

As we come closer to our true selves we get in touch with incredible amounts of energy. We are amazing beings. I have worked with thousands of people, and every one of them has had a wonderful and powerful energy under all of their holding back and behavioral patterns. Our potential is so far beyond our imagination. We all have so much to give. When I focus on this energetic core in people, I see each of us as a gift, and that our purpose here is to give the gift that is us. Can you go through life looking for opportunities to give the gift of yourself?

Many people do not know what giving really is. When they give, they feel they deserve something in return. Many people's conditioning supports this way of being. Some people feel this more directly toward the person they think they are giving to, and others create a mythical bank account in their minds, that they feel they are depositing into each time they give, to collect credit for future rewards.

This is not giving, and does not have the good feelings, or beneficial effects of giving. This is doing business in an indirect and somewhat dishonest way, because the person you are doing business with may not know he or she is entering into a business agreement. Watch for this and choose not to do it.

Business is great. There is nothing wrong with choosing not to give and to do business instead. To live practically in the world today, business is part of life. In a later chapter I will write about doing business applying the Point of View and the Deep Living Practice, but for now, pay attention to the difference between giving and doing business, and be honest and direct when you choose to do business.

As far as the mythical bank account, this is a conditioning based belief with no basis in reality that will just cause pain. People who believe in this bank account tend to get angry when they don't get what they want, to be irresponsible with their anger, and to fall into blame. Blame is another rest-stop-on-the-freeway type of feeling that feels terrible and never goes anywhere. It is the epitome of being irresponsible. Choose against blame by allowing your anger responsibly which will probably lead you to see that you are believing in a mythical bank account and thinking the rest of reality will honor it.

Practice: Asking for What You Want

Many people have a hard time asking for the things they want. There are many reasons for this that usually involve resignation or

> *fear. A wonderful skill to develop is the ability to ask for everything that you want and to be totally fine with hearing "no".*
>
> *You can achieve this through your practices of consciousness, courage, and self-inquiry. Be aware of the things you want, have the courage to ask for those things, allow your feelings when you either get or not get the things you ask for, and explore why you want the things you do not get.*
>
> *In this practice, you will probably be surprised how often you get the things you ask for. You will also see that if you ask for many things and get some of them, it really doesn't matter that you don't get all of them.*

Many people choose not to ask for much of what they want and wait until they want something really badly to ask for it. Then if they do not get it, they get upset, because in their mind they think they hardly ask for anything. You can see that they feel this because they have created a reality where they think that what they think is right and they assume that other people feel the same way they feel. This is a mistake many people make when they are in the state of taking. They feel they are the center of the universe, and assume that other people must know what they are thinking and feeling.

The truth is that most other people are also in this taking state, and feel that *they* are the center of the universe and other people must know what they are thinking and feeling. You can see how this wouldn't work very well, but at the same time, it is going on in much of the social interaction that I witness. The antidote for this is to come into a state of giving. Once you have experienced this giving state, the effects of the taking state become quite obvious. You will also notice that in the giving state it is possible to be present with what is actually happening. Being in a taking state makes presence impossible.

Many people experience an empty place inside them that feels like a hole. Much human behavior is based around people trying to fill this hole within themselves. People try to fill their hole with relationships, work, sex, food, drugs, alcohol, entertainment, and all sorts of other things. Sometimes they can fill it for a brief period of time, but soon they will begin to feel this hole again. This hole is the result of a lack of self-acceptance and self-love, as well as the result of feelings of attachment. The only way to fill it is by finding your truth and letting it radiate out into the world. You must accept yourself, love yourself, and give of yourself. This will create the wonderful feeling I have been guiding you to.

Focusing on giving instead of taking, and finding a balance between giving and receiving, will help you achieve this amazing feeling. Do you want to be a sun, radiating your energy out into the universe, or would you prefer to be a black hole, sucking everything around you into that tight and compacted place inside?

–Chapter 39–

Relationships and Intimacy

The relationship to oneself is the primary relationship, and the one that forms the template for all our other relationships, but it is in relationship to others where we have the opportunity to have some of our deepest experiences of life's potential. In this chapter I would like to discuss some ways of looking at your relationships that may help you get the most out of them.

Most people are looking for a special relationship with *that* particular person. Our conditioning very heavily supports this idea as a primary goal in life. Songs, books, movies, magazines, and television constantly bombard us with stories about how important it is to find the perfect partner for a special romantic relationship who will give meaning to your life. Many people make the search for this special relationship the most important thing in their lives. Many people put their concerns about this relationship over their concerns about themselves. This is very unhealthy and I have seen how it places tremendous pressure on relationships, which in turn makes having a good relationship very challenging. Treating your relationships as if they were more important than you are degrades the quality of your life and separates you from your sense of personal power.

The feelings involved in these special romantic relationships are undeniable. They are very powerful, and we have been convinced that they are the ultimate goal of the human experience. Though you may not believe me when I say this, I find the sense of personal power, the deep self-love, the clarity, the availability for intimacy, and the ability to connect deeply without fear or judgment, a far more wonderful state than the head-over-heels in love, "I need you so much", "I can't wait to see you again", "I would die for you" feelings I experienced in the past. I encourage you to keep an open mind and consider what else might be possible.

Even though the good parts of the special romantic relationship feel very good, the bad parts feel very bad, and in most cases the bad parts far outweigh the good parts. The primary problem with this type of relationship is that it is deeply rooted in attachment. At the basis of it is the feeling that you need someone else in order to be happy. This underlying neediness creates many long-term consequences.

We talked about the word "love" before and how ambiguous it is. People use it to mean all kinds of different things. Expressing attachment, or a feeling of neediness, is one of the most popular uses of the word "love", even though the people who are using the word "love" this way are rarely aware that this is how they are using it.

Sometimes people use the word "love" to express their willingness to sacrifice for the other. When you consider this, sacrifice really doesn't have anything to do with love. If you love someone, do you really want him or her to give up something for you? My experience is that love is about wanting the other to be happy, so why would you want him or her to give something up?

Mistaking sacrifice for love has its roots in attachment. As we sink deeper into the longing for connection, we frequently get to a "I will do anything for you" feeling. This feeling is much more connected to the lack of self-love based in feelings of helplessness, neediness, and unworthiness, than it has to do with a healthy loving relationship.

Pay attention to your underlying meaning when you use the word "love", and restrict its use to the feeling of wanting what is best for the other person and enjoying it when he or she gets it. If you mean something else, use the word that best describes what you actually mean. This may seem strange as you do it, but it will create a much more honest relationship.

I have yet to see an attached relationship that I would call successful. At their best these relationships become extremely insular, and the people involved create a very closed reality that attempts to shut out the rest of the world. Attached relationships happen when two people who feel incomplete come together to try to create an experience of feeling taken care of. I find the alternative of two full people coming together to form something greater than the sum of their parts much more attractive. To reach this more attractive and far more beneficial state, we need to let go of attachment and our ideas about what relationship is supposed to be like. As we have discussed, letting go of attachment is a challenging project, so it makes sense to look at ways to be in relationship while we are still in the process of letting attachment go.

The best way to look at relationship is to realize that you have many relationships and to not make one the most important. Approach all of your relationships openly and look for what potential is there. Be conscious about the choices you make about limiting your possibilities. We have rather fixed ideas about what is possible in relationship. Open up to new possibilities in all of your relationships.

Many of us have a primary relationship that we choose to put much more time and energy into than others. Practically, this makes sense, but do this because it is the most rewarding use of your energy and try not to look at it as more important than the relationships you have with other people. Be careful not to let your primary relationship degrade the quality of your other relationships.

Also be careful about making your primary relationship your most important relationship because you feel you need that person. If you do feel this way, be aware of it, and realize that these feelings of attachment are affecting your perception of reality. It is extremely likely that these feelings are reciprocal and the other person in the relationship is attached to you, and not seeing you clearly either.

And, though you enjoy the relationship and choose to invest time and energy into it, resist the temptation to make it the center of your life. Keep your focus on being responsible for and taking care of yourself, while also staying open to other relationships that may enrich your life. Doing this will make you stronger and give you more to offer into your primary relationship. If your partner is doing this as well, instead of being totally focused on you and your relationship, you can create a wonderful, nourishing, enriching relationship that supports each of you to reach both your highest personal potential, and the greatest potential of the two of you together.

The choice to go through life in partnership with another person is very understandable, but it is an area of your life where conditioning is very strong, and one in which you need to be particularly aware. It is easy to get caught in patterns that do not serve you. One thing that creates many difficulties is the feeling you are responsible for the other person, and most particularly, responsible for how the other person feels.

The good part of taking 100 percent responsibility for yourself is realizing that you are zero percent responsible for anyone else. This may initially feel cold or harsh, particularly with someone you are very close to, but if you really love and want the best for this person, supporting him or her to take complete responsibility is a wonderful way to do this.

This doesn't mean you can't do things for or take care of other people. I simply encourage you to do what you do because you love them, or because you want to, and not because you feel responsible, or that you should, or have to. Many people get caught up in feeling responsible for their partners. This is the basis of codependent behavior. Although it may feel like what you are doing is *for* your partner, it is frequently supporting behavior that does not serve him or her when seen objectively.

Sometimes being brutally honest, strict, and demanding is the most loving way you can be with another person, particularly if he or she is involved in self-destructive behavior. We always want to bring consciousness to the underlying motives of our behavior as best we can. This is where our practices of honesty and self-inquiry lead us. The same act, done with different motives, has very different effects and consequences. A particularly powerful example of this is when things are done out of a feeling of responsibility instead of love or joy.

Attachment is frequently underneath our tendency to think we need to take responsibility for others. We want these people to take responsibility for us, so we feel we need to take responsibility for them. It is another of those dishonest unspoken business agreements. If you look at the deeper motivations under the feeling to take responsibility for someone, you will frequently find a desire to control him or her. By taking responsibility for someone, you are trying to take his power away from him, so look and see if this is what you really want to do in the relationship, and if so, why.

It is impossible for someone to take your power from you, and conversely, it is impossible for you to take power from someone. It is relatively easy, though, to get someone to give up his or her power. The choice is always in the person whose power it is, and even if you have made the choice to give up your power, consciously or unconsciously, you can always choose to take it back. Your power isn't just something you possess. It is who you are.

Relationship provides our greatest opportunities for growth and self-discovery. Look at relationship this way until you get a better sense of your truth. Realize that your conditioning and attachment have major effects on you that affect your judgment and perception. There is an old saying that goes, "Life is a bridge, don't build a house on it." Realize you are in a state of transition and choose to use your relationships to support your path, as well as being a source of pleasure and comfort.

Again, attraction is largely a function of your truth driving you into situations that will bring up the feelings you need to experience in order to confront the aspects of your conditioning that are keeping you from your truth. Once you realize this, you see that although you are telling yourself this is your perfect mate and you will love him or her forever, the truth is that you are actually attracted for some other reason. Perhaps you have to get over the influence of a parent if you are going to find yourself, and this person will trigger enough of these feelings in you that she can help you through this process. This doesn't mean that you can't enjoy each other, and take care of each other, through the process. Just the opposite. Find loving and supportive people who have also chosen to find their truths, to be in relationship with so you can grow together. And who knows, you may end up spending the rest of your lives together doing just that.

When I am considering spending more time with someone, or putting more energy into a relationship, I watch for two things. The first is if the person wants me to be different from who I am. If he or she does, this will put pressure on me that I do not enjoy. Even if I wanted to be the person she wants me to be, the pressure would eventually create resentment. I am looking for someone who will accept me as I am. If she supports me in growing and finding my truth, so much the better. Then she becomes even more attractive to me. The second thing is that the person has an open mind and is interested in finding her truth. It is not fun to be around someone who thinks she simply is the way she is, or things have to be a certain way. These become fixed points, and if I am in relationship with her, I will have to organize my life around her fixed points. This may be okay in the short term, but over time this will create resentment.

Many people feel that relationship is built on compromise. My experience is that troubled relationships are built on compromise. It is beyond most people's imaginations that you can be in relationship without compromise. The problem with compromise is that it always creates resentment. Even if at the time you tell yourself that you are happy to make the compromise to get something that you want, a deeper part of you will feel resentment, and this resentment will eventually cause unconscious behavior. Sometimes this resentment will make you say something mean to the person, even though when you say it, you think you are complimenting him; or being late; or letting the door you are holding for him close a little too soon, or "accidentally" breaking something he likes, or maybe it will be buying him a present that you think he will love as you buy it, but you will unconsciously get it a size too small. Frequently attractions to other people are really about hurting the one you are already in relationship with, and are caused by resentment due to compromise.

Experiment with being uncompromising in relationship and see how it feels. Notice why you think you have to compromise, and see how often attachment is behind the choice. If you have the courage to be uncompromising, this can be a lot of fun. If, as you are moving toward being uncompromising, you decide to compromise anyway, realize that it will probably cause resentment, and watch for it in your behavior. Becoming aware of the process can support your choice to change. A little note here: if you truly want to be uncompromising in your life, you also need to be unattached to what happens. We will explore this later when we look at our advanced Practice.

If you choose to live uncompromisingly in relationship, you will probably come to points where the other person does not want to do what you want to do, or is not able to give you some experience you want. This doesn't need to be a problem. Each of you can do what you want, or get what you want, from people who want to give it. The only thing stopping you is fear of how your partner will react. Yes, you may want her to want what you want, but this is unrealistic, and to try to make someone live up to your expectations is not very loving.

One of the problems of our conditioned special relationships is that out of our conditioning, we get ideas about whom we should be with. We decide what these people should look like, what they should do, how they should behave. Then we create composite images in our minds. This is who we look for as a mate. If the person we are attracted to is attracted to us, he will frequently try to be the person we want him to be. Over time the pressure of this will make him angry and he will stop trying. We will feel disappointed and be angry in return. This creates an entanglement, and these kinds of entanglements are common in attached relationships. Most attached relationships become hugely entangled after a while. These entanglements are driven by our ideas of how we think we want things to be, which are products of our conditioning.

These entanglements can be a major challenge if you are in an existing attached relationship and choose to find your truth. As the relationship probably began with projections, compromises, and varying degrees of dishonesty, it most likely continued with frustrations, disappointments, and blame. Even if on the surface there is the desire to be together, these underlying feelings can make things very challenging. As always, the continuing attachment makes everything stickier and more difficult. At the same time, your partner in this kind of relationship is probably the perfect person to support you in looking at what you need to look at, and if you were to leave the relationship, you would probably go find someone who would trigger the same feelings in you.

> *Practice: Life Starts Now*
>
> *The Point of View includes a valuable way of looking at the world with the concept we call "Life starts now." Through our conditioning and unconsciousness, we have all done things that we regret, or now understand were inappropriate. Pay attention to these things, learn from them, and make your future choices based on what you have learned. This is taking responsibility for yourself, and if you do this, your past becomes a valuable addition to your life. On*

the other hand, if you focus on regret, guilt, or blame, your past becomes a heavy weight that makes growth and transformation difficult, if not impossible, and your life extremely unpleasant. Adopt this "Life starts now" attitude in all aspects of your life. It is essential if you are going to try to disentangle attachment in a relationship.

The very nature of attachment makes this challenging because people tend to be attached to things staying the way they are. Change appears threatening. Often as I support people to make major changes in their lives, I see their relationship partners wanting them to stay the way they were, and not accepting the changes in them. If you remember our discussion of being in a state of sucking or taking energy, this is an example of an effect of that. If the people around you are in a sucking state, they will be more concerned about how your transformation affects them than whether it improves your life. This is also an example of attachment versus love.

As you transform, your reality will change, and your relationships will change. Often as you change, other people will seem different. Someone you found attractive may become completely uninteresting, while someone you barely noticed may become extremely attractive. I encourage you to keep your focus on finding your truth, living your life as deeply, fully, and honestly as you can, and then let your life and relationships organize around that. Remember, people are responsible for themselves and get to make their own choices. You make the choices that are best for you, and can encourage everyone else around you to make the choices that are best for them. Some relationships in your life will transform, some will fall away, and some new relationships may develop. No matter what happens, you will feel happier and more fulfilled if you keep your focus on living your truth.

If you want to maintain and disentangle an existing attached relationship, it is essential that both parties agree to this. Many people *want* attached relationships, and they have every right to have them. If you are with someone who wants such a relationship, I suggest you encourage him or her to find it elsewhere. It is hard enough to break attachment patterns without having someone who wants to remain attached close by.

It is important to not put the relationship or the other person above yourself. If you choose to stay together, and disentangle the relationship, it is also essential that you choose to support each other to do this. This is where we come to one of the greatest potentials of relationship, where two people come together to support each other to find themselves. When we do this lovingly, while taking care of each other, it is the most wonderful way to be together during this transitional state.

When we are in relationship, we are usually in one of three states. The first is when both people are conscious and present. This is wonderful, and the state in which you would ideally want to spend as much time as possible. The second state is when one person gets triggered. By "triggered" I mean that he or she has come into a reactive state. If this happens, and the other person chooses to support the triggered person to get back to a present and conscious state, it is also wonderful and very healthy. One thing to look for here, though, is that the relationship stays in balance. If one person is always supporting the other, she will begin to feel resentment, and entanglement will increase. If this is the case, look at why the non-supporting person is making that choice, and support him to change his mind. The third state is when one person gets triggered and then the other person gets triggered, too. This is where the entangled state tends to take us, and if you remain in this state, you will only become more entangled.

Choose not to support this doubly triggered state. Here is a practice you can do when you fall into this kind of behavior.

> *Practice: Choosing Not to Support Entanglement*
>
> *As soon as either person in a relationship notices you are both triggered, have some words or a signal that calls a time out. Immediately separate, and spend time by yourself taking responsibility for what you are feeling. Remember, you are 100 percent responsible for what you are feeling, and you are incapable in this triggered state to see the other person clearly. Spend at least 30 minutes apart, then come back and tell each other what you have learned about yourselves. If you get triggered again, or start to blame, take more time. The important part is the decision that you are not going to spend any more time arguing or being angry at each other. Choose not to do it, and if you find yourself arguing, do whatever you need to do to take responsibility for yourself and stop it. At the same time, remember that this is a practice, and it may take you a while to get there. If you stay with it, you will be able to do it.*

If you feel the other person hurt you, realize that short of him or her doing you physical damage, it is your choice to feel hurt by the things that he says or does. Even if those things were meant to hurt you, and they quite possibly were, you still choose whether to feel hurt by them or not. If the other person physically hurts you more than once, you are making the choice to be with someone who hurts you. Look at this choice, take responsibility for it, and find what it is about you that made you choose to want to be hurt.

An example of this would be when you feel the other person is not seeing you or listening. Many people feel hurt by this. Why do you care? Why is it important to you that this person understands you? If you examine this feeling, you will probably see that it is about a parent or caregiver when you were a child, and you felt having your needs understood was necessary for your survival.

The other person can understand you or not. It doesn't need to upset your happiness. If the other person is incapable of understanding you, or pretending not to understand you because he or she knows you will choose to feel hurt about it, you may want to support her to look at this choice if she wants to, or consider how much time and energy you want to put into the relationship if she doesn't. On the other hand, most of the time when a person does not feel seen, my experience is that she is not really showing herself, so look for this first.

Occasionally it will not be worth the effort to stay together. You will come to see that you are too deeply entangled, that one, or both, of you is too easily triggered, and that disentangling the relationship is taking too much time and energy away from your practice of finding your truth, as well as making your life very unpleasant. Even though this person may be the perfect person to support your process, you may need to find another with whom you are not so entangled. Sometimes the lesson to be learned is knowing when to leave. Sometimes by leaving you can shift something that will be the most loving thing for both of you, even though you may not be able to be together to enjoy it.

Again, this is about putting your caring for yourself above your caring for your relationship. Before choosing to separate, it may be a good idea to get professional help. It is very hard to see yourself, or the other, with any clarity when you are in an entangled relationship. Be careful, though, because many people who work with couples are more focused on the relationship than on the individuals in the relationship. Make sure whomever you get to help you wants to support you to reach your goals and doesn't distract you with his or her ideas about relationship.

The degree of entanglement notwithstanding, many people are looking for commitments in relationship. Commitments give a feeling of safety and security. I am not attracted to commitments. Circumstances/situations change, other people change, we change, and we have no idea of what is going to happen or how we will be with it. I don't see how you can honestly say, at this moment, how you are going to feel, or what you are going to do in the future, unless you are willing to create a fixed point and live with the consequences of it.

At the same time, you may not be ready to live the fullness of your truth at this moment, and may need some sense of security as a support. For this it can help to make agreements in relationships. This may include agreements that restrict contact with other people or create definite times you will spend alone together. My current partner and I made an agreement early in our relationship that no matter what either of us was doing, the other was invited to participate. If you are in the midst of major change, you may feel you need to have a few things you can hold on to, and agreements can provide this. The goal of the Practice is to make your life as wonderful as it can be in the moment, and if making an agreement helps this process, go for it.

Remember that agreements are temporary. You are saying you will do something until you decide you don't want to do it anymore. Until you make that decision, there doesn't need to be any concern over whatever the issue is. Needless to say, at this stage in your Practice, you would not make an agreement, then break it and be dishonest about it. If you are still capable of doing this, you really need to step up your practices of honesty and courage.

While agreements can be useful in developing relationships, be careful about making them. They are fixed points that you will be organizing your life around, so be sure you really want to do what you are agreeing to, and keep checking if it is still appropriate for you. Sometimes, after a while, you will realize that the agreement is no longer necessary, either because you are ready to explore the area the agreement was keeping you insulated from, or sometimes you will have changed, and in your new state the agreement is irrelevant.

An agreement I often encourage couples to make is to not be mean to each other. It may seem strange, but I see people in relationships choosing to be mean to each other very frequently. This often comes from entanglement, and has to do with resentment around compromise, or revenge for perceived transgressions, and, as I mentioned, frequently the person being mean is totally unconscious about it, and thinks he or she is being supportive. I often see the person who is being mean arguing with the person who he is being mean to, telling her he is not being mean. If someone tells you that you are being mean, you probably are, and at least take the time to tune in, empathize, and get a sense of why she is feeling the way she is feeling.

When we are interacting with people, we are frequently interacting with their behavior. It is important to remember that people are not their behavior, and I suggest you don't take people's behavior seriously. Of course, many people think they *are* their behavior and take it extremely seriously. Behavior is an artifact of the conditioning, patterns, and strategies that make up the person's ideas about him or herself, and by looking for, understanding, and connecting with the deeper motivations underneath the surface behavior, and the truth of the person beneath that, you create the possibility of a much more satisfying relationship.

This brings us to intimacy. Intimacy, like freedom, is both desired and feared. The desire for, and fear of, intimacy are two of the major motivating factors in relationships. Intimacy is simultaneously very challenging and extremely gratifying. It is one of our primary goals of being in relationships with other people.

Intimacy hinges on your willingness to be vulnerable with another person. We've discussed vulnerability before. We are taught that we are weak when we are vulnerable and that it is dangerous to allow this state. This is one reason why people find intimacy so frightening. Even though our vulnerability is where we are actually the most powerful, the fear is still there. Ultimately our practice of courage is about allowing vulnerability, and intimacy is a great way to practice this.

Many people feel they need someone else to be intimate with in order to be intimate, and use this as an excuse to not allow intimacy. My experience is that this is not true. You can practice being open, available, and vulnerable any time you choose. It does not matter what the other person is doing. You will see that people frequently get uncomfortable if you are being significantly more intimate than they are. This is an example of how vulnerability is powerful.

So often we hold back and use the other person's fear as an excuse. You can choose not to do this by practicing allowing intimacy as fully as you can. It may be too much for some people, but others will welcome it. If you are holding back, you are very unlikely to find these people, because you are spending your time with the people you are holding back for, and probably blaming them, and getting angry at them, instead of choosing not to hold back, and attracting people who are interested in deeper levels of intimacy.

We tend to be attracted to people who want roughly the same degree of intimacy we want. In a relationship, what frequently happens is that one partner wants a bit more intimacy than the second, and the second does something to avoid the intimacy. This continues until the first gets frustrated and pulls back. Then the second does something to create intimacy, until the first gets lured in and opens up again. The cycle repeats in a continuous dance that maintains approximately the same degree of intimacy. Much of this plays out unconsciously, as we are telling ourselves all kinds of reasons to justify our actions. If we look deeper, we see that we learn how to regulate the amount of intimacy by learning what to give and withhold from our partners in order to create a state we are comfortable with. The key word here is "unconsciously".

Intimacy is one of the greatest experiences available to us. My experience, though, is that if you want it, you need to actively pursue it, and that it requires honesty, courage, consciousness, and self-responsibility. Learning to be available for intimacy is one of the goals of the Deep Living Practice, and all of the things we have been learning have been leading up to this.

If we choose to practice intimacy in a relationship—by practice I mean breaking out of the unconscious dance that maintains the current degree of intimacy and actively choosing to deepen the intimacy—it is virtually invariable that feelings will arise. It is our willingness to allow and expose those feelings that deepens the intimacy. It is in practicing intimacy that relationships are such wonderful vehicles for growth.

One of the first things to realize is that intimacy is not about sex. Sex can be very intimate, but sex can also be extremely lacking in intimacy. As I said, intimacy is about allowing the feelings that arise as you expose yourself to another person. These can be, and usually are, all kinds of different feelings. They are frequently very surprising feelings, and frequently feelings that you don't want to have.

Allowing intimacy is about becoming vulnerable and exposing yourself. Through intimacy you will find your truth. What makes intimacy so powerful is that you are exercising it with another person. It is even more powerful if he or she is experiencing it with you as well. I previously said that you don't need the other person to practice intimacy, and this is true, but to get the deepest experience and greatest benefits of the Deep Living Practice, being intimate with someone who is being intimate with you opens up one of the greatest potentials that is available for us.

Exercise: Intimacy

You can practice intimacy anytime, anywhere, but here is a way to focus the early stages of your practice. Find someone who wants to support you, and sit on the floor facing each other. Sit far enough apart so both of you feel comfortable. Close your eyes for a few moments and connect to your pelvis and your feelings. Open your eyes when you feel ready to begin.

When you have both opened your eyes, look at each other and experience how you feel about the person. Disconnect from what you know about him or her, and who you think she is. Just feel how you feel in relation to her in the moment, and notice if you have any impulses.

As feelings arise, you may have the impulse to stop the exercise, or even to leave the room. Don't allow this impulse. You may also want the person to go away or stop what she is doing, and as the feelings intensify, you might want to lash out at her or do something to make her go away. Avoid these impulses as well. These are part of our fight or flight response, and we are interested in what happens when you do neither of these and just stay with what you feel. The feelings will probably be fairly mild at first, but can become extremely powerful as you continue. If they become overwhelming, take a break, and come back to the exercise later when you feel more resourced.

Allow your feelings and impulses as honestly as possible. If you are not feeling much, move a little closer. As you do, feelings will arise. If you feel empty or numb, realize you are resisting what you are feeling. Allow the resistance, and look for what you are resisting. Resistance is very common in this exercise. If the feelings of resistance persist, go back to practicing feeling your feelings in a less challenging environment until you are able to feel feelings other than resistance, or maybe try with another person. This exercise will be different with different people, and some people may bring up feelings that are more challenging than others. At first some people may be harder to practice with, though eventually the ones that are most challenging will be the ones that are most beneficial.

As you feel your feelings and impulses, share them with the other person. She can share her feelings and impulses with you as well. As you hear what the other person says, tune in to how it makes you feel, and share that. Be ready for your feelings to shift quickly in ways that don't make sense. When we get into the world of feelings and intimacy, nothing makes sense.

If the other person has an impulse, imagine her doing whatever her impulse is, and share with her how imagining it makes you feel. If you both want to, follow your impulses, and do the things you want to do. Do these things very slowly, and agree that either person can say "stop" at any time, and if either one does, that you both will stop whatever you are doing immediately. If you stop, examine what each of you is feeling before deciding to continue or discontinue the exercise.

When you are following impulses, it is not about doing the thing the impulse is about. It is about feeling the feelings the impulse brings up in both parties. Frequently the feelings are strongest right before, or just as, you start doing whatever the action is. Be careful to not go over the top of your feelings in order to complete the impulse.

Use getting physically closer, sharing feelings, thoughts, and impulses to slowly reveal yourself as honestly as possible in relation to this person. What do you want to do with her? How do you want to be with her? What do you want to say to her? What do you want her to do to you? Be as honest as you can. Actively look for the little flashes of feelings at the edge of your consciousness. Allow whatever comes up slowly and consciously, while keeping your attention on the feelings involved.

Usually a clear dynamic develops between the two of you. Frequently it is more challenging for one person to allow feelings than it is for the other. It is at this point that most relationships get stuck. If at this point, the person who doesn't want to allow her feelings chooses to allow them, the dynamic changes, and the other person is more challenged by what is happening. If both people keep choosing to go deeper by having the courage to allow whatever impulse or feeling he or she finds challenging, the dynamic will continue to shift, and the resistance to the next step will continue to bounce back and forth between the two of you. Sometimes one person is available for a greater depth of intimacy, in which case that person can support the first to allow what he or she is feeling, and continue to do this until he or she feels challenged.

As you stay with this practice, you will go through many aspects of yourselves as you come closer and closer to your truth. Feel free to stop at any time and come back to it later. Notice how your relationship changes as you go deeper. This will eventually lead you to a state where you fully accept yourself just as you are, fully accept the other person, and come into a state of togetherness that is beyond description. You stop being an "I", and you become a "we". Another part of intimacy that people find challenging is, that to reach the depth of intimacy, you need to let go of your sense of self and really join with the other. Many people find the thought of this frightening, but I can assure you that the experience of it is one of the most fulfilling available to us.

Realize that you can always come back to yourself. People become afraid they may get stuck in the connection, but this is not the case. Another wonderful aspect of intimacy is that when you do come back to yourself, you are frequently less attached to your sense of self. You are much more clear that you are not the center of the universe, and at the same time, you are not alone.

As you practice intimacy, you need to be ready for anything, willing to accept whatever you are feeling, and share it. Intimacy supports our practice of self-love, and self-love supports our practice of intimacy.

Many people think it takes a long time to develop intimacy. This is not true. It depends on the willingness of the people involved. If both are open and available, you can drop into deeply intimate states in a few moments. People also feel that you need to know someone well to be intimate. This isn't true, either. It is only the participants' willingness to be vulnerable, and if the willingness is there, intimacy can happen with anyone anytime.

When you first begin practicing, you may want to choose whom to practice with, but you don't have to limit intimacy to a special few. Why limit the potential of most of your relationships in favor of one relationship? The only reasons are attachment and fear. You may end up putting the vast majority of your energy into one relationship, but because you want to. Be careful with this, though, as it is very easy to lie to yourself about your motivations. Your life will be so much richer if you remain open and available to what is possible with everyone you meet.

If you love another person, you will want him or her to get what he or she wants, and if you love yourself, you will also want to give yourself what you want. There is no reason both of you can't be happy. Making a relationship with someone else more important than your relationship with yourself does not create good relationships, either for yourself or for the other person. Let go of your ideas about how relationship should be, and create the kinds of relationships that work best for everyone involved.

Frequently this means getting some things you need from people outside your primary relationship. This is challenging because our conditioning about love and relationship runs so deep, and the feelings caused by attachment are so painful and powerful. It does not mean you have to exclude, or be against, the person you are in relationship with.

One of the challenges is that many people are attached to attachment. They really want an attached relationship, even though they understand everything I have been discussing. If this is the case with you, just dive into the attachment as deeply as you can.

Practice: Exaggerating Attachment
Remember, if you can't shift something, exaggerate the pattern. You can do this with your current partner, if he or she is available for it, but it is also interesting to notice that you can allow

attachment with anyone who is willing, if you choose to. This is another indication that the attachment is not about the person, but something that exists within you.

You can do this in a controlled setting for a short period of time, but it can also be useful to do it in life for a longer period, such as a few days. Allow yourself to go completely into your feelings of attachment. Be needy. Be clingy. Put your full focus on your object of attachment. This process takes much honesty and courage. Follow your impulses. Let yourself do all the things you want to do, and say all the things you want to say, but do and say them slowly enough so you feel all the feelings involved with them. Give yourself the experience of attachment as fully and deeply as you possibly can.

At first, the person supporting you should accept you completely, and be there for you exactly the way you want him to, so you can experience what it is like to have your longing for someone to take care of you fulfilled. Once he feels you have experienced the fulfillment of your longing, he can start to be a bit more demanding, offering you the comfort that you want, but making you do something for it. The goal is to support you to get into an "I will do anything for you" feeling, and then to use that feeling against you.

When you give up responsibility, you give up your power. The supporting person's job is to help you feel this as fully as possible, by using the promise of always being there for you as an incentive, while making the price for it increasingly steep.

When you make a choice to go into a process like this, be careful not to come out of it too soon. When the first resistance comes up, you will want to stop, but don't. Stay with it and practice being conscious with your feelings. Wait for the deep and powerful feelings to arise, and allow them consciously, until they shift. This is obviously a challenging practice, and I encourage you to become proficient in your basic practices before you try this.

Some things we just need to experience, and this may be one of those experiences for you. Letting go of attachment and taking responsibility *is* the choice to grow up. I've said before that it is never too late to have a good childhood. Give yourself all of the things that you've yearned for so you can have the experience of getting them. Frequently this is necessary before you are ready to let them go. At the same time, it is never too late to grow up. As soon as you are ready to completely accept yourself and take responsibility for yourself, you can enjoy the freedom, power, self-love, and self-determination that will allow you to both have an amazingly brilliant experience of life, but also come into deep and satisfying relationships with others.

We have seen that this conditioned romantic special relationship is not your highest potential, but what is? Many people are experimenting with many different ways of being together. I, too, have also experimented with this, and have had many experiences and ideas that I will include later in the book, but for the moment, begin experimenting yourself. I know of no successful working template. Many new and wonderful ways of being together are possible, and your input and experiences are just as valuable as anyone else's. If you approach all of your relationships with honesty, courage, consciousness, and self-responsibility, they will be gratifying, fulfilling, and wonderful, no matter what form they take.

-Chapter 40-

Sexuality

Sex is a primary focus for many people. For some it becomes an obsession. Our relationship to our sexuality and how we express it is strongly affected by our conditioning and what happened to us when we were children.

We are animals, and our sexuality is connected to our animal nature. Through our practice of self-acceptance, we embrace these animal aspects of ourselves. We eat. We breathe. We eliminate. We sweat. We reproduce. We grow old. We die. All of these things are part of living in a human body. To not accept them is essentially making a choice to be unhappy.

At the same time, we have consciousness, and our consciousness is capable of making choices that override our animal needs and instincts. Sometimes we do this in ways that enrich our lives, and sometimes we do this in ways that degrade our lives. Part of the Deep Living Practice is to make the choices about our relationship to our bodies, and our sexuality, that will be the most enriching for us.

Often, our conditioning about our bodies and sexuality is not very supportive. Many of us are taught that sex and bodily functions are taboo, and must be kept private and secret. You shouldn't even think about them, much less talk or be open about them. When these subjects do come up, it is frequently in some kind of derisive way, or people become very uncomfortable, and either change the subject or avoid their feelings with nervous laughter. How we are taught about sex, and what we learn from our contact with our parents, and primary caregivers, is at the root of this dysfunction.

Some of the greatest taboos in our culture are around body functions, childhood sexuality, and incest. These taboos have become so powerful, and our reactions to them so unconscious, that they have an extremely detrimental effect on us, both individually, and culturally. I've met very few people who are open, accepting, and comfortable with their bodies and their sexuality. Most of those who are had to explore their relationship to their bodies and sexuality, and alter their conditioning, in order to become that way.

If we want to address our relationships to our bodies and our sexuality, the first thing we need to do is make a distinction between sex acts and sexual energy. Sex acts are specific acts involving the genitals. Many people make broad generalizations and either accept or create, right/wrong, good/bad, allowed/not allowed categories, then use them as guides for what they will or will not do, or what they will or will not allow themselves to even think about. When we start to examine sex acts, we see they fall into two categories. Those sex acts that are done for reproduction, and those that are done for sensation or experience.

Our biological drive toward sexuality is based on reproduction, which occurs through unprotected intercourse between a man and a woman. This is a very powerful act that can have major consequences, so it is understandable that we have developed such a charged relationship to it. It feels appropriate that we approach it with concern and awareness. But there is no reason to have such a charged relationship to other acts that we do for pleasure, or because we want to experience a sensation.

To keep us from recklessly approaching the act of reproduction, our conditioning about our bodies and sexuality has become blown out of proportion, and is creating massive consequences, though it is not even being very effective in creating a conscious relationship to the act of reproduction. Most people are extremely reactive in relation to bodies and sexuality, and there seems to be a general consensus that it should be this way. We need to learn to look at our relationship to our bodies and our sexuality with much more consciousness and clarity.

A hygienic aspect to some sexual acts and body functions also includes the possibility of spreading disease. This is something else we need to be aware of. But if you look at it, you can see that how we have been taught to be in relation to these things is not with care and consciousness, but more with avoidance, secrecy, judgment, disgust, guilt, and fear. It is very much like when a parent lies to a child to get him to do something, like telling the child that there is a monster in the basement if the parent doesn't want him to go there. We have been taught to be reactive to these things instead of being responsible, and this reactivity is detrimental and self-perpetuating. It is time to begin the process of changing this culturally by taking responsibility individually.

Now, let's make a distinction between performing sex acts and having sexual energy. Sexual energy is a particular quality of feeling. Different people experience it in different ways, but no matter what specific ways it may be experienced, it has certain traits. Sexual energy has a feeling of being connected to the body, and it radiates out into the world. When someone is allowing sexual energy, you can definitely feel his or her presence. Sexual energy also has a quality of potential and availability. It feels like the person is open for something to happen, and that there is an invitation for something to happen.

Sexual energy is deeply connected to creativity. I experience sexuality as an aspect of creative energy, and it frequently arises in creative acts. I've spoken of the feeling centers in our bodies, and our genitals are very powerful feeling centers. When we allow sexual energy consciously, we are very aware of our genitals, and can receive much information through them.

Although sexual energy tends to arise when we are performing sexual acts, sexual acts are not required to have sexual energy. Having sexual energy does not mean you have to perform sexual acts. Sexual energy exists independently of any sexual act. This is a very important distinction to make, and one that our conditioning tends to guide us away from.

Your sexual energy is a vital part of your power and who you are. You can allow it at anytime with absolutely no commitment to perform a sexual act. Part of the Deep Living Practice is learning how to allow your sexual energy consciously and responsibly. Your sexual energy is part of who you are. Allowing your sexual energy is part of the practice of self-acceptance leading to self-love. It is part of the practice of getting in touch with your power and of living your truth. And, for some people, it is one of the most challenging parts of the Deep Living Practice.

People tend to go into unconscious behavior around sexuality. At the same time, it is the primary focus in many people's life. The basis behind this is that sexual energy is discouraged and disallowed when we are children. Children are sexual beings. Sexuality is part of who we are. By ignoring sexuality, and suppressing it, we create the dysfunctional relationship to sexuality that exists in our society. We need to openly allow sexual energy, sexual feelings, and curiosity about body functions and sexuality, so we can begin to move toward much healthier relationships.

When our sexuality is repressed, our natural development is interrupted. This results in the wide varieties of fixed attitudes, judgments, fears, obsessions, and perversions that exist around sexuality. This is a very challenging area to work in, because our conditioning is so intense. Similarly to how out of proportion our relationship to sex acts is, because of the need to be conscious and aware of reproductive and health issues, our relationship to childhood sexuality and incest has also become extremely reactive in a way that has ceased to serve us.

All cultures came to understand that reproducing with close family members is to be avoided for genetic reasons. We can see how extreme conditioning has developed to prevent this from happening in a world where many people are behaving irresponsibly and unconsciously, but the taboos, fears, and judgments have developed in a way that they are creating as many problems as they are solving. My experience is that most sexual dysfunction can be traced back to how our sexuality is repressed when we are children.

When our sexuality's natural development is interrupted, we are left to develop our ideas and relationships to our bodies, and sexuality, through whatever means are available to us, such as; things we are told that reflect the teller's ideas and relationships, which serve as a transmission of whatever they have been told; things we are exposed to in the media that reflect cultural opinions; conversations with our peers that are frequently driven by rumor, misinformation, or fantasy; and whatever other information we happen to come across. When we chance upon some sexually explicit information, or experience, it frequently has a huge effect on our development that is based on whatever form of sexuality it encompasses. Many parents, uncomfortable themselves with the topic, avoid it as much as they can, with the possible exception of a "birds and bees" conversation that usually comes too late, is extremely awkward, and rarely contains useful information.

We are left to learn by experience, but our experience is guided by all this misinformation as opposed to our natural sexual energy, which we have been taught to repress, but is still there and creating impulses and urges. We try to hold it back, because we've been taught that it is wrong, but it is coming up anyway, and we don't know what to do with it, besides hold it back as much as we can, until we let it out in a way based on these ideas we received about what it is supposed to be like, through which our natural sexual energy has been transformed into a distorted version of what is true for us. This results in whatever preferences, desires, obsessions, repulsions, judgments, perversions, fetishes, fantasies, or whatever else we experience in relation to our sexuality. It is not our truth, but the incredible power of our sexual energy is driving us to confront these aspects of ourselves in ways that seem almost impossible to deny.

So where do we go from here? We live in a world where all of this exists, and where many people don't want to be conscious and responsible enough to make broad or sudden changes in how they relate to their bodies and their sexuality. The Deep Living Practice offers a path to live our greatest potential while being conscious of what is happening around us. Through this, our lives will be the most wonderful they can be, and we will be contributing a positive energy into the collective reality. If you are living your truth, you become less encumbered by others' beliefs and reactions. Let's explore some of the ways we can shift our relationship to our bodies and sexuality, as through this, we will be doing our part, as best we can, to stop perpetuating the sexual dysfunction prevalent in our culture, and, by this, contribute to transforming the relationship to our bodies and our sexuality into ways that are more supportive to create a greater experience of happiness, freedom, and joy, both individually and culturally.

We will start by looking at gender roles. Obviously there is a biological difference between male and female, but our conditioning has such a large effect on how we relate to our gender that it can be extremely difficult to see where gender related aspects of our behavior originated. If you explore your ideas about gender roles, you will see that they are usually combinations of ideas you are in agreement with, and ideas you are rebelling against, largely affected by your gender specific role models.

One man I studied with focused on gender roles and encouraged exploration into the deep essence of male and female energy. He had found that a powerful dynamic develops when someone who is deeply in male energy connects with someone who is deeply in female energy. I learned a lot about gender and gender roles through experimenting with his ideas, but as I continued with my explorations, I discovered that we all have a deep inner truth that exists beneath our ideas about gender and gender roles.

Sometimes a person's core energy has qualities of gender, but sometimes it doesn't, and sometimes the quality of gender is not in line with the person's ideas of their genetic gender. It was through these explorations that I began to see how our ideas about gender roles are affected by culture and upbringing. I saw the benefit of supporting whatever core energy people have, and supporting their relationship to their genetic gender to develop as it will, without regard to conditioned ideas of gender roles.

Different ways of being in the world exist, and they are not only possible, but far preferable. To find them, we need to accept ourselves as we are, explore our conditioning in relation to gender, and make choices based on coming closer to our truth, while interacting with the world around us. To support this, I will refer to some traits that are typified as male or female. You can explore these ideas, and through these explorations, become clearer about your relationship to your ideas about your gender role. At the same time, don't take these things too seriously. Your deepest truth may be totally independent of these ideas, and your relationship to them only a transitional phase.

Consider the possibility of becoming less attached to gender roles, and being open to accept whatever is there, both in yourself and in others. Even the fact that we have separate bathrooms for women and men supports this separation and sexualizes bodily functions. So much in our culture has become sexualized due to the repression of sexual energy.

I am a huge advocate for touch. Part of our animal nature includes the need to be in physical contact with each other. Touch is extremely nourishing for us, particularly skin-to-skin contact. It is also extremely resourcing, though many people have become so reactive that they are very challenged to allow it. For many people, touch has become so sexualized, particularly skin contact, that they are unable to allow touch without their conditioning about sexuality becoming involved. Then their patterns of avoiding touch become so ingrained that they don't even realize that their aversion to contact is based in sexuality.

This becomes even more intense in relationship to our genitals. Our genitals are parts of our body, and we long to be touched there as well. My experience is that non-sexual touch of the genitals is not only possible, but also extremely nourishing, beneficial, and frequently even resourcing, once we let go of the reactivity caused by our taboos. But this reactivity is huge, and part of what makes consciousness so challenging in relationship to sexuality. For many people the idea of non-sexual genital contact is beyond their imagination, and culturally we accept this as normal.

This is also true for being naked. Most people feel shame or discomfort if they are not wearing clothing, but my experience is that most people are actually more comfortable without clothing, once they let go of their cultural conditioning about it. In fact, many people feel more resourced and secure without clothing, than with clothing, but are usually quite surprised to discover this. Here is an interesting experiment that demonstrates this.

> *Exercise: Sing Naked*
>
> *Learn a song. Get a recording device. Record yourself singing the song while dressed. Take your clothes off and record yourself singing the song naked. Listen to the two recordings. Most people's voices sound much more free, clear, and open when they sing naked.*

We accept, and forgive, unconscious behavior in relationship to sexuality, and in many cases we even condone it. People often feel their sexual urges are uncontrollable, even though they are not, no more than substance abuse in an addict is uncontrollable. To address these kinds of issues, we need to identify, then shift, the underlying motive for the behavior, and with sexuality it is usually about the repression, and interruption, of the natural development of sexuality. In terms of our Practice, we need to allow whatever sexual desires or fantasies exist, in a slow and conscious way, so we can experience the feelings involved. As we do this, we can work through the distortions in our sexual energy, until we get in touch with its original state.

We tend to become quite attached to our sexuality. Many people identify themselves in terms of their sexuality. Men tend to do this more than women. Their self-esteem is connected to their sexual prowess, and they judge others by the same standard.

Sexuality becomes the primary focus in many people's lives. If this is the case for you, please consider the hypothesis that a much happier and fulfilling state does exist. Sexuality is just one small part of what is available to us. By putting such an intense focus on sexuality, you are missing out on the vast majority of what is possible for you.

Sexuality and intimacy are two different things. They can happen simultaneously, but they can also happen independently, and sexuality can often get in the way of intimacy. I find that intimacy is the far more preferable experience, and I encourage you to choose to move towards intimacy, and allow sexuality as it arises. When we have such an intense focus on sexuality, and are attached to a sexual outcome in a situation, we create a fixed point that limits our possibilities.

Both men and women tend to do things they really don't want to do to get the things they want sexually, and it creates much entanglement and consequence in relationships, both with the other, and within the self. Through conditioning, women frequently allow their desire for closeness, physical touch, and intimacy, more than men, and often feel they need to be sexual in order to get these things. This is an intense form of compromise that consists of them selling themselves to get what they think they need.

Our non-accepting and judgmental relationship to our sexual energy is frequently a key component to self-hatred. We feel inherently dirty, bad, or wrong because we want things that we have been told are dirty, bad, and wrong. This is frequently connected to a feeling of needing to be punished that creates unconscious superficial behaviors that might make people angry with you, keep you from being successful, or create unpleasant experiences in your life, because deep down you feel you deserve it.

If this applies to you, it is a very challenging aspect to address, and, while I highly encourage you to look at it, because the effects of this in one's life are significant, I also encourage you to approach it slowly, with firm resourcing, and the support you need. Often this path includes going into highly reactive states and very intense fantasies of perverted sexual acts you want to experience. The clash between our true sexual energy, what we think our sexuality is, and our reactions to cultural opinions about sexuality, create the feelings and ideas that are behind what is considered perverted sexual behavior.

When I use the term "perverted", I am not meaning bad, though many people may give it this connotation. I feel "distorted" is probably the more accurate term, but I am using the word "perverted" as it is the term in common usage. I use it for clarity, even though it tends to cause negative associations.

Through the effects I have mentioned, our true sexual energy gets distorted, twisted, or perverted, and this creates these behavioral patterns, like obsessions with particular people or things, or sexualizing acts that most would consider non-sexual. A goal of the Deep Living Practice is to untwist these perverted and distorted relationships between our ideas about sexuality and our natural sexuality in order to clearly connect with our true sexual energy.

Although it may seem counterintuitive, the path to self-love is to accept any feelings and desires, no matter how strange, or wrong, they might seem, and allow them, as well as the feelings that accompany them. The key is to do this slowly and consciously. Most people who are experimenting and participating in the world of perverted sexuality are doing so unconsciously. They have made a courageous step by allowing these deep desires, even though cultural conditioning is against it, but after this initial courageous step, many of them indulge in unconscious and compulsive behavior. They focus on sensations, which are frequently very powerful, and tend to get addicted to them, but they are going over the top of the underlying feelings that are behind their desires.

My experience is that if you move toward these underlying feelings slowly and consciously, while deeply allowing the feelings related to them, they will transform. One of the challenging aspects of this practice is that frequently they will transform into something that you judge as even worse, and is more challenging to accept. It takes a lot of courage to go down this path, but I can tell you from personal experience, that though it may seem futile and endless, you can reach bottom, and at the bottom is self-love, clarity, and freedom.

Not all of us have this deep self-hatred, but most of us have some degree of reactivity in relation to our sexuality. This is even further intensified by the power imbalances and hierarchical structure of our society. Almost everyone I work with, when we start to explore their more honest feelings about themselves, finds a desire to either be controlling or be controlled in relation to sexuality. There are a huge variety of reasons for this, such as young boys who are raised by women who are giants in comparison to them, overwhelming them with their energy, so they equate love and nurturance with dominant women, or young girls whose fathers don't know how to react as their sexuality begins to arise, so the father becomes afraid and avoids close contact, then the daughter feels she has to suppress her sexuality and become submissive in order to make men feel safe. For most people, these kinds of experiences cause confusion, imbalance, and in some cases trauma. The vast majority of these kinds of experiences are taking us further away from our true sexuality instead of closer to it. The more extreme versions of these kinds of experiences can bring us into the realm of childhood sexual abuse.

Childhood sexual and physical abuse is extremely prevalent in our culture, and in my experience it is much more widespread than acknowledged. There are many different degrees of abuse and there could be much discussion as to the line where you would call something abusive or not. I have a good deal of experience working with victims of abuse, and no matter if you call what happened abusive or not, what interests me the most is how whatever happened is affecting the person's life in the present, and how I can support the person to mitigate, or eliminate, that effect. These effects can be massive, frequently altering the person's perception of reality. The good news is that this is not a permanent condition. We can heal from the effects of childhood sexual and physical abuse, and the Deep

Living Practice is designed to support that process. If you feel you were abused as a child, remember to focus on resourcing yourself first, and to get professional help if you feel you need it. Something fascinating I have found is that in most cases of abuse, the emotional fallout of the abuse is frequently more damaging than the abusive act or acts. The feelings of betrayal, the mistrust, the guilt, the secrecy, the fear of repetition, and the way relationships change all have major effects and should definitely be considered if you are working on clearing these types of experiences.

One of the saddest aspects of child abuse is that it tends to be self-perpetuating. It is very likely that the abuser was abused, and it is also likely that the abused becomes an abuser, or needs to shut down emotionally to avoid the possibility. This is usually happening unconsciously and is a tragic effect of the changed perception of reality, extreme reactivity, and compulsive behavior that is a result of the trauma of abuse. It is so wonderful to clear the effects of this from your system in that you will feel so much more stable and clear as you are interacting with others, as the abuser may change in your perception from a threat to a fellow victim that you can feel compassion for, and that you will also be able to allow a degree of intimacy with others that felt impossible before.

Intimacy does not exist when there is secrecy. Far beyond the effects of past trauma, our non-acceptance of what we are feeling sexually gets in the way of intimacy. To be truly intimate we have to be honest and open about all aspects of ourselves, and our feelings.

If we have ideas about our sexuality that are manufactured out of our conditioning, these will also get in the way of intimacy. People have learned how to be sexual, and when they become sexual they do the things that they have learned. It is as if they turn on their "sex tape" and go on autopilot. This is another example of automatic behavior. There is very little consciousness involved. Watch for this, and practice consciousness during sexual acts. If you do this, it is very likely that something else will happen besides the sexual act you thought you were going to perform.

If you remember, attraction exists because the person you are attracted to will help you find a feeling in yourself that will get you closer to your truth. This may have to do with being sexual, or it may not. Be open for any possibility. You can use the Intimacy Practice from the last chapter to see if intimacy with this person in question includes sexuality. Here is a way to focus the Intimacy Practice on sexuality.

Practice: Checking for Sexual Attraction

If you would like to find if your attraction to someone is sexual, it is very effective to do the Intimacy Practice naked, in bed, lying close and looking at each other. If the other person is open to this, it is a very quick way to see if there is a sexual aspect to the attraction.

Do this with no attachment to outcome. Just lie close to each other naked, and feel what you are feeling. Share your feelings as openly and honestly as possible. One at a time, try touching each other and feel how it feels. If you choose to go further, try holding each other with your bodies pressed together or kissing. If there is sexual attraction it will be very obvious by this point. Remember, at this stage the practice is more about allowing feelings and sharing them than completing any act. If you decide there is sexual attraction, it is up to you what you do next.

This practice may seem outrageous to you, but as I have said, very often our ideas of who we are, and are not, attracted to, and the things we are attracted to do with him or her, come from our conditioning and do not reflect our deeper feelings. Most people are unaware of their deeper feelings, to the degree where they have sexual relationships that are totally driven by these conditioned states. Obviously, it takes a certain degree of awareness and impulse control to do this kind of practice, and you will want to do it with someone who you feel will behave responsibly, but once you have developed these skills, this practice is an extremely effective way to shift your deeply ingrained conditioned ideas about attraction, sexuality and gender roles.

Many people go into unconscious behavior around sexuality, and through this they develop powerful impulses to perform sexual acts. As we have discussed, there are some impulses that we want to allow, but others that we do not want to support. Sometimes impulses are a way to avoid feelings. Often people perform sexual acts as a way to get rid of sexual energy. Because of their affected relationship to their sexuality, they are very uncomfortable with the feelings that arise with their sexuality, so when they begin to feel sexual energy, they feel like they need to do something about it. It is like yelling when you are angry or crying hysterically when you are sad. Sexual acts are sometimes a way to *avoid* feeling sexual energy, and can be looked at as a form of collapse. We want to learn to have our sexual energy, without feeling we have to do something to disperse it.

Our conditioning strongly supports irresponsibility around sexuality. Many people, men more frequently than women, feel that if they allow their sexual energy, they have to have sex. Some even feel they have the right to, to the degree where they will get angry with a woman if she allows her sexuality and then doesn't have sex with them. This goes to the absurd degree where in some places men are barely punished, if at all, for rape. Later in the book we will look at the state of relationship between men and women, and male energy and female energy, in a broader context, but for the moment, we want to focus on the possibility of allowing sexual energy independently of a sex act. When I was young, I was taught that if I became sexually aroused and didn't have sex, my testicles would start to ache, and they did. Later I learned that this wasn't true and my testicles stopped aching. This is an example of the power of our minds and our conditioning.

When sexual energy first begins to arise, we tend to avoid it by shutting it down. If we do allow it, we tend to feel like we have to do something with it, like having sex or masturbating. Experiment with allowing sexual energy without doing anything with it. Through this, we can start to get in touch with our true sexual energy.

Another way we can get in touch with our natural sexual energy is through the Letting Someone Hold You Exercise. Almost invariably, as part of becoming relaxed and comfortable while being held, sexual energy will start to arise. If you can allow this sexual energy, you will see it frequently has a childish quality. If the person supporting you is available for it, you can take this opportunity to explore your natural childish sexuality, and allow it to develop slowly and consciously. In this case, the person holding you can best support you by lovingly allowing you to do whatever you want, but not initiating any actions him or herself.

Many people have backed up sexual energy that can make it challenging to approach sexuality consciously. There are so many ways they have been holding back, they can't be aware of the more subtle feelings under all of their pent up desire. If this is the case for you, just go for it. Have sex. Have lots of sex. Have sex every way you ever considered having sex. Explore. Have fun. Take care of reproductive, health, and safety issues, but besides that, allow this backed up energy so you are no longer distracted by the effect of holding it back. This can be an extremely freeing experience.

One of my teachers was mostly concerned with teaching consciousness, but found it impossible with all the backed up sexual energy in the room. Through encouraging people to explore their sexual energy, he got the reputation of running sex groups. To some extent, this was true, because he created such a safe place to explore sexuality. But in the long run, I came to see that this was a necessary step on the path of learning to become more conscious. You may want to look for some kind of similar situation where you can safely allow your backed up sexual energy.

This is a particularly good time to consider shame as well. Shame is directly connected to your conditioning, and if you want to break free of your conditioning you need to stop allowing shame to control your behavior. In your exploration of sexuality, look at all the things you are ashamed of, consider doing them, and then try actually doing them, slowly and consciously. You will be surprised at how you really feel about the things you think you are ashamed of.

Allowing your sexual energy and moving through the world available for intimacy is a very powerful and exciting way to live. But remember, just because you are open to allow your sexual energy, and are available for intimacy, doesn't mean you have to do anything. You can choose what you want to do and when you want to do it. Over time, you may find that you are less attracted to people, and situations, where it is necessary to hold back. Letting go of the past is part of the process of creating a future that is closer to your truth.

In an earlier chapter I mentioned saying "yes" to your "no". I find it essential to be able to say "no" firmly and decisively before you can really relax into your "yes". Many people's conditioning makes it very hard for them to say "no". If this is the case for you, you can address this issue by creating situations where you can practice saying "no" and exploring the feelings that arise in the process. You need to fully allow the force of your "no" before you can find the power of your "yes".

Here are two practices that will help you become more aware of your sexual energy.

> *Practice: Bring Consciousness to Your Genitals*
>
> *The most obvious way to become aware of your sexual energy is to bring your attention to your genitals. Pay attention to how they feel several times an hour. Most people ignore their genitals most of the time. It is as if they leave them at home when they go out. Think of your genitals as an antenna that is tuned into sexual energy. Remember, just because you feel sexual energy doesn't mean you have to do anything with it, and that your sexual energy is an essential part of you all of the time, not only when you are involved in an overtly sexual act. You can perceive much information about the world around you if you are paying attention to your genitals.*

> *Practice: Consider the Possibility of Intimacy or Sexuality*
>
> *Consider the possibility of an intimate or sexual connection with everyone you meet. I found this practice extremely transformative. As I became more courageous, I began approaching people who I found sexually attractive, but thought I had no chance with. Besides finding that they were usually open and receptive, I also found that frequently there wasn't any sexual attraction after all. It was just my cultural conditioning that had told me that I should be attracted to these people. When I opened up to consider all people, I frequently found intense attraction with people I would not have approached because I could not even imagine being attracted to them. Through these contacts, I learned much about myself, started to come closer to my truth, and had some incredible experiences as well.*

I want to say a few words about boundaries. Sexuality is one of the most popular areas for people to create boundaries. Be conscious of this. Boundaries are substitutes for consciousness, and keep us from reaching our truth, and potential, by keeping us away from the uncomfortable situations that will bring up the feelings we need to feel in order to find our truth and potential. Use boundaries if you feel you need them, but practice letting them go as you feel you are ready.

If you are in a close relationship with someone, you are probably concerned with him or her having intimate and sexual relationships with other people. Jealousy is an incredibly powerful feeling and is deeply rooted in attachment. Although we address attachment in the Deep Living Practice, it is quite challenging, and can take some time, so people in relationships frequently make agreements about how much sexuality and intimacy is allowed outside the relationship.

Don't allow the agreements you make let you ignore your attachment issues, but instead use them to support you to explore and clear these issues by giving you the freedom to allow your attractions without having to be concerned of extreme consequences because you have agreed not to act on them. Share everything you are feeling and be as honest as you possibly can. Secrets destroy relationships. Make agreements as you feel you need them, keep them until you choose not to, but don't let them become fixed points that create resentment.

Use your self-inquiry to examine your true feelings and deeper motivations. Many people are extremely triggered if their partner wants to be sexual with another person. Really examine your feelings about it, and see what it actually is that bothers you. Is it the act? Is it the intimacy? Do you feel excluded? Are you comparing yourself badly? Is it the motivation behind the act?

Try not to let the power of the feeling hijack you into the blindness of a reactive state, and if it does, look at these things when you settle down. As in all other aspects of our Practice, we can break this down into addressable parts, and clear them one at a time.

There is no right way to be in relationship. Many ideas exist about it, but as with all ideas, they are just that, ideas, and they don't have anything to do with what is happening with you in the moment, beyond your choice to let them. How you want to be with your relationships and your sexuality is a work in progress. Use the skills we have been discussing to make it as wonderful as you can in each moment, and continue making it better by identifying and addressing any choices you are making that are degrading your relationships.

Look at whether you are energetically giving or taking in regard to your sexual energy. If you are feeling needy, or horny, you are in a state of taking. You are creating a hole that can never be filled. It can be temporarily sated, but soon the emptiness will return, and no amount of sexual activity will ever change this. The solution is to find your true sexual energy, and allow it to radiate out of you. These holes need to be filled from the inside, and you radiating your sexual energy out into the world will create the feeling of fulfillment you are craving.

An interesting aspect of sexual energy, and sexual acts for that matter, is the feeling of penetrating or being penetrated. This also relates closely to intimacy. The feeling that you are inside another person, or that the other person is inside of you. There are obvious physical manifestations of this in various sexual acts, but this also happens energetically. It can be extremely intimate. Sometimes it is greatly desired, sometimes greatly feared, and often both at the same time.

Many people disassociate at the moment of penetration. Watch for this, and approach penetration slowly, consciously, and with the Rhythm, while allowing space for all the feelings involved, whether you are doing it physically or energetically. In our typical gender roles the male energy is penetrating and the female craving penetration, but my experience is that there is a deep longing to both penetrate and be penetrated in all of us, regardless of gender.

The power of our sexuality is in the energy, not in the act, and this energy is always available to us. It is important to support our children to allow their sexual energy, and let it develop naturally. Yes, it is a dangerous world and we need to create a safe environment to do this, but we do need to do it. If we don't, we are not supporting our children to reach their potential, and are perpetuating the problems caused by sexual repression. Children need to learn about sexuality from their parents and caregivers. Don't let your fears about cultural taboos keep you from supporting their growth and curiosity. The most powerful way to teach children to allow their sexual energy responsibly is to learn to do it yourself.

The final issue about sexuality I would like to address in this chapter is the connection between sexuality and creativity. I talk about finding the truth of who we really are. I experience this truth as a creative energy. When we drop beneath all these ideas we have about ourselves, we *are* a creative energy that has the possibility of radiating into the world and contributing to the joint creation of reality. The more we accept, and allow, this energy, the more wonderful and fulfilled we feel. We are an act of creation, and our sexuality is the grounded and physical aspect of this creation. This is an essential, and natural, part of who we are, and if we don't allow it fully and completely, we are missing our creative potential.

At the very heart of this sexual creative energy is the ability to create life. It is the ultimate act of intimacy and creativity. I led a very active, though mostly unconscious, sexual and creative life, having had numerous experiences of many varieties with many different people. The most powerful experience though, was to look in someone's eyes and say, "Let's make a baby," then have her say, "Yes, let's make a baby." What happened after that was a wonderful and joyous experience, which far overshadows any other sexual or creative experience I have had and, gratefully, the consequences of that experience continue to this day.

-Chapter 41-

Family and Children

For most of us, families are the source of the vast majority of our behavioral development and conditioning. For many of us, though, much of the influence our family has on us does not support our truth or happiness. For a wide variety of reasons, including personal problems, relationship problems, financial problems, personal history, past trauma, and self pre-occupation, our parents, siblings, and extended families frequently create an environment that is not conducive to our healthy development into responsible adults, but instead leads us to make choices that create patterns and strategies which support attachment, reactivity, irresponsibility, fear, doubt, confusion, fixed ideas about ourselves and the world, and all manner of other things that keep us from our maximum potential and the experience of the joy of our true selves.

The first thing to realize is that was then and this is now. The things that happen in our first few years of life have a powerful developmental effect, but they are no longer happening, they are not fixed, and we can change them if we address them.

We tend to project our parents onto other people in our lives, but there is an even greater tendency to project our parents onto our parents. As children, we create versions of our parents in our minds based on particularly influential events, and these become the way we see our parents. These versions contribute to our internal dialogue and become the voices in our heads that tell us how to behave, and what is and isn't allowed. We want to identify these versions of our parents that only exist within our minds, and do what it takes to have them stop affecting our lives.

Practice: Transforming Negative Effects of Your Parents

My experience is that it is not effective to try to work through your parental issues with your actual parents. The relationships are usually very entangled, and this can create many additional obstacles. Both parents and children tend to revert to old states when they come together. This can make resourcing very difficult.

It is easy to find other people who are good parent projections for you, as you will tend to be either attracted to or repulsed by them. Find some who are open to supporting you. When you approach others with openness and vulnerability, many people are not only available, but also happy to have an opportunity to help. If this proves difficult, find professional support.

Resignation frequently plays a major role when approaching family issues. If you feel resigned, look for the longing beneath your resignation. This is frequently the longing for connection or being held. As you allow your longing, frequently anger or lust will arise. If lust arises, allow the sexual energy. This is all you need to do with sexual energy. Just allow it. Skin contact can help, and maybe some caressing or rubbing, but in this childish state, that is usually all that is required to support sexual energy.

It is extremely likely you will eventually feel anger. Anger is what you need to transform the patterns, so allow it when it arises. This can be challenging for several reasons. One is that our feelings toward our parents are usually mixed. There are probably many ways that they were extremely nourishing and supportive; many things that they did and sacrificed for you. They gave you life. This is all well and good, but for the purpose of clearing your system, you need to put all the good parts of the relationship aside for a few minutes and focus on the parts where you felt repressed, denied, hurt, betrayed, abused, or whatever other aspects of the relationship that were not supportive. Another challenge is that a deep part of you probably still wants their love and support. You feel you will destroy any possibility of ever getting the love and support you crave if you allow your anger. Even though this may be true, you need to choose to allow the feelings you want to transform anyway. It may be challenging at first, but if you stay with it, you can learn to do this.

To permanently transform these childhood patterns, you have to allow more than just anger. My experience is that to get these childhood effects of our parents out of our system, we must reach a killing rage. Of course, we need to do this consciously, and without going over the top into catharsis. It is as if we are killing the version of our parent that is in our memory that is having the negative effect on us. Sometimes it can be supportive to act out the killing. To do this, the person supporting needs to keep the person killing very present, usually with eye contact, offer some resistance, let the killer win when he is deeply in the feeling, and pretend to die after the killer has been in the rage state for 20 to 30 seconds. Remember, it is not about acting out or going over the top, it is about feeling the feeling without doing anything else. There is an art to supporting people through this kind of process, but I have seen untrained people supporting each other in these kinds of processes to great effect.

Frequently, after the killing, the killer will feel deep love, and the process usually ends with the supporter holding the killer to help him feel this love. Sometimes the killer will get the feeling of, "Who's next?" and will want to kill someone else. This will be the case if there are several aspects that need to be transformed, or possibly some other people, such as the other parent, brothers, sisters, grandparents, or other primary caregivers who had negative effects that the killer feels ready to address. If he has the energy, you can repeat the process one or two more times, but usually it is most effective to wait a few days to allow his system to reorganize after the first process, and for the energy to build up again. Usually subsequent processes happen much more quickly and easily.

When you clear the negative effects of your childhood out of your system, you will be much closer to your truth. It is also amazing how this affects your relationship with your actual parents. Most people find a much deeper love than they have experienced before. They also start to see their parents as actual people, instead of being lost in their parent projections.

We've already said that it is never too late to have a good childhood. Create situations that allow you to get all of the experiences you wanted as a child. It is important, though, to let go of the desire to get these experiences from your actual parents. If you have reached adulthood without getting what you wanted from your parents, the possibility of getting it from them now is relatively small. Having childhood desires fulfilled through other sources also helps to break the intense focus we tend to put on our parents. It may be hard to believe, but it really feels just as good from another source. Realizing this is part of letting go of attachment.

Our feeling that we have to get everything we need from our parents is an aspect of the nuclear family that does not serve us. The nuclear family creates extreme pressure on the parents. Many parents do not react well to this pressure. Their unconscious resentment comes out in their behavior, much to the child's detriment. As well, when we only have one male and one female role model, it leaves it up to them to give us all our information about life and gender. This leaves the child with a very narrow view of his or her possibilities. It would be much healthier to create situations where more people are available to both support giving the child the things he or she needs, and to offer the child a variety of role models and sources of information from which to choose. It would be very beneficial to support children to get away from the feeling of, "this is how it is," but instead see that there are a variety of possibilities, and learn to make choices that are appropriate for whatever situation they are in. This, of course, would require us to look at major changes in family structure, and how we raise our children.

A key aspect in family structures is the concept of responsibility. What works best is to take 100 percent responsibility for yourself, and no responsibility for anyone else, including family members. This does not mean you cannot love them, support them, nourish them, or take care of them. The relevant point is why you are doing whatever you are doing.

If you are doing what you are doing out of a sense of responsibility, you will feel resentment and it will affect the relationship. Many people feel stuck with family relationships. If they work for you, wonderful, but if they don't, why continue them? By continuing them we frequently create dysfunctional, and sometimes abusive, relationships that repeat generation after generation. This is a very challenging point for many people, but my experience is that the most responsible thing to do is to be responsible for yourself.

This can be even more challenging in respect to children. They, too, are responsible for themselves. Yes, they are not able to take care of themselves for quite a while, but the sooner we can start to teach them self-responsibility, the happier their lives will be. Ultimately they *are* responsible for themselves. They make their choices, and experience the consequences.

If we approach our children with love, and take care of them because it brings us joy to take care of them, while at the same time teaching them self-responsibility, we will have the best possible relationship with them, while supporting them to have the best possible life available to them. By taking responsibility for them we take their power from them, we force our ideas on them, and we create the resentment and reactivity that exists on both sides of so many child/parent relationships. Yes, there may be times you don't want to take care of your children, and that our family and social structures don't allow for this inevitable possibility is part of the reason we need to transform these structures into more functional models that provide more support and healthier, happier outcomes for both parent and child. This is a huge subject that deserves a book of its own, but for the moment, let's practice self-responsibility and teach it to our children.

My final word on family in this chapter has to do with choice. Many people think there is no choice in family matters, and this is not true. If your family works for you, that is wonderful. If working on making your family relationships better brings you joy, this is also wonderful and I encourage you to have fun with it. But if you are longing for a family relationship you are not getting, create it for yourself. Find people who want to live the way you want to live, and create a family with them. You do not need a genetic connection to create the experience of family.

Our increasing consciousness allows us to override aspects of our animal nature that are not working for us, and this includes these genetic familial bonds. Let's stop putting energy into families that are oppressive and dysfunctional, and start creating families that are supportive and wonderful. Genes are not a valid excuse for bad behavior. The most loving way we can support family members is not through codependence, but by helping them experience the consequences of their behavior, so they can make a responsible choice about whether they want to continue it or not. Let's create loving, supportive, nurturing families that take care of each other by supporting each member to take care of him or herself.

–Chapter 42–

Deepening Your Practice

As you continue with the Deep Living Practice, it will deepen and transform. The basic aspects will continue to develop, but will become effortless. Your Practice will become a way of life, and you will see opportunities to integrate it into your daily activities. Let's look at some ways that this can happen.

We've talked about the importance of vulnerability in relation to personal power and intimacy. To begin the practice of vulnerability, we allow insecurity. Much of our behavior is based on doing things to keep us from feeling insecure. Insecurity is the beginning of the path to your truth. We need to practice not doing the things that keep us from feeling insecure, but instead, stay present with our insecurity.

Information lies in the feelings that cause our insecurity. If we focus on interpreting this information, we are much safer than if we choose to not feel our insecurity and indulge in behavioral posturing instead. Most everyone feels insecure. Most people are just trying to hide it by pretending they are something they are not, though most of them are not even aware that they are doing this. As you allow your insecurity, you will feel much more in touch with what is happening around you, and your insecurity will transform into excitement. When we are not lost in pretending to be someone we are not, we feel vibrant, excited, and very alive.

As we integrate the practice of vulnerability into our lives, we can also practice intimacy. Opportunities for intimacy abound in day-to-day life. As you approach the world available for intimate connections, you will project a very powerful presence. Your life will also become much richer, as you have spontaneous deep connections in unexpected places. There is so much available for us that we are not taking advantage of because we are holding back.

Another aspect of practicing intimacy and vulnerability in everyday life is living transparently. Most of us hold our face in a mask, and don't allow our feelings to show. This also extends to the quality of our voice and our posture. Allow your true feelings to show through. Share what you are feeling with the people around you.

Many people have a secret self that they don't show anyone. By this stage, it is time to let go of your secrets. This may be a long-term process; probably starting with the secrets you keep from yourself. As you become more honest with yourself, become more honest with other people as well. The only way to feel truly free is to live boldly and transparently.

This brings us to the topic of automatic behavior. Most people behave automatically most of the time. We say the same things, or we behave in a predictable manner, in response to what is happening around us. This connects to how we allow choices we have made in the past, and then become unconscious of, to control our behavior. One of my teachers used to say, "You are all robots!" This is the result of a mixture of unconscious and fear-driven behavior. When you begin to let go of your automatic behaviors, you begin to see how incredibly predictable most people are. It is a paradox, because the root of automatic behavior is fear. When we look at deeper motivations, we see that people believe their automatic behaviors are keeping them safe, when the truth is that their behavior's extreme predictability makes them easy to manipulate and puts them at risk. We will see over and over again how by allowing our fear to control us, we get the exact result we are afraid of. Watch for automatic behavior and choose not to indulge in it.

So many people use what other people do, and feel, as an excuse for their behavior. Watch for the tendency to do this, and let it go. This is not to say that you should not pay attention to what other people are feeling. As your Practice develops, it will transform and primarily become a practice of consciousness. This includes choosing to be conscious of what is going on around you.

Integrate your practice of empathy into your life. Pay attention to what the people around you are feeling. You may be concerned that if you do this you will let what they are feeling affect your behavior, but you will see that you have a choice, and learning to exercise that choice is another very valuable skill to learn. This connects to our practice of feeling the difference between fear and what is appropriate. When you are fully available to do whatever you truly want to do, and are also conscious of the effect you are having on your surroundings, a wonderful regulation happens where you don't feel like you are holding back, and your actions are perfectly appropriate to the situation. We will discuss this state more in future chapters, as it is a primary goal of the Deep Living Practice.

This brings us to allowing impulses. As our practice of intuition deepens we will start to feel impulses to do or say things. This is an extension of our practice of following attractions. Getting in touch with these kinds of pure impulses that come from our truth is a wonderful part of the Deep Living Practice. This is where you can really start to allow your inner truth to guide your actions, and start following your impulses in day-to-day life. At first, do it slowly, or even talk about doing it before you do it. Many impulses seem absurd, or totally out of context, like saying or doing something that seems totally inappropriate or that you feel might be terribly offensive, but when you do them, you will see that they were perfect beyond imagination.

Make sure that you separate reactions from impulses. They feel entirely different, and they have very different consequences. As you follow your impulses, be aware of their consequences. Learn the difference in feeling between an impulse and a reaction. We want to learn to allow our impulses, but make notes of our reactions so we can clear them from our system.

We also want to separate impulses from desires. Desire comes from the feeling that something is lacking, and is ultimately based on a choice to be unhappy. Strong desires can arise and be confused with impulses. There is no feeling of need with an impulse. It does not feel good to block impulses, because you are blocking your energy, but there is no feeling of disappointment when you don't follow them, like you get when a desire is not fulfilled. You frequently feel excitement at the prospect of allowing impulses. Allow your impulses, and examine your desires and reactions, as you will find useful information in the motivations beneath them.

As your Practice deepens, you will become more powerful, clear, and stable than many of the people around you. You will start to see their fears, insecurities and behavioral posturing much more clearly. You will probably be more available for intimacy and connection, and more courageous in action than most people. As this happens I suggest you start offering your impulses before allowing them. Many of those things you think of saying or doing that your conditioning tells you that would be not allowed, wrong, or inappropriate are the exact things the person wants to have said or done on a deeper level. Something you may consider an insult or even abuse will reflect how he truly feels about himself, or something he fantasizes about having done to him. Of course, the person may be resistant, and you need to approach things slowly and with care, but if you do, you will touch a more intimate part of the person and reach a deeper and more honest connection.

The first step is to ask the person if he or she is available for what you are offering. This could take a form like, "I have something I would like to say to you. Would you like to hear it?" or, "There is something I would like to do with you. Would you like to hear about it?" The second step is to offer the impulse as clearly and directly as possible. If you know the person, you may not need the first step. If you do this, you will not feel like you are holding back whether she accepts your offer or not.

Offering your impulses becomes important, because as your Practice develops you will become aware of how uncomfortable it is to hold back or be dishonest. Most people live with this discomfort, disassociate from it, and integrate it into how they think it feels to be alive. As you continue the Deep Living Practice, and liberate yourself from these kinds of discomfort, and realize that life can feel better than you thought possible, you will be much more sensitive to how unpleasant it feels to hold back or be dishonest, and you will not want to let those feelings return. By following your impulses, or at least making the invitation to allow your impulses, you will feel wonderful no matter what the other people around you are doing, though you will probably want to find people who accept your invitations, as they are much more fun to be around.

Potential for you exists in whatever situation you find yourself in. If you find and live that potential, you will feel much better than if you choose not to look for it and pursue it. Allowing your impulses is one way to find that potential. Here is a practice that can start to guide you to your potential in whatever situation you may be.

Practice: Finding Your Place in the Room

In whatever situation you are in, there is always the perfect place for you. Find it. Experiment with sitting or standing in different places and notice how some will feel better than others. Don't necessarily look for the most comfortable place in the room, although sometimes that might be your place. Also consider the most exciting place, as this is frequently where you will find your potential.

Realize that your place is not static or fixed. Your place will constantly change with the dynamics of the situation. If you stay aware of your place, and occupy it, you will always feel much better than if you don't.

One of the most frequent concerns of the people I work with is that they feel like they do not know what they want to do in life. Here is a direct way to find the answer to that question.

Practice: Finding What You Want in Life

Make finding the answer to the question, "What is my role in life?" or "What do I want in life?" your top priority. Sit in a quiet room and consider the answer to this question. Feel free to write, journal, dialogue, draw, or do anything that supports finding the answer to this question, but do not do anything else you don't need to do. Get meals quickly. Use the toilet when you need to. If you have to work, go to work, but come home and get back to the question as soon as you can. Don't see friends, read, listen to music, or do any of the many distractions you usually indulge in. Choose to stay with this question until you find the answer.

This practice, like so many others, may seem too simple, but everyone I know who has done it has found their answer. The key to this practice is actually doing it. By now you should understand that all the practices are about the underlying choice, and this one is no different. By making the choice to find what you want to do in life and staying with it, the longest I have heard of it taking is three weeks, and for most people it takes less time. If you consider the importance of knowing the answer to this question, it is well worth the time invested.

When the answer comes, you will probably resist it at first. Keep your mind open to any possibilities. Remember, your truth is frequently beyond your imagination.

As your Deep Living Practice develops, I encourage you to become more playful and experimental. Remember not to take things too seriously. As children we have a wonderful capacity for play, and my experience is that the joy in play never goes away, we just stop allowing ourselves to have it. I find role-play a wonderful way to experiment with different ways of being in the world, and exploring what brings us joy. By exaggerating certain aspects of our selves, we can come closer to what is true for us, or become clear that something is not part of who we are.

The key to being truly free is understanding that nothing really matters, and through play and experimentation we can experience this directly. Role-play also helps when supporting each other in processes. We are all capable of being mean, violent, or abusive. If we can choose to allow an aspect like this consciously, we will see this aspect is a part of ourselves that we can access if we want, and in seeing that we can allow it if we want, we can learn to choose to not allow it if we don't want. By experimenting with this you can start to learn to live your life, as opposed to your life living you. If we embrace, and accept, all aspects of ourselves, they become part of our power instead of bursting out unconsciously in moments of reaction.

Speaking of reaction, you will want to continue noting when you are reactive, and finding the source of your reactions and transforming them. One advantage of this is that life is so much more enjoyable when you stop being reactive, but there is another deeper advantage. We have discussed how the primary role of your subconscious is to protect you, and how it uses past experience to create an illusion of safety. As you get further into your practice of eliminating reactivity from your life, your subconscious will begin to experience that paying attention to what is actually happening is a much more effective way to keep you safe and secure. This will encourage your subconscious to support your practice of consciousness, which will help you stay even more present. In time, all the different aspects of the Deep Living Practice will come together to support each other, and then your Practice will become even more effective and you can have major results in very short periods of time.

By becoming responsible with your anger, it will become the resolve that allows you to move through many of the challenging aspects of the Deep Living Practice. As your Practice continues, you will see how anger transforms into passion. What was once a feeling to be repressed and avoided will become the energy that fuels the most exciting and touching experiences of your life.

If you have not addressed the effect of shame in your life, it is time to do this. Shame is a consequence of your conditioning. If you want to break free of your conditioning, you need to break free of shame.

> ### Practice: Clearing Shame
>
> *Approach this practice the same way you approached the Fear Practice. Make a list of the things you are ashamed of, and start to do them slowly and consciously so you can feel the feelings involved. You want to reach a state where shame does not control your actions.*
>
> *If you do this, you will find that some of the things you were ashamed of were things you actually wanted to do. With other things you will have a neutral feeling, or it will be clear why you don't enjoy something, like it hurts, or it is unhealthy. In these cases, you will then know why you don't want to do the thing, as opposed to being told by your conditioning that you are not allowed, or not supposed, to do the thing.*
>
> *It is important that you actually do the thing, so you are making your choice based on experience as opposed to what you think your experience will be, as they are rarely the same. Frequently people choose not to do something they are ashamed of, telling themselves that they really don't need to. This is shame controlling their behavior, although they are unconscious of it.*
>
> *Doing this practice takes the power away from your conditioning and returns it to you. Frequently at the moment the shame goes away, it seems funny that you made such a big deal about it, and you deepen your experience that nothing really matters.*

Patience becomes an issue for most people by this stage. The best way to support patience is to take the time to look at the gains you have already achieved in your Practice. If you have been practicing for a while, life will be easier, and your relationships will be better. It can be hard to notice this while you are involved in whatever you are currently involved in, so take the time and be grateful with yourself for what you have achieved. Remember to do this when you are feeling impatient.

Keep your Practice focused. I've talked about many things, and made many suggestions. Focus on one thing at a time, clear it, then move on to the next. The way to choose the next thing to focus on is either what is causing the most unpleasantness in your life, or what you can't avoid. They are frequently the same thing, but if not, don't try to avoid what you can't avoid. This is life giving you a message.

When you have cleared something, there is frequently a brief pause while you enjoy the freedom and clarity from having let the thing go, and then the next thing to look at will start to become obvious. If you are looking for it, it is quite easy to see. It is like peeling layers from an onion. Avoid the temptation of working on too many things at once. It is much less effective, and creates frustration.

A key aspect of the Deep Living Practice is accepting who you are, and what is happening in the moment. Remember, there *is only* perfection, and if you don't like what is happening, focus your attention on figuring out what is perfect about whatever is happening. Sometimes the answer will come easily, and you get important information about the consequences of the choices you have made. Sometimes you won't get it in the moment, but later it will be very clear. Sometimes you never understand it, but what does happen is by looking at life this way, you stay engaged in a productive way, and stop wasting your time not liking something that you have no power over in the moment and were probably part of creating in the first place.

By this stage in your Practice you will start to experience some moments of joy and clarity beyond anything you have previously experienced. This is the Deep Living Practice's goal, and as soon as you start to have these kinds of experiences, you will want to focus on creating more of them. At the beginning of the Practice most people are lost in their behavioral patterns, and focus on transforming the aspects of their behavior that don't work. As soon as you start to have deep and wonderful life experiences, we want to shift our focus to what does work. Look at these experiences as states, and do what you need to do to get back into the states you want to be in. Staying in these states becomes the heart of your Practice.

You can look at being in these states as being directly on the path to your truth. The more time you spend on this path, the closer you get to your truth. I like to look at it as a laser beam guiding you to your truth. While you are on it, enjoy it. If something knocks you off, notice what knocked you off, make a note to address it, and do what it takes to get back on the beam. If you stay with this, you will find that you get knocked off the laser beam less and less frequently, when you get knocked off, you don't go so far off, and you are able to get back on much more quickly and easily. This is when all the energy you have put into your Deep Living Practice starts to pay off in ways that exceed your imagination of what is possible for you.

-Chapter 43-

Deepening Consciousness

As we progress with the Deep Living Practice, consciousness becomes the main focus, and, as well as with other aspects of our Practice, we want to look at how to integrate our practice of consciousness into our daily lives. As I mentioned in the last chapter, a key aspect of doing this is to bring your attention to your choices' consequences. Keep an open mind, because as your practice of consciousness develops, you may see that there are things to be conscious of that you were unaware of previously.

As your consciousness expands, you will become more aware of what is happening energetically, and you will begin to perceive energy. This may seem like we are leaving the practical and entering the esoteric, but my experience is that becoming aware of what is happening energetically is extremely practical. I have found we can perceive what is happening energetically both within someone, and between people, and that this information is as reliable, and frequently even more useful, than the information I perceive with my traditional senses. I have gained the reputation of seeing people extremely clearly, and this is because I have learned to read their energy. This is not a skill I was born with or that came to me magically. It is a skill I developed doing the Deep Living Practice, and you can learn it too.

When I am with people, I experience them as energetic phenomena. I experience their deep inner truth as a certain quality of energy and all the behavioral layers on top as various fixed points, diversions, competing energies and other factors that are keeping their truth from expressing itself in its pure and natural form. I've found it useful to look at these energetic phenomena in terms of vectors.

A simple way to look at vectors is to imagine rowing a boat across a river with a strong current. You paddle directly to the opposite shore (one vector) but the current of the river (another vector) pushes you sideways as you paddle, so you end up some way down the riverbank (your outcome).

I have found that looking at things in terms of vectors and understanding how vectors affect an outcome is one of the most valuable skills I have developed in life. I developed this skill long before my search for happiness and my study of consciousness. I was studying electronic music, tai chi, and stage lighting at the same time, and suddenly realized that they all worked on the same principles. Different amounts and qualities of different energies come together from different directions and create a predictable outcome. The way the different energies come together and react or respond to each other usually behaves in a similar manner, no matter what field you are working in.

Learning this at a young age served me well throughout my life. I was able to learn new things very quickly because it was just a matter of seeing how whatever it was I was learning fit into this relationship of vectors. I encourage you to start paying attention to vectors and looking for patterns. Learning to read vectors and see and interpret patterns is an incredibly powerful skill. You may already be doing it and not be aware that you are doing it.

If there is a subject you know well or something you do well, see if you can perceive the effect of vectors on whatever it is. It applies to everything, from riding a bicycle to cooking. Once you can see the effect of vectors in something you are familiar with, start to look for how things work in relationship to one another in areas you are not familiar with. Seeing energy behaving the same way in many different situations will help you understand the basic principles behind how vectors work, and then you can apply them to any situation. It is not something I can explain, or I would, it is something you need to experience to get a true understanding of.

Here, we are interested in how vectors pertain to your life. You are a truth that wants to express itself in a particular way. We can look at this as a direction, and refer to it as your path to your truth. Then you can look at all the other influences and effects in your life and consider them as vectors that affect your travel on your path to your truth.

Practice: Identifying and Shifting the Vectors in Your Life

Sit with your notebook and, to the best of your ability in the moment, identify what you want to do in life. We will consider this as the direction of your truth. Now list all the other things that affect your life. The list will probably be quite long. Each of us will have a distinctive list, but some examples of things that might be on your list are self-doubt, indecision, fear of confrontation, curiosity, desire for relationship, creativity, sexual drive, effects of family, commitments you have made, or physical conditions. Open your mind and consider anything that affects you moving in the direction of your truth.

Now, go through your list and identify what effect each of these things is having on your life. Are they supporting the direction you want to go? Are they blocking you? Are they weighing you down or do you have to drag them behind you? Are they diverting you? Some examples of this might be; my creativity pushes me forward, my fear of confrontation stands in my way, I have to drag my mother's opinions behind me, my desire for an attached relationship diverts me, or my relationship to money is like a huge weight on my shoulders.

Use this list to see which energies are having the greatest effect in keeping you from reaching your truth. Then do what you have to do to either eliminate these vectors, or alter them so they are supporting the direction of your truth. When you start to line up your energy to support your path and stop fighting yourself, your life will become much easier and eventually effortless.

I've offered exercises to support becoming more conscious, but eventually consciousness is best practiced in daily life. Pay attention to what you are doing. Focus on specific actions. Feel the glass in your hand. What is the temperature? How tight are you holding it? Could you hold it looser without letting it slip? Put it on the table. How fast are you moving it? What is happening with the liquid inside? Where on the table are you going to put it? Is it the perfect place? Why? Notice the contact as the glass is set down on the table. How do you draw your hand back from the glass? Where are you going to put your hand? Why? Putting this level of consciousness into simple activities is an excellent practice. If you are in a situation where you are waiting for something, choose to practice consciousness instead of waiting. Also, try doing it when there are distractions. We want to learn to be as conscious as we want, of whatever we want, whenever we want.

Next we want to look at the automatic "no." This is an example of the automatic behavior I mentioned before. Most people have a defense system in place where whatever is said to them, or presented as an option, gets stopped and examined before it is let in. In effect, we are saying "no" until we check it out, and decide whether we want to let it in and let it affect us. The problem with this is that we can only check new things out from our conditioning's perspective, so through doing this, we get our conditioned response instead of our honest response, and we may miss opportunities. As part of your practice of consciousness, watch for this tendency, and practice being open and available for whatever comes at you. You can always choose not to do something, but let it touch you first. This will deepen your experience of life.

This brings us to trust and mistrust. The whole construct of trust and mistrust is connected with memory and the past, and is ultimately about mistrusting ourselves to be able to stay present with what is happening and make the appropriate decision in the moment. Use your practices of consciousness and self-inquiry to examine trust and mistrust, and see if you can pay more attention to what you perceive in the moment than what your mind is telling you. It is through practices like this that we can achieve true presence.

I would like to spend a few moments looking at collapse. I have used the term to apply to times when we go into extreme unconsciousness, like when we start crying hysterically, get lost in self-pity, or start yelling at someone in anger. You have a choice in these moments. You don't need to go into the collapse, and by choosing not to collapse, you can affect your reality in a much more supportive way. As you deepen your practice of consciousness, refine your definition of collapse so it covers smaller and smaller lapses into unconsciousness. Consider that anytime you involuntarily lose consciousness of what you are choosing to be conscious of, as a form of collapse, and practice staying present in those moments. As you deepen this practice, you can learn to choose against the tiniest collapses, and learn to stay rock solid in your presence.

I would like to mention here that you have no obligation to be present with someone, or something, if you don't want to be. After a day of staying very present with a variety of people, I often enjoy sitting by myself and letting my mind wander. The key is to learn to have the choice. To be as conscious as you want to be, of what you want to be, when you want to be. It is a skill to develop, not an obligation. The whole point of the Deep Living Practice is to teach you to enjoy your life. By becoming more adept at consciousness, we learn to consciously create our reality. By now you probably see that you are creating your experience of reality whether you want to or not. You might as well do it consciously. It is much more fun and rewarding.

−Chapter 44−

Stepping Stones, Traps, and Diversions

I would like to say a few words about obstacles you may encounter on your path to your truth. First, consider what helped you reach whatever state of peace and happiness you have in your life now. Whatever got you to this point, though you may be exceedingly grateful that it brought you here, will eventually keep you from moving on. Think of climbing a ladder. You reach up, grab the next rung, and it takes you further on your way. Then you reach with the other hand and grab the next rung and that takes you even higher. But when it is time to reach for another rung, you need to let go of the rung you are holding on to in order to keep moving.

Many people I have worked with have found practices and teachers that have vastly improved their lives, and that they have become quite attached to. The trouble is, that no matter what you learn, unless it is *your* truth, it will never be what you are ultimately looking for, even if it helped you reach a state you enjoy much more than what you were experiencing before you started. It can be very challenging to let go of something, or someone, who has given you so much help and support. If you are totally happy where you are, there is no need to, but if you were totally happy where you are, you probably wouldn't be reading this book.

We can look at all the things we have done as stepping stones. You wouldn't have gotten to where you are without whatever teachers or practices have helped you obtain your current state, but if you really want to find your truth, you need to leave whatever it was behind. One of my teachers encouraged me to be a finder instead of a seeker, and I encourage you to be the same. You can continue looking for the rest of your life, or you can choose to find your answers, and then find them.

I've designed the Deep Living Practice to be your last stepping stone. Everything else has gotten you to this point, and this can take you to the end, to yourself, to your truth. *You* are the answer to all of your questions. The whole purpose of this Practice is to lead you to the point where you can trust yourself, listen to yourself, love yourself, and be your own guide.

Many paths talk about surrender. It is to your self, and to your truth, that you want to surrender. The challenge with this is that your conditioning considers itself as the truth. This is a trap, and I encourage you to be cautious of it. Anytime you hear yourself saying, "This is my truth", it probably isn't. It is probably your conditioning expressing itself loudly and clearly. This is challenging to let go of, and many people get stuck here. Your actual truth has an expansive open feeling with a quiet power that goes beyond knowing. If there is any contraction, or force, or idea that you are right, in what you are thinking, or feeling, it is not your actual truth. Remember, we don't know anything. Finding your truth includes coming to peace with not knowing.

In part, the Deep Living Practice was developed to give you a path to follow that is an alternative to your conditioning. The Point of View gives you a way to look at things, and be in the world, that supports you to reach the point where you can jump off of this last stepping stone into the unknown of your true self.

I lived very wonderfully with the Point of View for several years. I have yet to have a client come to me with a life situation where I could not show him or her how to use the Point of View to feel better and be guided toward the honesty, courage, consciousness, and self-responsibility that it takes to make that final leap to where you let go of the Point of View and surrender to yourself.

The Point of View provides a transition between who you think you are, and who you really are. It is a substitution for the guru process. The guru process can work as well. In it, you give up your responsibility for yourself to your guru, and you follow everything he or she says. By doing this, you can let go of who you think you are. The dangerous part of this is that you are giving another person a huge amount of power over you, and if you look at the history of gurus, you can see that it is often abused. Gurus can help people improve their lives, but, unless they are guiding the student to find the student's truth, not the guru's truth, they are not guiding the student to his or her maximum potential.

An important moment in my process was when I decided to totally follow this Point of View as it was being described to me by one of my teachers. It was clear to me that what I was doing in my life wasn't working, so I knew I needed to try something different. I had been studying with him for over a year, and my life was getting better, but I was still listening to everything he said through the filters of my judgment and conditioning. I was agreeing with some things, disagreeing with others, and adjusting some to make them more comfortable for me. Eventually I realized, as long as I continued to compare what he was telling me to what I thought was true, I would not be able to let go of who I thought I was. In that moment I decided to make all of my choices based on what he said, instead of what I was saying to myself in my mind. I told myself that no matter what he said, I would consider it the truth, and I would do everything he told me to do to the best of my ability.

It was the best choice I had made up to that point of my life. That teacher had many people studying with him, and though most everyone who worked with him received great benefit, very few changed at their core, and found their truths. It was in large part through making this radical choice that I achieved the happiness and fulfillment that I live in today. An interesting aspect is that I never told him I was doing it. He probably would have discouraged me, as he had bad experience with gurus, and had no desire to be one himself.

Several years later, through a combination of his influence and the Deep Living Practice, which I was in the process of developing, I made a deep connection with my truth and started to allow my truth to guide me. At that point, I disconnected from his influence, which was a process that took several months. Disconnecting from his influence was not very challenging compared to disconnecting from my conditioning, which had seemed impossible. The Point of View is a pathway out of who you think you are. Use it as a tool.

Another thing to watch for is rigidity. There is a fine line between actively pursuing your Practice and becoming too serious about it and pushing yourself too hard. The many challenging aspects of the Deep Living Practice require you to apply a certain amount of will, or you will simply not do the Practice, but at the same time, we want to be careful not to become rigid about what we are doing. Don't start believing that this is the right way, or the only way. If you do, it will become a fixed point, and start to work against you. I've already started to point out the paradoxes that become apparent as you get more deeply into the Practice, and this is another one. Can you have a belief system that you don't believe in? My experience is that you can. Avoid rigidity in everything you do. It is not effective, it takes a lot of effort, and it sucks the fun out of life.

Some people, as part of the search for their truth, have created identities for themselves that are not their conditioning, but are also not who they really are. I call this being on a "trip". They have usually greatly improved their lives by adopting their different way of being, but I find this can become a huge obstacle to them actually finding their truth. People who have done this have a tendency to be extremely attached to their new identity. My experience is that the people have merely traded beliefs, usually for beliefs that are more fun, but that still keep them from their truth. We need to let go of everything that is not our truth, if we are going to find our truth.

People who are on these kinds of trips tend to resist letting them go, because, for most, these trips are a vast improvement over their previous lives. The thing to consider is whether are you absolutely happy with your current life or not. If you are not, whatever you are doing is not the answer.

Some people change their names or take on new spiritual names as a way to separate from their conditioning. I found this valuable and it was very effective in my process, but it was also part of me being on a trip, so be careful. If you choose to experiment with taking another name, I suggest you look at it as a stepping stone, and not get attached to the new name. If you find you do, change it again. I got as much out of letting go of my spiritual name as I got out of taking it.

Also, there is no truth in emulating another culture. It may have helped you break away from your conditioning, but you were born into this culture. Participate here, and put your energy into contributing to make this reality wonderful, instead of trying to be someone else. Your truth is always with you, you don't need to go anywhere to look for it, although going somewhere can help you get away from influences that are keeping you stuck in your ideas of who you are.

Many people mistake staring into someone's eyes for being present. Frequently the inability to look someone in the eye, or hold their gaze, is a sign of fear, and is interesting to note and explore, but on the other side, I know many people who fix a gaze with someone, and feel they are having an intimate moment. My experience is that this is very rarely true. The participants may be having a meaningful moment, but it is usually with themselves. When I witness people doing this, which is quite often, I see very little intimacy. I refer to this as getting lost in someone's eyes. If you notice you are doing this, find other ways to connect, such as sharing how you are feeling, if you actually want intimacy, instead of settling for this substitute for presence and intimacy.

People also tend to be attached to the past. We find the familiar non-threatening, even if it isn't supportive. Feeling nostalgia can be touching, and bring up strong feelings, but these feelings are rarely healthy. Presence is now in the process of becoming what's next. It is vibrant, alive, and exciting. We need to let go of the past to be in the present. Remember, life starts now.

We've talked about saying, "I don't want to…". Remember to not use "I don't want to…" as a life direction, but instead as the beginning of an exploration of your conditioning, because your desire to not do whatever it is, is probably rooted in your conditioning. If in exploring, "I don't want to…" you find laziness, look some more. Laziness invariably has a deeper motivation connected with you doing something that is not in line with your truth. By this stage in your Practice you want to shift your attention to what you do want, instead of what you don't want. If we are in the realm of what we do want, laziness disappears.

When we are doing what we want, we are excited and full of energy. If you are feeling lazy, you probably need to make a radical shift in what you are doing. The same is true for depression. If you are feeling depressed, it is very likely that you are not allowing yourself to do something that you really want to do. Laziness and depression are signs that you are far from your truth, and you need to make a major change.

"What's the point?" or "I know what will happen anyway", are manifestations of either resignation or dishonesty. Either way, don't fall into this trap. If you become aware that you are indulging in these behaviors, look deeper for what is really going on. If it is resignation, look for the longing underneath. If it is not resignation, remember how easy it is to deceive yourself about why you are doing what you are doing, and what the outcome of your actions will be, and look for where you may be being dishonest with yourself, and if you are trying to avoid anything. When you say "What's the point?" or "I know what will happen anyway", you will notice that it is usually said with very little energy. Use your self-inquiry to look at why you don't want to do the thing. You will find a much more energetic reaction to whatever the reason is, and this is where to put your focus. Put your attention where the energy is.

Now I would like to give you a word of caution. When you are in the process of breaking away from your conditioning, your unconscious mind can sometimes act out. This can manifest in a variety of ways. I previously mentioned the feeling of nausea that frequently precedes intense feelings. This is one example, but there can also be other manifestations such as headaches, backaches, dizziness, and sometimes even more physical manifestations, such as rashes. I have found the best recourse in these situations is to accept whatever is happening and look for what the cause might be. With acceptance, the conditions usually pass quickly, and if you find the underlying cause and shift what needs to be shifted, the symptoms will frequently disappear immediately.

I would also like to warn you about a deeper level of acting out. Sometimes in the latter stage of the process, as you are really starting to disconnect from your conditioning, you will watch yourself do something self-destructive, and it seems your body is out of your control as you do it. This can be a shocking moment, but it is also a very valuable moment. We have all done stupid things where we can't understand why we did them, or had "accidents". You are finally becoming conscious of this kind of self-destructive acting out that you were previously doing unconsciously.

Definitely use your self-inquiry to explore the motivations behind your actions, but realize that by being aware of it happening, you are getting close to stopping this kind of unconscious reactive behavior.

It is likely that you will get stuck or diverted as you progress with your Practice. The key is to keep remembering why you are doing your Practice in the first place—because you want a wonderful life. If you are happy with your life there is no reason to change. If you are not happy with your life, there is no truly valid reason not to change.

The Deep Living Practice was designed to help you find exactly the life you want. Many people use it to shift something in their life and then choose to not go further with their Practice. Each of us chooses what we want in life, and what we want to get out of our Practice. If you have what you want, enjoy it. If at any time you decide you want something more or something else, you can always restart your Practice. Life is not about a goal. It is a series of experiences. Do what you want, when you want, to create the life you want.

–Chapter 45–

Getting Help

I look at the Deep Living Practice as a personal practice, and the majority of the work you do, and benefits you receive, will be from what you do on your own. It is by embracing it as a personal practice, and taking responsibility for yourself, that you will get the greatest results. At the same time, some aspects are very challenging to do on your own, and there will be times when you feel you need help. It is also very supportive to have other people practice with you, as the sense of community, and shared experience, can greatly enhance your Practice and your life.

One of the wonderful things that happens with the groups I give is that the participants frequently stay in contact and support each other to continue their Practices. In the places where we give many groups, communities start to form with people who attended different groups enjoying each other's company and support. Many long-term relationships begin in the groups, and through these, communities. Once you have begun the practice of honesty, courage, consciousness, and self-responsibility, it is wonderful to be with people who are practicing these things as well. It also becomes uninteresting and frustrating to be with people who are not practicing these things, as you begin to see more clearly how they are choosing to allow fear to control their behavior, and how their beliefs and fixed attitudes limit their possibilities. I highly encourage you to find other people to practice with, either by sharing your Practice with others, sharing this book, or taking advantage of social media to connect with other people who have similar interests.

Once you develop a circle of peers, you can support each other in the exercises and practices that require more than one person. It is a great way to spend time with other people, and creates the opportunity for deep connections. In my groups, I constantly have untrained people supporting each other with effective results. By supporting other people, you will get a deeper insight into the Practice that will, in turn, support you. Just remember to do everything slowly, and as consciously as possible, and if things begin to get unconscious, stop what you are doing, and focus on resourcing and bringing your attention back to your pelvis.

A great way to start getting people together is by creating a sharing group, as we discussed in our Internal Dialogue chapter. Sharing your internal dialogue is a great way to start connecting, and finding people to support you in other aspects of your Practice. Allow the group, and relationships created in the group, to develop in any way that they might. Don't be fixed that the group only be about sharing internal dialogue. Let it develop in any way that supports your Practice, or the Practices of the other participants. I once rented a house with people I knew from sharing groups, and we lived together for about six weeks giving each other feedback about each other's behavior the entire time. It was an incredible experience that changed my life. So much is possible; you just need to create it.

One thing to be aware of in these situations is that when most people are giving you feedback, it has as much to do with them as it has to do with you. This does not mean it is not valuable, it just means you include the source of the feedback in how you interpret it. It is also useful to notice that if something someone says to you makes you angry, it is probably true, and it is time for self-responsibility and self-inquiry, not for blame.

One of the challenges of doing the Deep Living Practice on your own is that it is very hard to see yourself clearly, and most other people see you through *their* filters. Most people tend to be lost in their sense of self. The metaphor about describing water to a fish is apt here. If something is all you remember knowing, you have nothing to compare it to, which makes it very hard to perceive.

People who have learned to see others more clearly can be helpful if you can find one, but there are also people who think they see you clearly who don't, or pretend to in order to take advantage of you. Once you learn to feel your feelings, you can trust them to guide you. Whether it is when people are giving you feedback, or if they are telling you how they perceive you, there are times when you feel a deep resonance, and you know what they are saying is true. Your feelings can also guide you if you do not have the support of someone who sees you clearly. This is why it is so important to get in touch with your feelings, and learn to let them guide you. They will show you the way to your truth more reliably than any other source.

Some things are very hard to do by yourself. If you have had extreme trauma, if you are subject to panic attacks, if you are involved in addictive behavior, or if you are in an entangled attached relationship, it can often be extremely difficult to avoid getting lost in behavioral patterns, and to see yourself clearly enough to find your way out. In these situations, you may need to get trained or professional help. If you choose to do this, take care in choosing whom to help you. Avoid those who have a strong agenda, and look for people whose main focus is listening to you, and being guided by your needs. The ideal person to support you will be open, available, vulnerable, and unshakable. Be sure he or she is comfortable working in whatever area you want to work in. Don't be afraid to ask her questions to make sure she is the right person for you. If she is not open to you questioning her, or is too attached to things being a particular way, she may not be the right person for you.

That said, it can be very hard to find this quality of support. Don't let the lack of the ideal person to help you slow you down. I used everybody I could find, and took what I could get. Focus on getting the support you can from whomever is available, and not on where they are lacking. Also, look for opportunities, and choose to take them. My experience is that when we make a choice, the opportunities will arise if we have the awareness and the courage to take advantage of them.

How much is finding your deepest truth your priority? How important is it for you to know exactly what you want in life, and to be able to get it? How important is it to wake up every morning excited about your life and to experience happiness, joy, and fulfillment all day long? If you make these things your top priorities, you will do whatever it takes to get the help you need. In my process I gave up everything—twice. The first time to start my search, and the second time was when I found a teacher I realized could really help me change my life. I gave up the things I had done and learned up to that point, and followed him around the world. I had decided I was going to find my truth, and did whatever it took to learn what I needed to learn from him. If you make finding your truth your priority, you will find the way to find it.

−Chapter 46−

Some Final Words on Your Practice

Here are a few more ideas to help you in your Deep Living Practice. The first is to realize that your Practice moves in a spiral. It simultaneously circles and deepens. You will find yourself coming back to the same issues again and again, but as you do, you will see that your relationship to them has changed. Some people get frustrated at frequently looking at different aspects of the same issue. Being frustrated doesn't help, and only gets in the way of you addressing all aspects of the issue and eventually clearing them from your system.

The first time you approached whatever the issue was, you may have taken care of 80 percent of it. This is wonderful, but the 20 percent that is left is now 100 percent of what you have to clear to find your truth. It does not support your process to waste time and energy not liking that you did not clear 100 percent of the issue the first time you addressed it. When you address the issue the next time, you may clear all of it, or you may clear 90 percent of it, in which case, the 10 percent left will be 100 percent of what you need to address when the issue arises again. Take the time to notice that as you clear parts of an issue, your reality changes, your behavior changes, your conditioning has less of a hold on you, and your experience of life improves. You are making progress.

At some point, as you continue with your Deep Living Practice, you will know what you need to do much better than I do sitting here, some time in the past, writing to an imagined version of who you might be. When you find your path, make your Practice your own. I am offering what I have done with the information I got from my teachers. Let this get you started, but when you are ready, follow your own path. I call this becoming self-activating. This is a significant point in your practice of self-responsibility. Just make sure your choices are coming from a deep and expanded place inside you, and not from your conditioning or fear. These feel very different.

You may consider supporting others in their Practices. It is one of the most powerful ways of advancing your own Practice. If you really want to learn something, teach it. If you can explain it to someone else, you really know it, and frequently by explaining it, you make it your own. Supporting others is also a way to come into a state where you are giving energy, which feels great. Supporting those around you to be more honest, courageous, conscious, and self-responsible is not only a caring thing to do, it makes them more fun and exciting to be around, and creates opportunities for meaningful and intimate relationships.

I've talked about your Practice being like a mountain. Once you truly choose to embrace your Practice, you will be on the downhill side. Your Practice then becomes about accepting and relaxing into your truth. There is nothing to achieve, and nothing to gain. It is about relaxing into self-acceptance and self-love. It is about coming to the realization that everything is perfect, whether you understand that perfection or not. It is about accepting what is happening, and taking responsibility for creating what you are experiencing.

It is time to keep your focus on where you want to go, and what you want to do, instead of what you don't want, and what isn't working. When you really find your "yes" to life, your "no" fades away, and rarely even affects you, because you are so focused on your "yes". Your internal dialogue may still be running, but it will be easy to ignore if you want to, and the idea of making life choices based on what it says will strike you as absurd.

At this stage of your Practice, you may be experimenting with allowing your energy without holding back. As you do, stay aware of the effects you are having on the world around you. As you stop holding back, you can reach the point where you are not able to stay conscious while allowing your energy. It may feel too exciting, and too wild, for you to stay present with. Your Practice becomes about being more conscious, so you can allow more energy consciously, and continues with alternating steps of more energy, then more consciousness, then more energy, then more consciousness. This part of the Practice may last for a while. It is where your true self starts to emerge into the world, and your life starts transforming into something wonderful that is frequently beyond anything you might have previously imagined.

Some long-term practices to stay present with are letting go of conditioning, attachment, and our deep-seated beliefs. Examining your ideas about "good" and "bad" supports all three of these practices. Can you let go of the idea that some things are good and others are bad? Can you see that everything just is? Choices have consequences that directly create our experience of reality, but whether something is good or bad is a matter of perspective. I always take note if I use the words "good" or "bad", and realize that they are very subjective and only relate to my personal sense of truth, or to some aspect of my conditioning that I have not yet addressed.

There are parts of my conditioning that I haven't addressed, as they cause no unhappiness in my life. If they ever do, I will address them. For many years my Practice was my top priority, and this made all the difference in my life. But after a while, my life was incredibly wonderful, and I made enjoying my life my top priority. Whenever something gets in the way of me enjoying my life, I make looking at whatever it is my top priority until I have cleared it from my system, then I get back to enjoying my life. It is a lovely way to live.

As you continue living deeply, your sensitivity, intuition, and empathy will continue to develop, and you will become more adept at interpreting your feelings. This makes life much richer, and much easier. You will see what is happening around you with much greater clarity. Doubt and confusion become a thing of the past, and life becomes simple, as you are clear about what is appropriate and inappropriate for you, and can make the choice to always move toward what is appropriate. You will have learned to make the distinction between suppressing something, and not supporting something, and be able to make your choices easily. You will come to see that from the conditioned mind's perspective, there are many paradoxes, and that from the conditioned perspective, many of the things I have described should not work, but they do. Experiencing this helps you let go of your last connection with letting your beliefs of how things should be control your choices. You will see that you can be absolutely confident and certain, while at the same time realizing that you do not know anything for sure. You will see that you can be totally uncompromising, but at the same time be completely unattached to what happens. You can be extremely relaxed and happy, while you are totally insecure. You can be responsible without being serious, and caring without feeling responsible. These states are indescribable from the conditioned mind's perspective, but the experience is wonderful, easy, and flowing. You will come to see that so much of our conditioning was created by people's discomfort with paradox, but as you accept paradox as life's nature, you enter a very different experience of reality, and embrace these paradoxes with joy. You experience that living in paradox is exciting, like riding a wave that never has to end. The possibilities are infinite.

Everyone makes choices that include and exclude certain possibilities, and through this they create the realities that they live in. The problem is that most people create rather unpleasant realities for themselves. Create a reality that is wonderful beyond imagination. The trick is to stay conscious of other people's realities, and not be rigid, fixed, or exclusive.

As you deepen your Practice, you will become more aware of energy, and energy is all about flow. Create a flowing reality and ride effortlessly through life, interacting with other realities as opportunities arise, affecting them, instead of choosing to let them affect you, unless, of course, you want to let them affect you.

You have just as much right to live, and do what you want to do, as anyone else on this planet, and no more right, so make your choices accordingly. As you have become responsible with the energy of your anger, and moved through the process of using it as determination to support you finding your truth, you will see that your anger becomes your power, and your passion. Live powerfully and passionately.

You will have let go of your ideas of who you are; shattering your sense of self in the process. You will have addressed the negative effects of your conditioning, and rid yourself of the controlling voices in your head from your memories of parents, or other strong influences, by learning to ignore, disobey, or even kill their effects in your mind, if that's what it takes. You will have transformed reactivity into responsibility, and learned to not allow fear, or shame, to control your behavior. You will reach a point where you can say "I don't know", and it will be coming from deep honesty instead of avoiding your truth. You will bask in the freedom of knowing that nothing really matters, and that you are here to have an experience, so you might as well have the most wonderful one possible, which will invariably include you giving your true energy into the world, and participating fully in this joint experience we call life on planet Earth.

There are times in the Deep Living Practice where you feel like you are going insane or you are going to die. Where we are going with the Deep Living Practice *is* insane from the point of view of your conditioning, so go there. It is a highly functional and enjoyable form of insanity, most likely much more so than the form of insanity you are letting go of. The times when you feel you are dying are times when some aspect of you that is not your truth is dying. It feels just like death, though if you stay with it, you will not die, but instead feel reborn, as you move closer and closer to what is real for you. You will likely have these kinds of feelings as you approach the final stage of the Deep Living Practice, which is to become your truth. When you become your truth, it is time to let go of your witness.

You are a creative energy in the process of manifesting a reality. The closer you are to the experience of this, and the goal of the Deep Living Practice is to get you ever closer, the more wonderful you will feel. When you finally become this, embrace it, accept it, surrender to it, allow it, you will see that everything else you have been doing in your life has just been an arduous attempt to avoid your truth, and you will wonder how you ever could have thought it was a good idea. Finally you can relax into yourself realizing that your truth was always with you, you just weren't paying attention to it. In this state, you *are* happiness, you *are* fulfillment, *you* are the answer to everything you have been looking for.

-Chapter 47-

Living in the World

The purpose of this book is to support you to develop a personal practice to bring you closer to your true self. This will bring you to an experience of happiness and fulfillment beyond description. Frequently, when I am working with people, and am encouraging them to be extremely honest, or to allow their energy without holding back, they will ask me how they could possibly live like that. The answer is ... exceptionally well. As you get further into the Deep Living Practice, you see life more clearly, you know your direction in life, and life becomes exceedingly simple. You know where to put your energy, and where not to, and are able to see what the consequences of your choices will be, and make your choices accordingly. Let's look at some ways that our Practice relates to living in the world.

As you become more honest, courageous, and conscious, and you choose to participate responsibly by allowing your energy to radiate into whatever situation you are in, you will become much more attractive to the people around you. As you become more solid and grounded, people will perceive you as trustable. I've talked about how you create your reality, and as you start doing it consciously, you will create a field around you that is extraordinary. Some people may feel intimidated by you, and some may resent you because you are allowing things that they are still repressing, but they will still be attracted to you and be positively affected by you.

As you come closer to living your truth, it becomes very easy to operate in the world. People will feel better when you are around. You will go somewhere and the atmosphere will improve. You will be sought after for advice and support, and be in a position to give it well and easily. There are many rewards to living this way.

You will be able to interact with the conditioned world easily. You will be able to clearly see what needs to be done, and how to do it as simply as possible. Without reactivity, attachment, and childish stubbornness, you will see situations for what they are, and know how to navigate them in a way that achieves the objectives you want to achieve as easily as possible.

We all have things we have to do; bills to pay; taxes; government regulations; social expectations. I refer to these things as the "practicals". These are the things you need to deal with in the practical world. Look at your practical concerns clearly with the sense that if you choose to live in this house, city, or country, these are the things you need to take care of ... and then just take care of them. If you don't like them, you can live somewhere else, and deal with the practicals there. Every place you go will have some practicals that you need to address. Choose where you live carefully, so it supports your joy. If you can see your practicals for what they are and take care of them as they arise, the practical part of your life can flow easily.

Choose *everything* in your life with care. The place you live, the clothes you wear, the things you use, what you eat, the places you go, the ways you spend your time, and the people you spend your time with. They all have a huge effect on your experience. Tune in and make choices that create a reality that brings you joy. Don't allow habits and preconceptions to affect these choices. Create your life exactly the way you want it.

A trap that many people fall into is comparing themselves to others. Don't. Be yourself. We are all unique and wonderful in our own way. Be yourself as fully and completely as possible, and don't create pain and suffering in yourself by trying to be something that you are not. There are ways to be, and ways to do things, that have developed in our culture that, though they may work for some people, do not work well for others. I work with many people who are trying to be something they are not, and feel great stress from the expectations they put on themselves. We don't need to do this. There are many ways to be in the world outside of the accepted standards, and many people are creating innovative ways to be in the world. You can do this too. Find your truth, live it, and let the world organize around your joy. You may think this is impossible. It is not. It may just be beyond your imagination in this moment.

Let's look at gender roles and stereotypes. I have, for example, worked with many women who have been taught that to be successful they need to act like men. Some achieve success with this, but they are not truly happy in their success, and feel the stress of trying to emulate a masculine role. I've worked with many men who are not comfortable with what they have been taught their role as a man should be, and allow the inner conflict between their true energy and their expectations on themselves to create doubt and confusion that virtually paralyzes them. As long as we behave according to expectations, we support things to stay the way they are. It takes great courage to break out of these expectations, but with this courage comes joy.

I have worked with many people who think, and have been told, that they are stupid. They are not stupid; their minds just work in a different way. By trying to think the way other people tell them to think, they create much frustration and unhappiness, both in themselves and the people around them. I have always found that there are other ways they can operate in which they are happy and can still be very functional. It is just a matter of letting go of expectations.

Create a way to live in the world that allows you to be the way you are. It not only brings you joy, it is the responsible thing to do. The trick is to give energy. Our conditioning tells us that if we don't play by the rules, and do what we are told, we will fail and be rejected. My experience is that this is not at all true. The ones who live differently become our artists, innovators, and role models. If you are giving energy, if you are actively participating in life, living your truth, and giving your gift, you will be rewarded. Everyone I know who lives this way lives a brilliant life. The key is to be giving.

Many people ask me questions about making money. Money is a convenient way to store energy. Life is all about energy, and energy is all about flow. This is why it is so useful to be able to perceive energy; it really gives you a huge advantage. If you are giving energy, energy will want to flow back into you. Many people block the flow of energy into them, frequently in the forms of money, support, or love; out of fear, self-hatred, or some other reason. The Deep Living Practice is a way to support us to shift these patterns, so we can let our energy flow in and out unimpeded. If you are having financial problems, look at where you are either not allowing your energy out, or where you are blocking the flow of energy to you.

Just as many people don't allow themselves to feel loved, many people do not allow themselves to receive energy from others. This includes financial energy. Something in their past has made them choose to feel that they don't deserve to receive things, they feel they have to do everything on their own, or they have some other reason why they can't let support in. Many people are actually afraid of success and unconsciously sabotage any chances for it they might have. Some people's conditioning has taught them that life is hard, so they create hard lives for themselves. When people are lost in their behavior, these ideas will create outcomes that they *think* they want to change, but no matter how hard they try, nothing seems to work. By realizing that it is impossible to do something that the majority of yourself does not want to be doing, using self-inquiry to find the cause, and the tools of the Practice to shift the pattern, you will be able to live the life of ease, grace, and abundance that you deserve.

We are incredibly fortunate to live in a time and culture that allows so many of us to live so easily and abundantly. This is not true for everyone, but most of you who are reading this book have the luxury of being able to focus on having a wonderful life. I went to an introductory talk once, with a man who was to become one of my significant teachers. At the end of the event, he said, "When given two options, take them both." I decided to try out this concept and found that my life immediately became much fuller and more abundant. It was not always possible to take both options, but it frequently was, and it opened many possibilities for me that I had previously felt I could not allow myself. I saw how frequently I was making choices to deny myself things that I really did not have to make. I was only making them because I thought I was supposed to.

There is nothing wrong with needing money. Needing to make money motivates me, and gives me focus, but I never make decisions based on money. If I need money, I think about what I want to do, and then I do it in such a way that I earn money for it. The way most of us relate to work is part of our conditioning. We feel it is something we have to do in order to make money, we do it until we retire, and *then* we can enjoy ourselves. This is crazy. Do whatever you want to do, find a way to get paid for it, and keep doing it as long as you want to. Don't allow your conditioned beliefs about what is possible to keep you from finding your unique way of life.

Remember that while you are working on your Practice, you are in a transitional state. You will know that what you are doing is not your truth, as you have not yet found it. Realize that until you get deeper into your Practice, your choices are coming from your conditioning, so you need to make your Practice your priority, after doing what you need to do to survive. Look at how you spend your time, and make sure that you are not spending large amounts of time doing things that don't support you finding your truth. Decide what you need to survive and live comfortably, then find the easiest way to get what you need, that will leave you the most time for your Practice. Integrate your Practice into whatever you are doing to earn what you need. If you do this, you will move through this transitional stage quickly, and then you can find more satisfying long-term solutions.

If you are more conscious than the people around you, you will stand out, and be rewarded for it. If you become more empathic, the people around you will appreciate you. When I was in business I did very well because I understood what the people I worked for wanted, and gave it to them. This made me more valuable than people who were just there to do a job, or came to work with a sense of entitlement that was frequently rooted in a parent projection.

The Deep Living Practice supports you to tune in to whatever situation you are in and—by seeing people's deeper motivations and understanding vectors and their consequences on the outcome of the situation—add a valuable contribution to the desired outcome. When you can do this, you become a very useful person. As you begin to perceive energy and the effects of vectors, you will learn how to line your energy up with other energies in order to get things done in a very efficient way. This is an extremely valuable skill, whether you are working for someone and choosing to line your energy up with theirs, or creating your own business, and hiring and managing people to help you achieve your goals. When we can see, and understand, people's deeper motivations, it becomes extremely easy to interact with them productively, instead of getting caught up in their behavioral projections and strategies.

I encourage you to focus on what's next. Let go of what you don't want, and what you are against, and focus on what you do want, and what the next step is to get you closer to it. My experience of presence is that it is a very dynamic state of what is next in the process of forming. Can you always be fully with what is, while also being open to, and participating in, the creation of what is next? This is an exciting way to live.

The Practice I have presented in this book is designed to get you out of the behavioral patterns that make it very challenging to be conscious of much more than what is going on in your mind. Once you get out of your behavioral patterns, amazing things are available to you, and you will perceive this area of behavior as narrow and constricted compared to all that is available, though when you are in it, it seems like it is all there is. The Deep Living Practice is not the end, but the beginning of the deep, rich, wonderful life that is rightfully yours.

–Chapter 48–

A Revolution of Consciousness

Since I was a little boy, and began learning about life and the world, I couldn't understand why things were the way they were, and why people behaved the way they did. I remember constantly thinking, "It doesn't have to be this way."

I became very angry and reactive, and indulged in a lot of self-destructive behavior. To channel these feelings, I started making art. My art was also angry and reactive, and the underlying theme was still "It doesn't have to be this way." I felt this very strongly, but at the time I had no idea how the world *could* be. When I was young, I explored a variety of religions and belief systems, but none of them worked for me, and in resignation I used drugs and alcohol to numb myself enough to function in the world.

In my early forties I gave up trying to continue life as I had learned to live it, and searched for answers. I found them, and have offered some of what I learned with you in this book. What I have presented is the basis of how to find your truth and happiness in life, but there is also a much broader application of the things I teach. I've found a way to live in the world where everything feels like it is the way it is supposed to be. I've found the answer to the question, "If it doesn't have to be this way, how could it be?" I don't have a final answer, or a concrete picture of how the world would be if everyone lived this way, but I have found a direction to move in that feels wonderful, responsible, and makes me happy to be alive, and to be participating in the joint creation of the reality we are all sharing.

In this final chapter I would like to write about some of what I have learned and perceived about how the world is, and how adopting the Deep Living Practice and the Point of View might move the world into a reality that may keep future children from saying, "It doesn't have to be this way," but rather feel nourished, supported, and happy to participate in a world that makes it easy for them to reach their maximum potential and live joyous, fulfilled lives.

One key is self-responsibility. I've come to see that self-responsibility is social responsibility. By taking complete responsibility for yourself, you will come into the state where you have the most to contribute to those around you. As long as you are supporting your conditioned state, you are perpetuating and deepening the way our culture controls and disempowers the vast majority of its members. The real key is consciousness.

By becoming more conscious, we can no longer ignore and deaden ourselves to all the things in our culture that do not work. If you are conscious of what you are feeling, you will experience that it does not feel good to be unfair, to be dishonest, to take advantage of others, and to witness suffering, much less to cause it. You will feel motivated to be responsible, and contribute to a solution instead of contributing to the problem. This motivation will come out of your truth and depth, not out of any sense of guilt or responsibility for others, and it will most likely manifest in ways that surprise you.

Some people think they enjoy being unfair, dishonest, greedy or cruel, but my experience is that the motivations behind these behaviors are related to the conditioning, strategies, and experiences of these people, and the rewards they receive are minor compared to the potential of finding their truth. Many people are very lost in these behaviors, and will probably not change in this lifetime. Don't become resigned because of this. If you can look underneath your resignation, and get in touch with your longing for a more wonderful way of being in the world, your experience will vastly improve, and you will start to contribute to change. It does not matter how things are. All that matters to you is how you are with how things are, and if you are participating to create a more wonderful reality. If you focus on that, you will feel wonderful, and be doing your part.

Earlier in the book I described a practice to find what you truly want in life. When I did this practice myself, it took about ten days before I had the thought, "I want to be a revolutionary." Then I immediately thought, "No, that's too much, I could never do that." Over the next few days though, it became inescapable. It was what excited me, it was what felt the most expansive, it was what brought me joy.

In my youth, I was against almost everything, I was full of hate, and I had the desire to destroy. But now I have learned that being against things doesn't work. If you are against something, you are part of it. This revolution is not about tearing something down, but instead is about creating something wonderful, and letting the things that don't work fall away. I came to see that the revolution that I am dedicating my life to is a revolution of consciousness. The sessions I give, the groups I run, this book, are all my way of supporting this change in consciousness that I feel is so necessary. This is where I find my joy and fulfillment.

The way I am encouraging people to live is very different than what we have been taught. Some people will say that it isn't normal. There is no such thing as normal. Normal is a myth. Normal is a concept held over your head to control you. If you look at the world you will see that there are so many different ideas of what is normal, for so many different people, that the idea of you allowing some group of people's concept of normal to control you is ridiculous. It becomes a social contract that you agree to for acceptance. But is it worth sacrificing your happiness and joy? My feeling is that it is not. I tried quite a few different normals in my life, and none of them brought me happiness and fulfillment. It is time to create new normals that support and enrich us instead of keep us controlled, striving, and unhappy.

What would it be like to have a culture that was not driven by fear, a culture that put cooperation over competition, a culture that didn't support dishonesty or greed, a culture where people were aware of what the people around them are experiencing and let it touch them, a culture where people grew into responsible participants contributing what brings them joy, and then the culture organized around those contributions?

I'm not advocating taking apart what we have done so far. Let's focus on what is next. Everything has come to a point where we have both the luxury of and the necessity to create something new. We have developed technology that makes life extremely easy for many, but it also ignores many. In the future this will probably be known as the Petroleum Age, and we still have enough of this remarkable substance to create a reality that doesn't need it. The key is to start making our collective choices based on what will support each and every individual on the planet to become responsible participating members. For each of us individually, this begins with making the choice to find, and live, our truths as honestly, courageously, consciously, and responsibly as possible.

What would it be like to live in a world where everyone was happy and doing exactly what he or she wanted to do? It would be a very different world. There would be many things that no one wanted to do, so they wouldn't be done. Much of what is being done is being driven by the momentum of progress, and relies on conditioned minions to make it happen. I imagine a world where everybody was doing what they wanted to do would be much simpler and much slower, but is that a bad thing? There would probably be many things we have now that we would not have, but are these things we really need? Remember, if our energy is moving toward feeling happy and fulfilled, we will feel happy and fulfilled no matter what we are doing. Or we will do what it takes to feel happy and fulfilled.

Our conditioning tells us that other people are lazy, and won't do their part, but my experience is that when people are doing what they want to do, they have no problem giving energy. It is also my experience that each person has a unique energy, and is happiest when he or she can give it. Could we create a culture that is made up of people giving the gift of their unique energies, and allow the result of the culture to organize around the sum of the gifts being given?

If everyone contributes what brings them joy, what joyous things might we create? We have a strong base to start from, and if we make this our goal, line our energy up to create this, and adapt and change as we must to realize this, there is no reason we cannot achieve it in the same ways that we achieved all the other things that seemed impossible before we did them. My experience is that, for the individual, moving in this direction feels great, no matter what everyone else is doing. Who knows how far we will get, or how things will turn out. What's important is that you are having a wonderful experience and are doing your part to create something wonderful.

What is going on inside of us radiates out into the world. By bringing consciousness to this we can affect change from the inside. We need to let go of our beliefs, and ideas, of what is right and wrong, and let our inner truth be our moral compass; let our collective truths guide us to a new reality. Can we let go of our ideas about gender roles, ethnic, and racial stereotypes, national identities, and even the idea of our supremacy as a species? Can we realize that we are part of something much bigger than ourselves, or our species, and that we are active participants in creating a much bigger reality than we are aware of? Can we behave responsibly while considering the consequences of our actions, on as large a scale as we are capable of being aware of in the moment?

Media has a huge effect on our conditioning. I suggest you simultaneously become aware of how most things you see, hear and read are perpetuating aspects of the culture that do not serve us, and consider creating media, conversation, or at the very least, thoughts, that support a more supportive and empowering way of life.

Our culture has become very fragmented. One aspect of this is how children rebel against adults. It only makes sense, because what the adults are doing doesn't work. But by being against the established generation, the next generation makes its choices reactively, and creates something that is equally dysfunctional. We need to focus on creating a supportive reality that does not create rebellion, but supports a continuum where we can grow through building upon what comes before, instead of the reactivity, that creates gaps between the generations and pendulum swings between polarities of ideologies.

We need to stop taking behavior seriously, look for deeper motivations, and address issues where they really matter. We need to become aware of our energetic nature. We need to learn to identify energetic patterns and vectors, and learn that by aligning energy we can achieve things easily and effortlessly, instead of forcefully and with great consequence.

Can we bring consciousness into all aspects of our lives? Can we do business consciously and support conscious businesses? Can we realize that the experience of doing something is just as much a part of what we are doing as the result, and make sure to be conscious that both of them are as wonderful as possible?

If you feel inclined to participate in this revolution of consciousness, share what you have learned through your Practice. Let your energy radiate out into the world. Be responsible for yourself, and support those around you to take responsibility for themselves. Be the change you want to make.

The world is very stuck in many ways, but everything can change. It all begins within each of us individually. If you look at the exponential nature of change, you will see that something that starts very slowly, and works against incredible odds, can shift very quickly once momentum has developed. Don't succumb to resignation. Find your longing for a wonderful life and allow it to guide you.

We live in a world of limitless possibilities. Feel free to experiment. We know that much of what we are doing is not working, so experiment with your intuition and your impulses to create new things that do work, new ways to be in the world, new ways to be in relationship, and new ways to structure family. How can we come together, and line up our energy, to create wonderful new experiences of reality? Explore how we can come together in groups, join our energy for a purpose, and create results that are much greater than the sum of the parts. We can bring magic back into our lives.

All of this, and so much more, is possible. It is up to each of us to begin this process for ourselves by finding our truth. Like the flight attendant says: "Put your own mask on first." Until you find your truth, you are lost in your ideas about what is true. Once you find your truth everything is clear. Make the choice to find yourself. Live your purpose. Love your life.

List of Practices and Exercises

For more information about
Deep Living
and the work of
James Swank
visit
www.jamesswank.org

CPSIA information can be obtained at www.ICGtesting.com
Printed in the USA
BVOW071421210212

283453BV00001B/50/P

9 783000 360718